Chicago Tribune

Say It's So

The Chicago White Sox's Magical Season

PHIL ROGERS

TRIUMPH
BOOKS
CHICAGO

This book is available in quantity at special discounts
for your group or organization. For further information, contact:
Triumph Books
542 South Dearborn Street, Suite 750
Chicago, Illinois 60605
(312) 939-3330
Fax (312) 663-3557

Printed in U.S.A.
ISBN-13: 978-1-57243-870-5
ISBN-10: 1-57243-870-3

Text edited by Dan McGrath
Design by Chuck Burke

To Shelby and Dylan Rogers,
the greatest kids in the world

Believe It! We are all rejoicing because, yes, the Chicago White Sox are the 2005 world champions.

The ride from Opening Day through the final out of the fourth World Series game had really happened, but not until the celebratory parade through downtown Chicago did it really sink in that all the heroics performed by the 2005 White Sox resulted in their being crowned as champions.

My arrival in Chicago with the Sox dates to Sept. 14, 1970, when I was hired as general manager, along with new manager Chuck Tanner and pitching coach John Sain. I admit to being nervous flying into O'Hare Field realizing that we were being given the opportunity to work with this historic and storied franchise. The 15-plus years through 1985 brought hope, challenges, some seasons with excitement into September and some seasons where we barely survived the threat of a franchise move to Milwaukee, Seattle, Denver or Toronto.

But let's not dwell on the past. Let's enjoy 2005 as the type of season very few other clubs have experienced: a wire-to-wire, first-place finish in the regular season, and an 11-1 record in the postseason.

General manager Ken Williams dramatically changed the face of the 2004 club into one of the best balanced in the league heading into the 2005 season. I will forever marvel at how Ken accomplished this. Manager Ozzie Guillen expressed to Ken the type of club he would like to manage, and Ken provided it. The players responded enthusiastically and stayed positive throughout the season. They surprised the baseball world with their relentless pursuit of excellence.

I've been asked often how it feels to be part of this scene. Well, the emotions are felt in various ways.

First and foremost, you are happy for all current White Sox fans, but you find yourself thinking about all the people who have remained staunch Sox fans through all the non-championship years. I thought of John Allyn and Bill Veeck, who were custodians of the franchise through the '70s and strongly resisted overtures from other cities who wanted the Sox to leave their beloved Chicago.

All current and past members of the Sox organization have been pulling for Jerry Reinsdorf to be rewarded with a baseball world championship. To watch Jerry raise the trophy over his head and see the joy on his face is a memory that will stay with me.

I also greatly value my good fortune to have returned to Chicago in my current capacity, as a senior advisor to Ken Williams. What a thrill it has been to see so many of the fans, close friends whom I have known for 30-plus years, and some more recent friends being so happy beyond their wildest dreams. It's rewarding to know that this great game of baseball can be a source of inspiration, motivation, and tears of joy for people of all ages.

I have been lucky enough to work in baseball since 1951, and I can unequivocally say that my greatest and happiest day in the game was my birthday, Oct. 26, 2005. Incredibly, the Sox won Games 3 and 4 of the World Series on that day. Sox fans will forever remember Oct. 26, 2005 as the day Geoff Blum struck the winning blow with a line-drive home run in the 14th inning of Game 3, well past midnight. Later that day the Sox shut out the Astros 1-0 to win the Fall Classic.

That accomplishment resulted in an unparalleled act of togetherness for Chicago as 1.75 million people attended the parade to welcome our White Sox, World Series champions.

Roland Hemond
November 2005

EDITOR'S NOTE

Former White Sox general manager Roland Hemond is one of the most respected men in baseball, having spent more than 50 years in the game as an executive with the Sox and four other teams and as a special assistant to former Commissioner Peter Ueberroth.

Just because it's obvious doesn't mean it shouldn't be stated. A lot of people made this book possible, but none more so than the 2005 White Sox.

They seized their moment relentlessly, playing 27 outs a game—or 42, when required—with a cold-hearted efficiency, but they also had the grace and patience to share it with their city and with fans throughout North America and the world. That's where reporters come in. So from someone who has killed my share of clubhouse carpet, big thanks to Ozzie Guillen, Mark Buehrle, Paul Konerko, Aaron Rowand, A.J. Pierzynski, Don Cooper, Greg Walker and everyone else who gets it.

To the South Side soldier just home from Iraq whom I met in the upper deck before Game 1 of the Championship Series, what a way to come home from war. It was a privilege to cover this story in the pages of the Chicago Tribune and the chance of a lifetime to tell it again in the pages of this book.

Thanks to my fellow reporters at the Tribune, including Mark Gonzales, Paul Sullivan, Dave van Dyck, Rick Morrissey,

Steve Rosenbloom, David Haugh, Melissa Isaacson, Mike Downey, Ed Sherman and Philip Hersh. Also, thanks to others at the Tribune whose reporting contributed to our coverage and to this book, including Gary Marx, Hugh Dellios, Jon Yates, Brendan McCarthy, Tonya Maxwell and James Janega. Special thanks to the Dean, Jerome Holtzman, who inspires us all.

None of us could have done our jobs as well without the 1-2 punch of Dan McGrath and Bill Adee, who just might be the best combination of sports editors anyone ever put together. Also thanks to editors Mike Kellams, Ken Paxson, Tom Carkeek, Mike Sansone, Bob Vanderberg, Lee Gordon, Rich Strom, Mike Kates and Mark Jacob for their work.

Thanks to Mitch Rogatz and Tom Bast of Triumph Books for recognizing a story worth retelling. Special thanks to the Chicago Tribune, in particular Jim O'Shea, Bill Parker, Tony Majeri and Susan Zukrow, for allowing us to use the work of a great bunch of photographers—I still can't believe Phil Velasquez was in a bar in West, Texas, when Scott Podsednik, of West, Texas, hit a game-winning home run in the World Series—and putting the project on the fast track.

There are two great things about my job. One is that the late Marge Schott wouldn't have really considered it a job, because all I do is watch baseball. The other is that I'm around some of the best people in the world, especially at events like the World Series and the All-Star Game. Thanks to Phyllis Merhige, Katy Feeney, Tracy Ringolsby, Bob Elliott, Richard Justice, John Blake, Tim Kurkjian and, well, the rest of you know who you are. Thanks to the PR staffs of the White Sox and the Houston Astros, especially Bob Beghtol, Pat O'Connell, Jimmy Stanton, Lisa Ramsberger and Katie Kirby, for doing a great job during the 2005 postseason, as always.

And finally thanks to some of the others who played a bigger role than they know in helping me decide to write this book: Shari Wenk, Laura Giancola, Gene Wojciechowski, T.J. "Punchy" Quinn, Chris Devane, Rob Slesinger and, once again, the most enthusiastic man in show business, Dan McGrath.

Hitting Kelvim Escobar in the backside with a baseball is no mean feat. His rear end is almost as big as your average heliport. No wonder the Los Angeles Angels reliever uses
it as knights once used shields.

When A.J. Pierzynski hit a wicked one-hopper back to him,
Escobar twisted in front of the mound and put his massive ca-
boose in the way of the baseball. It dropped off his rear end and
rolled only a few feet away, making Pierzynski a dead duck.

As sure as the Chicago White Sox had thrown a World Series since they had last won one, Escobar was going to toss
the ball to Darin Erstad, and the White Sox's half of the eighth
inning would be over, the score still tied 3-3. But, no, this time
Escobar had another idea. He was going to do it all himself.
He didn't need no stinking first baseman.

Escobar, who is charitably listed at 230 pounds on a 6-foot-
1-inch frame, lumbered toward the first-base line, where Pierzynski was motoring toward the bag. Escobar was in position
to tag Pierzynski, no problem.

But there was a problem.

Escobar had picked up the baseball with his bare hand. As he ran toward the line, he pounded the ball into the palm of his glove but then pulled it out, still cradled in his massive fingers. He didn't want to collide with Pierzynski, so he took a little step to his right as Pierzynski ran past him. He tagged him with the glove, which was on his left hand, about a foot away from the ball, which dangled in the Southern California air in his right hand. That hand never touched Pierzynski.

The left hand didn't know what the right hand was doing.

Decade after long, disappointing decade, through the 1960s and into the '70s, '80s, '90s and beyond—and we don't even want to talk about 1919 and the misery that followed those dark days—that description had fit the White Sox, a franchise that sometimes seemed like such an afterthought it didn't even have its own curse.

Sure, the White Sox had gone 88 years since they had last won the World Series, two more than the Boston Red Sox had in 2004 when they captured the hearts of a nation—not to mention the ones in New England that had so often been broken—but they had no Curse of the Bambino to rally around. They didn't even have a Billy Goat Curse, the one that has followed their cross-town rivals since the 1945 World Series, when Cubs owner Philip K. Wrigley would not allow Sam Sianis' goat into Wrigley Field for Game 4 against the Detroit Tigers.

When the White Sox lost, they were just losers, nothing else. There was nothing lovable about them. And year after year, owner after owner, from the Old Roman, Charles Comiskey, to the widely vilified Jerry Reinsdorf, with Arthur Allyn and John Allyn and Bill Veeck in between, it seemed that when it came to running a baseball team, the left hand never knew what the right was doing.

But, hey, this time it was a good thing.

After Escobar tagged Pierzynski with his empty glove, umpire Randy Marsh called Pierzynski out, meaning Escobar didn't have to pay for walking Aaron Rowand with two outs after starting him out with two strikes.

Escobar and his teammates ran off the field toward the third-base dugout at Angel Stadium. But long before most of them got there, Ozzie Guillen, the firebrand who had played shortstop for the White Sox for 13 seasons and was now their manager, was on the field and in Marsh's face.

He had rocketed out of the dugout immediately after the call. Guillen was telling Marsh something that Escobar knew to be true—Pierzynski should be safe because he had been tagged with an empty glove, not one containing a ball.

"I knew I didn't tag him," Escobar would say later. "They got all the breaks in this series, but that could have been a break for us. I wasn't surprised."

Second-base umpire Jerry Crawford, who was the chief of the six-man crew of umpires, and home-plate ump Ed Rapuano quickly joined Marsh and Guillen. They huddled for a moment before waving him to first base.

The crowd of 44,712 roared, thinking the umpires were reaffirming the out at first base. But that wasn't it at all. They were saying Pierzynski was entitled to the base, that there were runners on first and second and two outs. That the Angels were going to have to come back out of the dugout onto the field, and Escobar was going to have to try once again to get the third out.

It's never a good thing to have to get the second out twice. The Angels had lived through one of the worst examples of that nightmare four days earlier in Chicago, when Pierzynski—according to Mark Whicker of the Orange County Register, he "comes up 11 percent of the time but is in the middle of the death scene 99 percent of the time"—had taken first base on Angels catcher Josh Paul's controversial dropped third strike and then watched the teammate running for him, Pablo Ozuna, steal second and score the winning run when Joe Crede smashed an Escobar pitch off the left-field wall at U.S. Cellular Field, the Sox's home park.

That stunning turn of events was so fresh that the Angels must have gotten goose flesh when the umpires put Pierzynski back on first base.

Angels manager Mike Scioscia wasn't going to risk an exact replay. This time he pulled Escobar and summoned Francisco Rodriguez, his closer, to face Crede.

Crede took the first pitch from Rodriguez for a ball, then the next for a strike. He swung and missed the next one but wouldn't go fishing for the next two, getting the count to 3-2. Not wanting a walk that would have loaded the bases, Rodriguez delivered a slider that lacked its usual bite. Crede went down and golfed it into center field, scoring Rowand to give the White Sox a 4-3 lead and take the last bit of air out of the Angels and their fans.

Back in Chicago, at trendy places like the ESPN Zone, at hard-core Sox haunts like Jimbo's on 33rd Street and at a few thousand taverns in between, celebrations were turning rowdy.

The White Sox were going to the World Series for the first time since 1959. The left hand did know what the right was doing. Both were raised in the air, all across the South Side, in the suburbs and even at a few resistance strongholds up north, in Cubs country.

◆

Seven postseason wins down: three against Boston, four against the Los Angeles Angels. Four more to go.

Four more to do what neither of Chicago's major-league teams had done since 1917, when Woodrow Wilson was in the White House: win the World Series. Guillen and his players were on one of the most amazing October runs in history.

You would have to go back to Cincinnati's Big Red Machine to find a team rolling through the postseason like these White Sox. But really there never had been one, as the Reds were a powerhouse team that was expected to dominate. The Sox were given the longest odds of the four American League teams when the playoffs began.

Yet before they were through, after first baseman Paul Konerko cradled the throw from Juan Uribe that defied the odds to arrive at first base before Houston's Orlando Palmeiro, they would match the best postseason record (11-1) since Johnny Bench, Joe Morgan, Tony Perez and their Cincinnati teammates swept the Philadelphia Phillies and New York Yankees to go 7-0 in 1976, some 19 years before the playoff field was expanded from four teams to eight.

The White Sox would outscore their opponents by 67-34 in the postseason, the biggest margin of any team ever. They earned this success with their talent, their sweat and their manager's daring, but they also got a lot of the good luck that had eluded them while struggling through a past filled with heartache.

Ozzie Guillen and his 25 players made history and, more important, they changed the baseball history of their city. This is their story.

Thrifty business

Operating on a shoestring for decades, Sox watch other teams win it all

If you were a White Sox general manager back in the day, you were multitasking before the expression had been invented.

Roland Hemond, the Sox GM from 1971 through '85, was in charge of a whole lot more than providing a 25-man roster for one of the most intriguing casts of managers known to man. In those years Hemond worked with Chuck Tanner, Paul Richards, Bob Lemon, Larry Doby, player-manager Don Kessinger and Tony La Russa, who was 34 when he was given his chance in 1979. Hemond also was in charge of Comiskey Park, a jewel at one time that was in irreversible decay, as well as elements of marketing, media relations, ticket sales and, on a given day, plumbing and groundskeeping.

A scene at Comiskey on a weekend in late August 1979 would seem out of place in the $4-billion industry that major-league baseball has become, but it was not that unusual at the time, especially not in Chicago.

Bill Veeck had twice come forward to rescue the White Sox franchise from ownership crises, first putting an end to fighting among the Comiskey family heirs in early 1959, when the team was coming off a second-place season and would wind up in the World Series, and again in 1975, when John Allyn wanted out and it appeared the team could wind up in Seattle.

Veeck was many things. A robber baron with bottomless pockets wasn't one of them.

Money was always an issue with Veeck, as it was with the White Sox owners who preceded him and those who would follow him. This was a working-class franchise without an O'Malley or a Steinbrenner, one that had to make a dollar before it could spend one. Consider it the legacy of Charles Comiskey, the Old Roman.

Comiskey had the vision to build Comiskey Park, which, when it opened in 1910, fit its billing as "the Baseball Palace of the World." But he ran his operation on a shoestring. The Sox often played in dirty uniforms as Comiskey saved on laundry bills. He gave his players only $3 a day in meal money, $1 less than the standard. He was notoriously tight-fisted in salary negotiations with his players, even stars like Buck Weaver, Joe Jackson, Lefty Williams and Ed Cicotte. He had promised players bonuses if they won the World Series in 1917 but delivered only a case of inexpensive champagne at the team party. His payback would come two years later, when a gambling syndicate got the ear of first baseman Chick Gandil and hatched a plot to have the Sox throw games in the 1919 World Series.

While it was the players who ultimately paid the price for baseball's most disgraceful chapter—eight players, including Jackson, Weaver and Cicotte, were banned for life by Commissioner Kenesaw Mountain Landis—the stain clung to the franchise, which stayed in the hands of the Comiskey family for almost 40 years after the Black Sox scandal.

Chicago had two major-league teams, sure, but never an

ownership group that would or could outspend rivals to build a championship club. The Cubs had the more stable ownership, with the Wrigley family running Chicago's National League team for 65 years before selling to the city's largest media group, Tribune Co., which owned WGN-TV and WGN Radio in addition to its newspaper. Fans could complain about the teams that were put on the field, but there was never a question about opening the door.

Those real-world realities of business were among the harsh facts of life for the White Sox, however.

So it was that Hemond found himself sweating a major financial crisis late in the 1979 season, which had been a lean one. Harry Chappas, a 5-foot-3-inch infielder, had made it onto the cover of Sports Illustrated in March but into only 26 games at shortstop. That was fewer than Kessinger, who served as player-manager until La Russa was promoted from Triple-A Iowa on Aug. 3, after a seven-game losing streak dropped the White Sox 14 games below .500.

Veeck, like every owner before and after him, understood the importance of maximizing revenues in the summer. Chicago's weather often limited crowds in the spring, and only the heartiest fans turned out to see the Sox play out the string in September. But there was a way to make money when the team was out of town: renting out the ballpark for concerts and other events.

The Beatles' visits to Comiskey Park in 1965 and '66 are still among the most talked-about concerts in the history of a city with a rich musical history. But Veeck didn't care if the acts were groundbreaking; he just needed them to be money-paying. In the summers of 1978 and '79, concerts called the Summer Jam series drew many more fans to Comiskey than the Sox did. The stage was generally set up at the edge of the infield, with fans allowed to sit or stand in the outfield grass, as well as the two decks of seating.

Rock bands had played at Comiskey while the White Sox, in their first month under La Russa, were off on a trip to Baltimore, Boston and Milwaukee.

Downpours, however, plagued the concerts. There was almost no grass left in the outfield, which more closely resembled a mud bog than a baseball field after the final loadout of the music series.

Downpours, however, plagued the concerts. There was almost no grass left in the outfield, which more closely resembled a mud bog than a baseball field after the final loadout of the music series.

Veeck, who had lost his right leg while serving with the Marines during World War II, was expecting good crowds for a weekend series against the Baltimore Orioles, who featured young hitting star Eddie Murray and were on their way to an AL pennant and the World Series. Hemond understood that this was a time when the most important thing was that the games be played, not how his team played in those games.

"When I went out on the field that afternoon, there was Bill in center field," Hemond said. "He had his shirt off, like he always did, and he was using a rake on the field. There were shovels, all kinds of tools all around the field. There was no grass on the field, none, not anywhere. It was just mud. Everywhere you looked there was mud. I went out there knowing we were in big trouble.

"Bill said to me, 'Roland, we've got to get the game in tonight. If we don't, I can't make the payroll.' He told me to go to the clubhouse and make sure none of the players came out on the field, to keep Tony [La Russa] and the players from seeing it for as long as I could. So I head back toward the dugout. When I looked back, I saw Bill's wooden leg was sinking into the mud. He was getting shorter and shorter, and I had to go back out there and help him get out of that hole. That's so funny now, thinking about it. But at the time I'm thinking I can't laugh, I can't even smile, because he'll kill me."

An owner stuck in the mud. What a fitting analogy for the White Sox franchise.

◆

As dire as the straits in which Veeck and Hemond found themselves during the late 1970s, there would come a time a couple of decades later when some would look back on those as the good old days for Chicago baseball.

The White Sox, at least, would provide periodic excitement for their fans. And as bad as things tended to be for them, they were often worse on the other side of town.

After the big tease of 1969, the Cubs wasted the opportunity they were given by the confluence of Ernie Banks, Billy Williams, Ron Santo and Ferguson Jenkins under manager Leo Durocher. Those teams had six consecutive winning seasons from 1967–1972, but there wouldn't be another one at Clark and Addison Streets until 1984.

Phil Wrigley, king of the gum empire, and later William Wrigley, his son, didn't seem interested in competing with Walter O'Malley, August Busch, John Galbreath and other NL owners. But a lot can change in 20 years.

Or nothing at all.

When Tribune Co. purchased 81 percent of the Cubs from Wrigley in the summer of 1981, Mike North made a living out of a hot dog cart. He worked ballgames in the summer, always rooting for his home team.

Like many of his friends, the opinionated vendor was excited when one of Chicago's most powerful companies put its

financial might behind a franchise that had become synony-
mous with losing.

"We had been through so many years of the Wrigleys," said
North, who finagled his way onto the air at WSCR Radio and
has become the city's top sports-talker. "With the Wrigleys
gone, we thought they would win."

That widely held assumption was reinforced when the
Cubs got within three innings of a pennant in '84, the third
season of Tribune Co. control. Between them, though, the
Jerry Reinsdorf and Tribune Co. ownership groups would go
a combined 47 seasons without getting to the World Series,
let alone winning one.

Between them, the two franchises had a collective losing
streak of 183 seasons through 2004: 96 for the Cubs, who last
won the World Series in 1908, and 87 for the Sox, who hadn't
won since Pants Rowland's team beat the New York Giants in
the 1917 Series.

Through 2004, 45 years had passed since the last World Series appearance by a Chicago team, that by the Go-Go White
Sox in 1959. In the intervening years, when America's sweet-
hearts went from Ingrid Bergman and Olivia de Havilland to
Julia Roberts and Angelina Jolie, 22 different franchises went
to the Series, including eight that didn't exist in 1959 and two
others that had moved between '59 and their World Series
appearances.

The Red Sox and the so-called Curse of the Bambino? Sorry, Boston had been to the World Series in 1967, '75 and '86
and to the league championship series in four other seasons
before winning it all in 2004. Chicago fans could only wish for
that kind of drought.

And what about all those expansion teams that swept in
and did what the White Sox and Cubs couldn't? The Toronto

Blue Jays won back-to-back World Series in 1992 and '93. The Mets, supposedly New York's laughable franchise, won the World Series in 1969, only their eighth season in business, and again in '86. They lost the Series in '73 and 2000.

Most galling of all for Chicago fans was the instant success of the Florida Marlins and Arizona Diamondbacks. Buying up proven free agents with a reckless abandon that was unimaginable for fans of the Sox and Cubs, the Diamondbacks beat the Yankees in 2001, their fourth year of operation. Their ownership group was headed by Jerry Colangelo, a Chicago Heights native. The long-suffering Arizona fans had endured only one losing season, the very first.

Then there were the Florida Marlins, who created the short-sighted model Colangelo followed to give his fans instant gratification. The Marlins won in 1997, only their fifth season, stealing Game 7 from the long-suffering Cleveland Indians. In 2003, when the Marlins used an eight-run eighth inning to beat Mark Prior and the Cubs in Game 6 of the National League Championship Series, there were 5-year-olds in Ft. Lauderdale who had never seen the Fighting Fish win in their lifetimes.

Imagine the inestimable disgust of Chicago fans watching the World Series in 1997, '01 and '03. Hard-core fans on both sides of town had given the Reinsdorf group and Tribune Co. their hearts, hoping, in some cases praying, that the end of their one-sided love affair would finally come to an end. Yet through 2004, when the Sox finished second for the seventh time in the last nine years and the Cubs stumbled down the stretch to miss a chance at back-to-back postseason appearances, the civic losing streak stretched to a combined 183 years.

"I'm disappointed we couldn't have won more," former Tribune Co. Chief Executive Officer John Madigan said. "We have the ingredients to win [the World Series]. I'm disappointed that we haven't."

Reinsdorf, partner Eddie Einhorn and their group of investors purchased the Sox from Veeck before the 1981 season. They got the team on the rebound, after American League owners had rejected Edward J. DeBartolo, paying the same $20 million price DeBartolo had agreed to.

At one point, when it looked as if the DeBartolo deal might fly, then-Sox President Andrew McKenna told Reinsdorf that Chicago's other team might soon become available. He knew Reinsdorf had grown up following his hometown Brooklyn Dodgers before attending Northwestern University Law School. He was a National League man, and he lived in NL territory. In those days, if Reinsdorf wanted to take in a baseball game, he usually did so at Wrigley Field.

So McKenna wondered if Reinsdorf would be interested in the Cubs. "I said to Jerry, 'You know, there's another team in town,' " McKenna said. "I had no knowledge at the time. I said that half in jest, not expecting anything could happen."

Less than six months after Reinsdorf's purchase of the Sox closed, control of the Cubs passed from the landmark building on the west side of North Michigan Avenue to the tower across the street. Estate taxes and the advent of baseball's free-agency era contributed to William Wrigley's decision to sell the ballclub he had inherited from his father, Phil. Tribune Co. paid $20.5 million.

"The afternoon the Cubs sale was announced, I got a call from Jerry," McKenna said. "He said, 'You were right.'."

McKenna now says there was no way Reinsdorf could have wound up with the Cubs. Published reports indicate that Reinsdorf owns only 12 percent of the Sox, which means he would have put in no more than $2.4 million when he assembled his investment group.

"The Wrigleys were very private people," McKenna said. "If they were going to sell, they would only sell to somebody who could put down a check for the entire team."

Both purchases have proved to be wise investments. In April 2005, Forbes magazine estimated the Cubs' value at $398 million, the sixth highest figure in baseball behind the Yankees, Red Sox, Mets, Dodgers and Seattle Mariners. The Sox, who had slipped from 16th in 2002 to 20th, were estimated to be worth $262 million.

When Reinsdorf and Tribune Co. joined the major-league fraternity, it consisted of 26 teams. The only other franchises not to win a pennant between 1981 and 2004 were Houston, Montreal, Pittsburgh, Seattle and Texas, and each of those franchises has had at least one ownership change in the last two decades.

Thus it could be argued that none of baseball's ownership groups had been as unsuccessful for as long as the two in Chicago.

Before the Cubs beat Atlanta in the first round of the 2003 playoffs, they and the White Sox had somehow combined to lose their last 14 postseason series, another mark of futility that caused Chicagoans to lose their lunch when New Englanders moaned about the Curse of the Bambino.

◆

Other than their proximity to Red Line "L" stops about 70 blocks apart, there is no common thread to the ownership groups behind the Cubs and White Sox.

Madigan says the Cubs have been run "like any of our subsidiaries." That puts them on the same level as the television stations and newspapers in a media conglomerate that has annual revenues in excess of $5 billion. The team's baseball executives currently report to Tribune Co. general counsel

Crane Kenney, whose existence is barely documented in the team's media guide. Dennis FitzSimons, Madigan, Don Grenesko, Stanton Cook and Jim Dowdle preceded Kenney in the role of overseer of the Cubs.

North calls it a faceless ownership. "The Tribune Co. becomes like Oz, like the wizard of Oz," he said. "They never knew there was really a man behind it."

Reinsdorf, on the other hand, had always been the face of his ownership group, the man clearly responsible for all that is right or wrong with the White Sox. He is a fist-pounding, cigar-smoking overachiever who sometimes has been longer on passion than resources. His appetite for success hadn't been sated by the six NBA titles that his Bulls won behind Michael Jordan. He wanted to somehow wring one trip to the World Series out of the Sox before selling them or turning them over to his four children.

"Ninety-five percent [of the investors] want to sell, but he doesn't want to sell," Jimmy Piersall, the former big-league outfielder and broadcaster, said in 2002. "He wants to stay in the limelight."

Reinsdorf picks and chooses his times to be interviewed. When the Tribune devoted its 2003 baseball preview section to a comprehensive examination of Chicago's two ownership groups, he was absolutely delightful company for a Tribune reporter at a Scottsdale, Ariz., restaurant. His passion for the sport was as evident as the rising price of beef and fine wine, and his encyclopedic knowledge of baseball's history was on full display.

But Reinsdorf had done what he often does: set ground rules for the meeting. He would not be quoted in any article. He felt he had been burned by reporters more than once, and in the process he had gone from being one of baseball's most accessible owners to one of its barely visible men.

That always changes when a team is winning, of course. At times like those Reinsdorf can't help himself. But on a daily basis, pity the poor reporter who needs a quote.

◆

While neither franchise had done enough winning before 2005, Reinsdorf and Tribune Co. had been responsible stewards for Chicago's two-team tradition, which dates to the founding of the American League in 1900. Reinsdorf preserved that heritage by putting it to its biggest test.

After concluding there was no way to make a go of it in the original Comiskey Park, Reinsdorf and Einhorn negotiated both a lease and a lucrative television package in St. Petersburg, Fla., in 1988. By demonstrating that relocation was more than a theoretical option, they squeezed a $137 million stadium out of the Illinois Legislature. It binds the White Sox to the South Side until 2010.

There's no one reason why Reinsdorf and Tribune Co. were so slow translating their success in other ventures into success in baseball. But the one event probably most responsible for continuing the teams' pattern of consistently coming up short is Tribune Co.'s purchase of the Cubs.

In 24 seasons under Tribune ownership, the Cubs have had winning records only eight times. The only franchise to perform as poorly in the regular season over that span is the Milwaukee Brewers, and they at least reached the World Series once, even if it was back in 1982.

Yet the business acumen of Tribune Co., combined with its ownership of Chicago's largest television and radio stations and newspaper, has played a major role in turning the city into a Cubs town. Along with a steady rise in player salaries, which have increased almost 500 percent in the last 20 years, that trend makes Reinsdorf's job more difficult with each passing year.

The balance of power between Chicago's two franchises was demonstrated most clearly in 2000. The Sox were the winningest team in the American League, claiming a Central Division championship with 95 victories, while the Cubs matched Philadelphia for most losses in the majors. Yet the Cubs drew almost 800,000 more fans to Wrigley Field—"their ivy-covered burial ground," in the words of the late Chicago songwriter Steve Goodman—than the Sox did to the new Comiskey.

It wasn't always like that. "I remember when the upper deck at Wrigley was closed for weekday games in the '60s and '70s," North said. "A foul ball would go up there and an Andy Frain usher would walk over and pick it up. You'll never see that again."

In 55 of the 65 seasons of Wrigley family ownership of the Cubs, the Chicago team with the better record also had better attendance. In 2005, the Cubs outdrew the White Sox for the 13th year in a row even though the Sox had the better record in eight of those seasons.

The competition between the franchises had become so lopsided that some denied it even existed.

"I don't believe the Cubs are our competition," Einhorn said in 2002. "We compete against ourselves."

Using the unexpected NL East title in 1984 as a catalyst, and undoubtedly helped by the gentrification of Wrigleyville and its trademark brownstones, Tribune Co. has done a masterful job in marketing losing teams. Vice President John McDonough and his staff have sold everything from sunshine to Sammy Sosa, and there has never been a shortage of customers buying.

Between 1997 and 2005, the price of Wrigley Field's bleacher seats increased from \$12 to \$34, but those seats have been in such demand the club was working to add almost 2,000 more of them for the 2006 season. The Cubs' average season attendance has climbed from 1.37 million in the last five years of the Wrigley ownership to more than 3 million per season in 2003-05.

Eight miles to the south, Reinsdorf watched the bottom drop out of his attendance in the second half of the 1990s. At times he has wondered if the fans would ever come back.

The new Comiskey Park opened with the Sox fielding strong teams, and fans came out to see them. In 1983 the Sox became the first Chicago team to draw 2 million fans, and they set a city record with their attendance of 2,934,154 in 1991.

That year they combined with the Cubs to draw about 5.25 million fans. The city's total had dipped to 4.55 million by 2001, with the White Sox responsible for the decline.

Reinsdorf had many factors to blame: The stadium site, fans' disaffection for the bland design of the new Comiskey, traffic and lingering resentment over Reinsdorf's role in the ill-timed strike of 1994, which probably cost the Sox their best shot at reaching the World Series since 1959. But underneath it all is a feeling that the club can't catch a break with the media, which Reinsdorf and many hard-core White Sox fans believe is biased in favor of the Cubs.

For years, the Sox's public relations staff counted the front-page headlines and column inches devoted in Chicago's newspapers (particularly the Tribune) to the city's two teams. While the editorial departments of the Tribune and WGN television and radio fiercely defend their autonomy, the corporate relationship with the Cubs is a conflict.

It's understandable that Reinsdorf feels slighted. "The Encyclopedia of Major League Baseball Teams" explained his dilemma after Tribune Co. purchased the Cubs:

"Not only had the media giant injected new money into the NL club, but it used its newsstand and radio-television broadcasting dominance to devote about 10 words about the Cubs for every one spent on the White Sox."

Making matters worse, Reinsdorf became a whipping boy for many Chicago fans. At times he has been seen only as the guy who broke up the six-time champion Bulls, not the one who helped build them. He has been booed loudly when introduced at sporting events, even celebrations like the Bulls' trophy presentations.

North is among those who believe the Chairman gets a bad rap. "I like Jerry Reinsdorf," North said. "I believe he wants to win more than the Tribune Co. wants to win. He wants to win it all."

Winning often relates directly to revenue in the modern era. The Sox's popularity, and ultimately their resources, were affected by two mistakes Reinsdorf and Einhorn made in their early years with the club.

After their first season in charge, they sacked Harry Caray's partner, Piersall, and prompted Caray to resign when they announced their intention to create their own pay-cable TV network and charge for telecasts that been on free TV for as long as most Chicago fans could remember.

Caray's departure might not have been so devastating had Tribune Co. not pounced on him for the Cubs. "Harry was one of the few announcers, him and Vin Scully, who drew fans to the ballpark," Piersall said.

For most of his career, Caray was brutally critical of the shortcomings of players on the teams he worked for. But Tribune Co. persuaded Caray to change his approach. He became such a cheerleader that he even invented a song for catcher Jody Davis, anointing him, "Jody, Jody Davis, catcher without a peer."

Caray and the Cubs were broadcast around America when WGN joined Atlanta's WTBS in achieving superstation status on cable, which was partly why Tribune Co. sought to buy the team. The Sox had been on WGN, too, but began to travel all around the dial after Einhorn, Reinsdorf and Fred Eychaner created Sportsvision, available only to fans who sprung for a converter box and subscription fees.

Einhorn's plan flopped. Reinsdorf crawled back to WGN in the late '80s, shortly after he, as chairman of Major League Baseball's ownership committee, had rejected Edward Gaylord's attempt to purchase the Texas Rangers because a TV station he owned (the Nashville Network) was deemed to have the potential to become a superstation. According to a highly placed source, Reinsdorf went back to the Tribune-owned WGN because "they were the only station that would put the Sox on the air."

In putting together a team, Reinsdorf has always spent what he took in from his fans. He says privately that he and his investors have basically broken even on a cash-flow basis, although it hasn't been easy for him, just as it wasn't for Veeck and the others before him.

When Marge Schott owned the Cincinnati Reds, she once asked why the team paid so many scouts since "all they do is watch games." But Reinsdorf always knew it was no accident that the beloved Brooklyn Dodgers of his youth were blessed with stars like Duke Snider, Roy Campanella, Pee Wee Reese and Gil Hodges.

His commitment to scouting and player development has been as consistent as it is wise. At the same time he was downsizing the major-league payroll by shedding Robin Ventura, who was both productive and popular, and the productive

Albert Belle, Reinsdorf approved more than $6 million in signing bonuses to stockpile young pitchers from the 1999 draft.

When longtime scouting director Duane Shaffer told him Stanford quarterback Joe Borchard could develop into a Mark McGwire-caliber power hitter, he signed off on a bonus of $5.3 million, which is still the biggest in draft history.

Reinsdorf might be the one major-league owner who would rather befriend a Double-A pitching coach than a young star on the rise. Forced to answer to his investors, he seems to battle players over every penny—Mark Buehrle, for instance, received only an $85,000 raise after he won 16 games and finished fourth in the AL in earned-run average in 2001.

Not many veteran players have left Reinsdorf's teams on good terms. He stayed in his Comiskey Park box the day the Sox retired Carlton Fisk's number. From Jack McDowell to Ventura, Ozzie Guillen to Roberto Hernandez, All-Star players have left Chicago disillusioned, if not angry.

"If I had one wish, it would be for a little more honesty," said Doug Rader, who managed in 1986 and briefly returned as a coach in '97. "If you're not going to be honest, you lose the faith of the players, the general public, everybody."

Rader was among those who were appalled when Reinsdorf cashed in the 1997 season by unloading veteran players with the Sox only 3 ½ games out of first place on July 31—the infamous "White Flag" trade. But even with the occasional capitulation, Reinsdorf has fielded winning teams in 15 of his 25 seasons through 2005.

His commitment to the minor leagues, along with shrewd management by Hemond in the early '80s, Ron Schueler in the '90s and Ken Williams in the 2000s, has helped produce an overall winning percentage of .518, third in the American League for that period. Only the Yankees and Red Sox won more games in those 25 years.

Reinsdorf's signing of Fisk and purchase of Greg Luzinski gave him and Einhorn some early credibility, as did an AL West title under La Russa in 1983, the "Winning Ugly" team. He has splurged on free agents when he thought they would help him win and bring fans to the ballpark, most notably the five-year, $55-million deal for Belle, but adjusted quickly when things didn't click.

◆

While Wrigley Field was gaining popularity as it aged, riding the crest of a retro-ballpark craze that began when Baltimore's Camden Yards opened in 1992, the new Comiskey was panned for having minimal appeal when the Sox moved into it in 1991. If Reinsdorf had had his wish, the park would have been built in the western suburbs, not across the street from the original Comiskey and across an expressway from public housing projects. He had purchased land in Addison, but a stadium measure there failed by a narrow margin. Then-Mayor Harold Washington insisted that the team remain at 35th and Shields if it was to play in a publicly financed ballpark.

"If the new ballpark had been built in Addison, they'd be drawing 30,000 a game," North says. "They would draw 3 million a year."

While Reinsdorf may have preferred to follow Chicago's growth to the northwest, he has done the right thing on the South Side. The Sox have a reputation for generosity in the community, building fields and giving away gloves worth more than the price of a ticket. Reinsdorf has put his beliefs on minority hiring into action, making the Sox the first team ever with an African-American manager (Jerry Manuel) and general manager (Williams). He hired Guillen to replace Manuel after 2003, which was Manuel's sixth with the Sox.

Tribune Co. inherited a good thing in Wrigley Field, and recognized it.

With the Wrigleys fielding mostly non-competitive teams after World War II, the late Jack Brickhouse used the ballpark as a drawing card. He encouraged fans to come spend their afternoons at the ballpark at Clark and Addison.

"Whoever came up with the 'friendly confines of beautiful Wrigley Field,' that was just a masterstroke," Hemond acknowledged. "Jack Brickhouse kept saying it, and people started believing it."

In terms of creature comfort, there's no comparison between the new Comiskey—known as U.S. Cellular Field since 2003—and Wrigley Field. But the fans and reporters who moan ad nauseam because Comiskey isn't a modern shrine like Camden Yards seldom say a peep about the claustrophobic concourses or Stone Age bathrooms at Wrigley.

"When I go to Wrigley, I see cramped concourses, aging seats and some ivy in front of a brick wall, which in itself is dangerous," Hemond said. "The batting tunnel, the clubhouses, everything is outdated. But people seem to love it."

The original Comiskey Park, built four years before Wrigley, was in such disrepair before Reinsdorf bought the team that Hemond recalls how Veeck enlisted children from nearby schools to paint murals, which he hung to hide cracks in the stadium walls.

Tribune Co., after purchasing the Cubs, vowed not to let Wrigley fall into the same condition. It pours money into maintenance every winter and has seriously entertained thoughts of moving only once, before it received approval to add the lights that went up in 1988.

"I think we have the finest ballpark for watching baseball," Madigan said.

Wrigley is only one of the advantages Tribune Co. inherited. Madigan credits P.K. Wrigley for understanding how television can help sell any product.

"Philip Wrigley was a genius at marketing gum and a genius at marketing baseball," Madigan said. "He made the decision to put all the games on television, so fans all over the Midwest could watch his team. Cable has allowed us to make it accessible for even more people. That has served us well."

From a balance-of-power standpoint, it's too bad the Sox weren't the first baseball team to give away Beanie Babies. The Cubs were. The marketing approach developed by John McDonough is both inventive and relentless, no doubt helped by advertising space and time in Tribune-owned properties.

"John has done many things to enhance our image," Madigan said. "We've had some exciting players. That's also helped us."

Winning never hurts either. But Tribune Co. has found that the won-lost record is not controlled as reliably as the balance sheet of its other subsidiaries.

Because fans come to Wrigley Field whether the Cubs win or not, it's natural to question the team's commitment to winning. "They're not a baseball team," agent Barry Axelrod complained after the Cubs opted not to re-sign first baseman Mark Grace. "They're a tourist attraction."

Pat Gillick has been the architect of playoff teams in Toronto, Baltimore and Seattle. He took his name out of the running for a job as the Cubs' general manager in 1987 after interviewing with the Tribune's Madigan and Grenesko.

"I didn't think the Cubs wanted to win," Gillick said. "That's part of the marketing plan. Some of the mystique of the Cubs is ineptitude. If they win, there might be an expectation level to win again."

Maddening for fans is Tribune Co.'s refusal to unleash its full resources to get the Cubs into the World Series. After all, this is a media giant that swallowed the Times Mirror chain for $8 billion in 2000. But only once has the Tribune engaged in a bidding war for an elite free agent, and its $100-million offer to Mike Hampton was rejected.

"When I look at George Steinbrenner, he's a fan, and I believe he'll do anything in the world to win," North said. "I believe the Tribune Co. wants to win, but they don't want to win at any cost."

After hiring Dusty Baker away from San Francisco following the 2002 World Series, Tribune Co. increased the payroll. It was at $103 million in 2005, which ranked fourth in the majors.

But some still complain that the Cubs aren't serious about winning.

"People are going to sing that tune even if our payroll is $148 million," Cubs President Andy MacPhail said. "It will never be enough."

Corporate interference is baseball's ageless battle between church and state.

Tribune Co. initially recognized the need for management expertise specific to baseball. McKenna, the Cubs' first president under Tribune Co., hired Philadelphia Phillies executive Dallas Green within four months of the purchase.

Green was given full control of the baseball operation. He and assistant Gordon Goldsberry overhauled the organization, putting it on sound footing at the major- and minor-league levels. But Green and manager Jim Frey were unable to follow up on their early success, largely because of injuries that decimated the pitching staff that had won the East title in 1984.

Madigan fired Green after the 1987 season, replacing him as GM with Frey, who had no experience in that position. He bypassed such candidates as Hemond and Dave Dombrowski, then a rising young executive who since has run teams in Montreal, Florida and Detroit.

According to Piersall, who worked in the Cubs' organization as a coach and instructor, losing Green and Goldsberry was the worst mistake Tribune Co. has made with the Cubs. Grace, who spent 13 seasons in Chicago before helping Arizona win the 2001 World Series, concurs.

Before naming Frey, Madigan assumed the title of Cubs chairman and restructured the team's chain of command to include Grenesko, who was Tribune Co.'s executive vice president. Madigan also told reporters he would take a more active role.

Green believes this involvement set the organization back for a decade. "I can tell you in no uncertain terms that they have very little feel for the game of baseball," Green said. "They have a lack of respect for people in baseball. That translates into bad decisions. It started with firing me and hiring Jim Frey."

Goldsberry's drafts brought the Cubs such future stars as Shawon Dunston, Greg Maddux, Rafael Palmeiro and Grace. But it would be a decade before talent would flow again. The organization became predictably impatient, a trend that began with Green going through six managers (including three interim managers) during his six years in Chicago.

Following Green, Tribune Co. tried three general managers and six managers in a seven-year period. The Cubs bottled lightning in 1989, winning an East title behind hunch-playing manager Don Zimmer, but that would be one of only two winning seasons in a stretch of 13 years.

"There were times they made mistakes," Grace said. "They let Larry Himes [the GM in 1992-94] completely screw the organization up. That was tough to recover from."

The low point in this chaotic period came when Himes failed to stop then-Cubs Chairman Cook from playing hardball with Maddux and his agent, Scott Boras. Maddux never should have reached free agency, but management essentially dared him, pulling a five-year, $25-million offer off the table at one point. Maddux, a certain Hall of Famer, left Chicago for Atlanta after the first of his four consecutive Cy Young seasons, raising questions about the Cubs' operational savvy.

"I don't want to go back and rehash it year by year, era by era," Madigan said when asked about Maddux's defection. "Over time, any company has changes, different needs, different times. We always tried to have the best people there we could, like we do in all our operations. If help is needed, the corporate office provides help. The needs ebb and flow."

MacPhail was bred on baseball. His father and his grandfather are in the Hall of Fame as executives. He helped Minnesota win two World Series as a general manager before taking over the Cubs.

With MacPhail in charge, Tribune Co. management receded into the background, which was no accident. Dowdle said his goal in hiring MacPhail in September 1994 was "to cut the cord between the Tower and Wrigley Field."

Under MacPhail, the Cubs finally moved into the modern era in scouting and player development, getting there long after the White Sox had established themselves. Reinsdorf understood that it's cheaper to grow talented players than it is to sign them after they have established themselves elsewhere.

In 2003, the most unlikely thing happened: The Cubs and Sox both contended into September.

It was the Cubs who captured the moment. They went 19-8 to steal the National League Central and then bounced the Braves in a five-game first-round series, with Kerry Wood winning twice. They took three of the first four championship series games from the Florida Marlins to get close enough to the World Series to almost touch the bunting but dropped Game 5 in Florida to Josh Beckett, which didn't seem like a bad thing at the time. It meant they could wrap up the pennant at Wrigley Field.

Mark Prior took a 3-0 lead to the mound with him in the eighth inning. The entire city of Chicago, save for Sox territory—more of an edgy, often angry, alienated republic than a traditional nation—was ready to break away from its moorings and go into orbit. Eight runs and an infamous foul ball later, the Marlins had tied the series and forced Game 7.

It's fair to say the mood at Wrigley was a little bit grim the next afternoon. But not for Ozzie Guillen, who served as third-base coach for Marlins manager Jack McKeon.

During batting practice, he stood near the on-deck circle, hitting ground balls and conversing, in his inimitable style, with some Cubs fans nearby.

"You scared?" Guillen asked. "You should be scared. You should have beaten us last night. Now we're going to beat you today. You had your chance. You blew it. Too bad. Too bad."

Guillen would stop hitting grounders with the fungo bat only to shake his head or bring his hands up around his neck, as if he was choking himself. "You guys should be scared," he said. "We've got a good team too. We're better than your team. You guys scared? You should be scared."

Guillen wasn't kidding. The baseball gods would grant no forgiveness for a team allowing eight runs in the eighth inning of an NLCS game. And when the Sox played the Cubs in interleague games in 2004, some fans showed up wearing Sox jerseys with the name "Bartman" across the back and "03" as the number.

Ozzie's wild ride

Guillen's 13 seasons with Sox feature ups, downs and a bitter farewell

Discovered by future Chicago Bulls general manager Jerry Krause while playing shortstop for Triple-A Las Vegas in 1984, Oswaldo Jose Barrios Guillen came to Chicago for the ride of his life.

A skinny Venezuelan with a smile as bright as daybreak over Siesta Key and a laugh infectious enough to put the Centers for Disease Control on alert, Guillen would be in the middle of the White Sox infield for 13 seasons, beginning with a Rookie of the Year performance in 1985.

Guillen caught Krause's eye with his instincts as much as his flair for making big plays. "He's as smart a young player as I've seen," Krause remembers writing in his report.

Guillen played with a passion that was evident from the scout's seats as well as the dugout. He didn't always seem to be the hardest worker, unless you could work and talk at the same time, but he was always in the right spot at the right time. He had a knack for making plays.

"There was a question about his arm," Krause said. "But I

always noticed that he threw out the fast guys by a step, and the slow guys by a step. He wasn't going to waste that arm. He was just so bright."

John Kruk, a teammate in the San Diego organization, says Guillen taught him more about playing baseball than the men the Padres were paying to be instructors.

"He's one of the smartest players I've ever been around," Kruk said. "When we were in A-ball together, he taught us all how to play."

◆

Guillen was acquired in a seven-player trade with San Diego that basically boiled down to Guillen for LaMarr Hoyt, an overweight Cy Young winner in 1983 whose off-the-field baggage would contribute to his pitching in his last big-league game in 1986, at age 31.

Jerome Holtzman, Chicago's dean of baseball writers, panned the deal when it was made, writing that the Sox were trying to dump Hoyt's $900,000 salary. He said the consensus from scouts was that Guillen was "a shortstop with some but certainly not overwhelming promise."

Guillen immediately dispelled the doubts. He hit .273 while acting like anything but a 21-year-old in his rookie season. He was famous for his trips to the mound to talk to pitchers, even visiting Tom Seaver when the future Hall of Famer was en route to his 300th win.

"Seaver got a kick out of that," then-Sox general manager Roland Hemond recalled. "Here's this kid trying to take charge of a future Hall of Famer like he was a veteran."

Guillen played with dozens of more gifted athletes and hitters during his time with the White Sox, but he was in the middle of everything. He might have had the greatest peripheral vision in the history of eyesight. He could be engaged in a conversation in one corner of the clubhouse, but he had a way of knowing exactly what was happening with every one of his teammates. He never missed a chance to get in a jab or the last word.

A Gold Glove winner in 1990, when he was 26, Guillen was never the same after destroying his right knee in an outfield collision with Tim Raines in 1992. He didn't have the same range or tremendous lateral movement. But he pushed himself hard, helped along by trainer Herm Schneider, and was back at shortstop for 134 games the following season, increasing his stature in the eyes of fans, teammates and Chairman Jerry Reinsdorf. The Sox won the American League West that year, 1993, and appeared on their way back to the playoffs in '94 before a player strike ended the season on Aug. 12.

For Guillen, it was downhill from there. The Sox weren't the same when major-leaguers returned in 1995, starting the season late because of the ongoing labor war. The '96 season was a continuation of the same disappointment, with the Sox once again getting pounded by the Cleveland Indians, who had somehow shot past them during the two strike-shortened seasons.

But Reinsdorf shocked everyone—his fans, his players, his fellow owners—with his attempt to jump-start the team in '97. He gave Albert Belle, a notoriously anti-social slugger who was the centerpiece of the Indians' lineup, a five-year, $55-million contract. Belle's personality had cost him the MVP award in 1995, but Reinsdorf figured the pairing of Belle with two-time MVP Frank Thomas would surely get the Sox back in the playoffs, either as a division champ or as a wild card. After all, they had combined for 88 home runs and 282 RBIs the previous season, Belle leading the league with 148 and Thomas seventh with 134. Between them they had drawn 41 intentional walks. That's respect.

In spring training, a playoff spot seemed almost a fait accompli for this collection of talent. Some players even talked about a 100-win season.

But, alas, this being Chicago baseball, there was a flaw in the plan. Two flaws, really. The Sox didn't have nearly as much pitching as the Indians, and the guy making the decisions about the pitching was Terry Bevington, who somehow had the trust of Ron Schueler, then the general manager, even though he was ill-equipped to handle the demands that came with being a manager.

Bevington seemed to have proved himself as a minor-league manager but was badly out of place under bright lights. He carried himself with an odd, eccentric, half-crazed manner, almost like the Billy Bob Thornton character in "Sling Blade."

T.J. Quinn, an investigative reporter for the New York Daily News, covered the mid-1990s White Sox for the Daily Southtown. He still makes Robin Ventura and others fall down laughing with his character "Sling Bev," in which he impersonates Thornton doing lines from Bevington, who had as much business being near a major-league team intent on winning as Roseanne Barr did singing the national anthem.

Game handling? Bevington once signaled to the bullpen for a relief pitcher even though he didn't have one warming up.

Running a clubhouse? Bevington decided it would help "unite" his team if he started riding the players' bus from the ballpark to the airport rather than the one carrying coaches and other members of the traveling party. Every player except one then switched to the so-called staff bus, leaving the politically correct Thomas and a red-faced, mad-as-hell Bevington riding alone on a bus from Kauffman Stadium to the airport in Kansas City, no short commute.

People skills? In his last conversation with longtime Chicago

Sun-Times baseball reporter Joe Goddard, who had stopped by to wish the fired manager the best, Bevington told the mild-mannered Goddard he hoped he'd "die a slow death."

This was the man who would be central to Guillen's life in 1997, a year that would be the low point of his career.

Guillen cried on the night in spring training when Ventura, who had played third base beside him for seven years, broke his ankle in a horrific slide at home plate in Sarasota, Fla. It was a harbinger of bad times.

The year would feature Guillen's worst night in the big leagues: July 29, 1997. He learned that Harold Baines, a close friend since Guillen had arrived in Chicago, had been traded. Then he dropped a most routine infield popup, the kind he had caught 10,000 times in his life. Finally, he took out his frustration and embarrassment on the clubhouse television, shattering the screen with his bat.

It was described as the best hit of the night.

Guillen characteristically joked about it the next day, but he would rather no one had known about the outburst.

◆

In addition to his choice of managers, Schueler had probably sentenced the White Sox to runner-up status with an all-time bad choice in the free-agent market.

Roger Clemens, cut loose by the Boston Red Sox after a 10-13 season, was most interested in returning to his native Texas, but neither his hometown Houston Astros nor the Texas Rangers made a strong pitch. He was open-minded beyond that, and his agents, Alan and Randy Hendricks, let it be known that Chicago appealed to him as a place to bring his family.

But Schueler wasn't buying. The Sox allowed Clemens to go to the Toronto Blue Jays, who gave him a deal worth about $31 million over four years. The Sox instead signed Jaime Navarro, giving him $20 million for four years even though he had won more than 15 games only once in his career. Schueler justified the signing by saying Clemens was more of a risk than Navarro.

Oops.

While Schueler took the responsibility for the decision, it's possible that the fault was with Reinsdorf's budget, which provided enough for Navarro but not Clemens. Either way, the Sox were screwed.

Clemens, a three-time Cy Young winner at the time, would win four more Cy Young Awards in the next eight seasons, including one that season. Navarro would go 25-43 over three seasons with the Sox, and they'd win a division title in 2000 largely because they unloaded him, getting Jose Valentin and Cal Eldred from Milwaukee.

Clemens wasted no time showing the Sox what they were missing. He beat them in the second game of the year in Toronto, throwing a complete-game six-hitter, and then won at the new Comiskey on April 9, this time with $5\frac{2}{3}$ scoreless innings. Those losses helped get the Belle-Thomas Sox off to a 9-18 start, which pretty much finished them before they started.

As the season went on, Schueler acknowledged it was possible the Sox would have to shed some salary to make ends meet. Fans had not warmed to the team, even though it had crawled back into a tepid race with Cleveland in the Central.

Still, it was shocking when one of the coaches told a Tribune reporter he had heard some big-name players being discussed in possible trades, among them closer Roberto Hernandez and 27-year-old starter Wilson Alvarez. Shortly thereafter, Reinsdorf told Sun-Times reporter Toni Ginnetti that "anybody who thinks we can catch Cleveland is crazy."

When a reporter approached Thomas in the tiny visitors'

clubhouse at Tiger Stadium to discuss the trade rumors, he expected Thomas to say management owed it to the veterans to keep the team together. After all, Ventura was about to return from a hurried rehabilitation for his broken ankle, and Cleveland had not been able to pull away. But Thomas talked like a member of management, saying he would understand if low attendance required Reinsdorf and Schueler to trim payroll. Spoken like a real company man.

The Sox were only 3 ½ games behind the Indians when they traveled to Anaheim on July 30, a day before the trading deadline. They were floored when they arrived at the ballpark the next afternoon to learn that Schueler, with Reinsdorf's blessing, had given away their chance to win. The Sox sent Hernandez, Alvarez and starter Danny Darwin to San Francisco for six minor-league players, the best of whom were shortstop Mike Caruso and pitchers Bob Howry, Keith Foulke and Lorenzo Barcelo.

It was a deal the Tribune tagged the "White Flag trade," a distinction Reinsdorf and Sox officials hated at the time but would later use in their own advertising campaigns.

"It's obvious we're disappointed with the way our ballclub has played this year, with our record, no question about it," Reinsdorf said. "We're faced with losing Alvarez and Roberto and getting nothing, as we did with Alex [Fernandez]. Now all of a sudden we add six players who if the scouts are right have a chance of being in the big leagues. Two or three have a chance of being stars. … If they're half right, we're in great shape."

In Hernandez, Alvarez and Darwin, the Sox sent the Giants a package that included a combined 31 years of experience, along with 258 career victories and 194 saves. The trio would help the Giants reach the playoffs, where they were swept by Florida in the first round. The Sox received one player,

Foulke, with major-league experience in return.

John Hart, then Cleveland's general manager, later said "there was dancing in the halls at our office" after news of the Sox's trade with San Francisco. The Indians had just finished a 4-10 homestand and were so desperate for pitching they added lefty John Smiley, who had a 5.23 ERA with Cincinnati.

Yet Reinsdorf was unapologetic. "This team had a chance and didn't seize it," he said. "It was hard to look at this team and feel very confident. I wasn't interested in finishing second in a poker hand."

Asked if a white flag should be flying in front of the Sox's dugout, Ventura said, "Any flag would basically mean the same thing."

The veteran third baseman had returned ahead of schedule from his broken right ankle in hopes of helping the Sox catch Cleveland. He told reporters he never knew the season ended on July 31.

"It's just disappointing, I guess, to think you have a team where everybody in here thinks you can still do it and you can't," Ventura said. "You'll never know what could have happened."

The Sox had only 22 players in uniform when they played Anaheim that night, adding rookie pitchers Scott Eyre, Alan Levine and Nelson Cruz the next day. That gave the already overwhelmed Bevington seven rookies on his roster.

Yet Reinsdorf was undaunted.

"Yesterday I said we had no chance of catching Cleveland," Reinsdorf said after the trade. "Today I'm not so sure."

◆

Guillen and his veteran teammates were sure, all right.

The last two months of the 1997 season turned into a farce, with players revolting against Bevington and doing everything possible to retain their sanity.

Ventura parodied the ceremony the Sox had held in 1993 when Fisk broke the record for games caught, one in which Bo Jackson had ridden a motorcycle in from center field as a gift for Fisk. Ventura presented a girl's bicycle to catcher Ron Karkovice, who almost never played and clearly was in his last year with the Sox. Ventura rode in from the left-field bullpen on a pink bike with a banana seat, catcher's gear hanging from the basket. He wore a sleeveless White Sox warm-up jacket with "Born to Ride" written on the back. "That bike cost me 10 bucks," Ventura said later.

Every day that September was like the last day of school. Ventura was so relaxed before one game that he went out onto the outfield grass for stretching puffing an enormous cigar.

This wasn't the way any of these guys wanted to go out, but they felt abandoned by ownership. It was a dark time for everyone involved, but especially Guillen, who had been so excited by Ventura's return that he commissioned an airplane to pull a banner welcoming him back.

In his 13 seasons with the White Sox, Guillen had always made people smile. He had posed for more pictures than Tyra Banks. But he had never forgotten that he was involved in a business, and now he knew he had something to worry about himself.

Guillen was earning $4.5 million in 1997, and he knew the Sox faced a decision at season's end: bring him back for $4 million or buy him out for $500,000. He hoped to work out a deal to come back and play two more years, giving shortstop prospects Caruso and Jason Dellaero time to mature.

But shortly after the White Flag trade, Guillen acknowledged he might be in his last season with the Sox.

"Right now, I don't think I'm going to come back," he said. "I hope I do, but we're talking about right now, and I don't think so. Maybe later on I will have a different opinion. Right now I am preparing myself mentally to not coming back here. If that happens, I am prepared for it. But I hope it doesn't happen."

Schueler had a one-on-one conversation with Guillen after trading away his friends. He made no promises.

"Basically I told him, 'Play hard until the end of the year, hustle, and we'll see what happens,'" Schueler said. "Right now I don't know what direction we're going to go."

After weighing all the factors, Schueler said it was "an easy call" to trade Alvarez, Hernandez and Darwin to San Francisco. The decision on Guillen, however, figured to be much tougher, maybe even heart-wrenching.

"It's definitely going to be tough," Schueler said. "Ozzie's been here a long time. The fans like him. The important thing is for him to finish strong."

The Tribune addressed his future in a story that pointed out how he was having the kind of season at the plate that Bevington and Schueler had expected. But his almost non-existent power and low total of walks made him a good investment only if he was a defensive specialist, and his reduced range would not permit that. Guillen didn't want anyone to make excuses for him.

"People talk about my knee being bad," Guillen said. "Hell, I got hurt five years ago; it's not like it was yesterday. Some people talk about me getting old. I'm younger than [Walt] Weiss, [Greg] Gagne and all those guys. The difference is I've played six or seven years more in the major leagues."

Age had become a sensitive issue.

"People don't think I'm 33," Guillen said. "But I don't give a damn whether I am 33 or 43. I feel like I'm 33. I wish I was in my 40s and could play like Paul Molitor. He plays like a 22-year-old."

The Tribune story concluded that this would probably be Guillen's farewell season, because he simply could not play well enough to justify being paid like a regular on a team that was watching every dollar. It had to be an unpleasant thing to read.

Guillen sought out the reporter the next day in the visiting clubhouse. "Hey!" he yelled. "Get over here. I read your story."

Uh-oh. But then Guillen's smile came out of nowhere.

"You're right," he said. "I'm horseshit."

◆

In the weeks ahead, Guillen more than once said he didn't want to "steal" Reinsdorf's money the following year. He said he wouldn't play anywhere if he couldn't get at least $2 million per season.

"I am not going to fly around the country every two days for $2 million," Guillen said. "I don't need the money. I will stay at home with my family. I will be a scout or a coach. Then I will steal Jerry's money. But I want to play as long as I can help some team. I know there are a lot of teams I can help. I know how to play the game."

The final week of the season, Guillen met with Schueler to resolve his contract status. He got the meeting under false pretenses, saying he wanted to bring his father and others from Venezuela to watch the last game, if it was going to be his final one with the White Sox. Then, after he had his answers, he laughed and told reporters that his father hates to travel, that he was never coming.

Schueler told Guillen the Sox had decided not to pick up the option. He had batted .252 with four homers and 52 RBIs that season.

"If I hadn't prepared myself for this, I would be crying right now," Guillen said. "This is not a broken heart, but I am unhappy. I am sad, but life still goes on. If this is the biggest problem a person is going to have, then shoot, he's a lucky person."

After seeing 11 teams look elsewhere for their regular shortstops, Guillen would sign with Baltimore after filing for free agency. The Orioles wanted him to back up Mike Bordick and were able to sign him for only $450,000.

It turned out Guillen loved wearing a uniform more than he had realized the September before.

"This is the first spring training that I don't have to teach anybody how to play the game," Guillen said. "It's fun.... They came after a lot of guys at the end of their careers. I think that's good."

Guillen's feelings about the White Sox also came to a boil over that winter, in large part, he now says, because they handed his job to Caruso, who had never played above Class A. In an interview with the Tribune at the Orioles' camp in Ft. Lauderdale, Guillen blistered his old organization.

"It's time for me to enjoy the game," Guillen said. "The last two years were miserable. I want to help this team. My enthusiasm and attitude will be good for this team."

The Sox had changed managers, firing Bevington and hiring Jerry Manuel, and Guillen knew Manuel would make a strong first impression.

"Anybody they get there, he'll look like a genius after that fiasco last year," Guillen said. "They could put [trainer] Herm Schneider there."

Among the strong (if predictable) opinions Guillen expressed about the Sox after they cast him aside:

On Ventura, who was eligible for free agency after 1998: "I hope Robin gets out of there as quick as possible. I know Robin doesn't want to be there."

On an infield featuring Frank Thomas at first, Ray Durham at second and newcomers Benji Gil or Caruso at shortstop: "That's going to be some kind of ugly.... The guys on our bench are better than the guys in their lineup."

On the loss of credibility with fans: "This team (the talent-laden Orioles) could be in Chicago, and they wouldn't sell any tickets either. The fans aren't going to believe they will keep the team together. They're not stupid. I'll tell you this, they lost 27 season tickets because of me—my season tickets."

Guillen said he had twice asked to be traded during 1997, once after Bevington ordered his sons out of the clubhouse early in the year and again after the White Flag trade. He said Schueler answered his trade requests with a promise he would be taken care of if he stayed quiet and kept playing hard. Guillen continued not only to be a good soldier in the clubhouse but to fulfill his usual obligations in the community.

In the end, he felt like a chump.

"They're all fake," Guillen said. "I deserved better—not because I had been there a long time, but because I did a lot for them. I did all those things when maybe I shouldn't have.... They talk about being fan-friendly, media-friendly, that's what I am. They give Albert all that money and he doesn't do anything for them. They won't give me $500,000, and that's my organization."

Guillen said he finished 34 plate appearances short of the total that would have vested his 1998 option because Schueler ordered Bevington not to play him as often in the second half of the season. He pointed to similar situations involving pitchers Jason Bere and Tony Castillo.

"Do you think Tony Castillo really wants to perform for them after they do that to him?" Guillen asked. "Do you think Jason wants to go out and do the job for them after they go into a six-man rotation to take money away from him?"

Yet at the end of the interview, almost as an afterthought, Guillen said he wanted to work for the White Sox when his playing career was over. He said that had always been one of his goals, and nothing had changed.

"I will," Guillen said. "I believe I can do that. I believe I can help kids."

◆

In the White Sox's new spring-training headquarters in Tucson, Ariz., the hallway walls were decorated with large action photos of current and former stars, including Guillen.

His photo was defaced by an unknown vandal after his comments appeared in print, and later was removed entirely. It was as if the Reinsdorf-Schueler management team was the Politburo and Guillen was some crazy capitalist whose very existence needed to be expunged.

Guillen's prediction about Manuel would prove correct. A class act and a good baseball man—possibly the only manager ever hired after preparing himself for his job interview with three days of fasting and prayer—he was received favorably in Chicago.

With Reinsdorf ratcheting the payroll down, Manuel had little choice but to play a lot of kids and unproven players. Some, such as Magglio Ordonez, Paul Konerko and Carlos Lee, established themselves as All-Stars or future All-Stars. The Sox had losing records in 1998 and '99 before using the addition of Valentin and career performances from James Baldwin, Cal Eldred and others to win 95 games and the division title in 2000.

But Lou Piniella, an unlucky draw for a manager in the playoffs for the first time, spun Manuel in circles as the Seattle Mariners swept the Sox in the first round.

Manuel would last three more seasons as the Sox's manager, winning 81-86 games a season, enough to call themselves contenders but not enough to get beyond mid-September with any real hope of eating at the big boys' table.

Something was missing. That something, it turned out, was the little shortstop who had gone away mad after 1997, the

New architects

Reinsdorf entrusts fate of the franchise to Williams and Guillen

Jerry Manuel, a leader whose Christian beliefs are a source of strength, prepared for his job interview with the White Sox in an unusual fashion. Ron Schueler, the general manager who hired him, had said "the room lit up" when Manuel walked into a hotel suite for his interview.

"It is my belief that was spiritual," Manuel said later. "When I went in there, I had a plan. God gave me a plan."

When Manuel was offered his first-ever interview for a managerial position, he spent one day at his desk, studying White Sox personnel and preparing outlines to show how he would run the team. Then he began to prepare his soul, spending three days in "fasting and prayer."

That's one way to do it.

Another, which Ozzie Guillen selected when Ken Williams was searching for Manuel's replacement, was to catch the next plane to Chicago and see what would happen.

Guillen's plan? Didn't have one.

After playing for the Sox for 13 seasons, he figured Jerry

Reinsdorf and others in the organization knew him as well as anyone. Either they wanted to hire him or they didn't.

And if they didn't, somebody else soon would.

After all, Guillen had spent two postseason runs playing for Atlanta's Bobby Cox, who taught him things he didn't know about winning baseball. He then coached for Jeff Torborg and Jack McKeon for three seasons after his playing career ended on skid row, with Jose Canseco and Dwight Gooden on the 2000 Tampa Bay Devil Rays. He knew he was ready to have a team of his own.

Guillen had watched one of his contemporaries, former All-Star catcher Tony Pena, win a Manager of the Year Award in his first season with the Kansas City Royals. That helped him believe in himself.

Williams now says Guillen wanted the Sox job "desperately," but Guillen didn't want it badly enough to try to figure out what Reinsdorf and Williams wanted to hear and then give it to them. He just acted like himself.

Reinsdorf and Williams have said that they had to be convinced Guillen had grown up some since his playing days in Chicago. They knew the passion was there, but they weren't sure about the self-control.

"I told him: 'Hey, you've got a lot of convincing to do,' " Williams said. " 'I love you like a brother, but you have a lot of convincing to do if I'm going to put my reputation on the line and give you this job.' And basically we started a 20-minute argument."

Guillen: "You know me. If you don't think I can do the job, let me know right now and I'll get up and go back to Miami. Don't waste my time."

Williams: "What did you come for if you're going to quit that easy?"

In the end, after an interview that lasted maybe two hours, Guillen did head to O'Hare for his flight home to Miami. While Guillen was in the air, Williams got Reinsdorf's blessing to offer him the job.

"If he's not afraid to fight me when he doesn't have the job, then we're going to make some good decisions together," Williams said. "He ain't going to tell me what I want to hear."

Guillen jumped at the job offer, coming back to Chicago for a news conference to be introduced before discussing salary. He let Reinsdorf fill in the number, saying he wasn't worried because he already had enough of Reinsdorf's money. He earned more than $23 million as a player and says Reinsdorf made sure he managed it wisely.

◆

One thing about Reinsdorf: If he likes you, he likes you for a long time. The prime example is probably Williams, the general manager who hired Guillen.

In his first 25 years overseeing the Sox, Reinsdorf paid a house call to only one draft pick. That was Williams, a two-sport talent who in 1982 was headed to Stanford University to play football.

"Roland Hemond told me we drafted a guy in the third round who had first-round ability," Reinsdorf said. "And we needed to sign him because he was going to play football at Stanford, so he asked me to go visit the family."

Williams' father, Jerry, grew up in Berkeley, Calif., where his circle of friends included Huey Newton, who would go on to be a founder of the Black Panther movement. Jerry Williams was a sprinter at San Jose State and close friends with teammates Tommie Smith and John Carlos, who were sent home from the 1968 Olympics because of their clenched-fist, black-power salute on the medal stand.

Carlos told reporter Ken Rosenthal that Jerry Williams was as fast as anyone in their group and "would have been in medal contention" if he had qualified for the Games. But Williams knew of the brewing protest and decided to steer clear of the Olympics. He was more interested in the well-being of his young family, especially his only child, who was 4 years old during the Mexico City Olympics.

"Even though I felt I was the fastest, I felt I had to have a silent protest or I would have been blackballed," Jerry Williams told Rosenthal. "I wouldn't have had the opportunity to get Ken where he is today. Nobody would have hired me."

Williams wanted to be a firefighter but battled discrimination in what for a long time was a closed society. He joined the San Jose Fire Department in 1972 only after filing a lawsuit alleging discrimation.

"It was ironic," Ken Williams said. "You had to sue for your right to risk your life to save others' lives."

Williams retired as a captain, but he faced constant battles, he said, because he was African-American.

"They gave me the job," he said. "I needed that job. But I had to go through—in essence, had to accept—all the hell and damnation they were dishing out in order to get that paycheck."

As he listened to Jerry Williams tell his story, Reinsdorf was captivated by the strength and intelligence he exuded. "He was impressive," Reinsdorf said.

And Kenny? He was working on his car in the driveway as his father and future boss charted the course of his life.

Reinsdorf was in his second season as a baseball owner. And he was so taken with Jerry Williams' story that he looked him in the eye and promised him he would take care of his son.

"My pitch to them was, 'Have Kenny go to Stanford and play football, and we'd like him to play baseball in the summertime, and if Stanford won't give him a scholarship, we'll pay for it,' " Reinsdorf said. "I told his dad that once he's in our organization, not to worry, because I promised I would take care of him."

Williams had enough talent as a football player that he could have made a living playing that sport.

"He definitely could have an NFL defensive back or wide receiver, maybe even a running back," said Paul Wiggin, who was Williams' coach at Stanford and now works for the Minnesota Vikings. "He was that good an athlete."

Williams' last football game was also the final game for John Elway at Stanford. It ended with archrival California scoring the winning touchdown on the infamous five-lateral kick return that weaved through the Stanford band. Williams was headed onto the field with the kick-coverage team when Wiggin pulled him back at the last second.

Williams went on to play six seasons in the big leagues with the White Sox, Detroit, Toronto and Montreal but never established himself as a regular. He can't help but wonder what would have happened had he stuck with football.

"Guys were saddened to see Kenny give up football for baseball because he was such a good person, good teammate and likable," Wiggin said. "But he also was one of those bright-light kids who knew what he was doing. If I read where he was stepping in to take over at Honeywell (Corp.), I wouldn't be surprised. You could tell he had that special ability to absorb information and get along with people."

When Williams' playing career ended in 1991, he found himself summoned to Reinsdorf's office in Chicago. He was seeking a job as a scout, and Reinsdorf hired him immediately.

"He was convinced he could find talent in the inner cities that nobody else was finding," Reinsdorf said. "He said,

'Everybody's afraid to go in there, and I'm not afraid.' Two years later he decided there wasn't as much talent there as he thought, but I liked the way he went at it and I wanted to teach him the business side of things."

With Reinsdorf as his mentor, Williams was only 31 when he was named the White Sox's farm director. It's as demanding and thankless a job as there is in baseball, with responsibilities including as many as six minor-league rosters and a staff of perhaps 30 instructors. The travel can be endless, and the lights not too bright in places like Hickory, N.C., and Prince William, Va.

While Williams' responsibilities stayed essentially the same, Reinsdorf gave him the title of vice president of player development in 1997. He began spending more of the summer in Chicago, watching games in Reinsdorf's box behind home plate at the new Comiskey Park.

Another longtime Reinsdorf staffer, assistant general manager Dan Evans, was at many of the same games but watched them in Schueler's box, not with Reinsdorf. That seating arrangement would prove telling when Schueler resigned unexpectedly after the 2000 run ended with three quick losses to Seattle in the division series.

Evans, a Chicago native and Hemond protégé, had been in the organization 19 years, literally working his way up from intern. He would go on to be the general manager of the Los Angeles Dodgers, but he wasn't Reinsdorf's pick. That was Williams, who quickly found himself on his own as Evans resigned in disappointment.

"We didn't just pluck Kenny out of thin air," Reinsdorf said. "We knew him and what a great job he'd done with the farm department. He wasn't a risk at all. He was the logical one."

Taking over a team that had won 95 games the year before,

Williams probably tried too hard to put his stamp on things at the beginning.

He picked up left-hander David Wells in a controversial trade with Toronto largely because Mike Sirotka, a 15-game winner for the Sox in 2000, injured his shoulder and never pitched in another big-league game. Williams said he went for Wells because he wanted to know who would start Game 1 of the playoffs.

Oops.

Williams also traded for Royce Clayton to play shortstop, which meant Jose Valentin moved to center field. He got excited about outfielder Julio Ramirez, a multitalented player he had acquired from Florida. The 2001 White Sox got off to a 7-15 start but recovered to win 83 games, eight fewer than first-place Cleveland.

Williams' worst move came before the 2002 season, when his desire for an established starter prompted him to trade young pitchers Kip Wells, Josh Fogg and Sean Lowe to Pittsburgh for Todd Ritchie, a veteran who had won 15 games in 1999 and made 33 starts in 2001. But Ritchie was pounded (5-15, 6.06) by the stronger American League lineups. The Sox went backward, finishing 81-81, 13 games behind Minnesota.

A year later, Williams sent Keith Foulke, who had wound up as a $4-million setup man for Manuel, to Oakland for closer Billy Koch. That deal backfired when Foulke regained his groove for the Athletics and Koch, who had pitched in 87 games in 2002, arrived as a shell of the guy who once intimidated the game's best hitters.

Reinsdorf never wavered in his support of Williams, which paid off when he plucked pitchers Freddy Garcia and Jose Contreras from Seattle and the Yankees in midseason deals in 2004. On Guillen's recommendation, he then broke up the lumbering, right-handed-dominant lineup that had won a division championship in 2000 but underachieved ever since.

"You know, Kenny never got his degree [at Stanford], but as it turns out he didn't need it," Reinsdorf, the promise keeper, said. "He's now in the upper echelon of baseball executives, and he's going to remain there for years to come. I'd say he's done all right."

◆

Guillen's first day as the White Sox's manager was the first day he had ever served as a manager. He hadn't gone to the minor leagues to learn his craft or even to winter ball in his native Venezuela. It was as if he had been born to be a manager.

Conducting one interview after another and chattering nonstop, Guillen seemed not to notice his players that day in Tucson, Ariz. The players certainly noticed him.

"You have Jerry [Manuel] on one end of the spectrum," center fielder Aaron Rowand said, "and you have Ozzie all the way on the other end."

Rowand, a habitually hard worker, had arrived early to get his feet on the ground as he tried to make sure he would be the regular center fielder.

"This camp feels a little looser," Rowand said. "There's a buzz around the team. People are excited, but this is probably only the beginning."

Reinsdorf was in high spirits as he wandered around on the back diamonds, watching Guillen's first workout. That said a lot, as Williams hadn't yet found a way to jettison Koch, leaving the Sox about $5 million over budget.

Reinsdorf was asked if camp felt different with a chatterbox and registered disturber of the peace like Guillen in charge.

"It's amazing," he said. "I don't want to knock Jerry. Jerry's a fabulous man. Ozzie's just different, has a different style. You can see it around the clubhouse. These guys are really going to have fun playing."

Fun? That had appeared to become a foreign concept as the Sox went through their motions, professional but oftentimes also lifeless, in Manuel's last two seasons.

"I will say that over the last few years ..." Reinsdorf began, then stopped himself. "No, it's not so important what has happened in the past, but I think the future is going to be special. Tony Pena has it, the same thing as Ozzie, and you could see it in what happened to the Royals. They started playing with a certain exuberance, with life. I think that's what we're going to get with Ozzie."

At the end of that opening workout, Guillen offered up a story from the year before, when he served as a coach on the Florida team that knocked off the Cubs and won the World Series. In June, the Marlins had lost to Boston 25-8, with the Red Sox scoring 14 runs in the first inning. Johnny Damon had three hits before the Marlins could get three outs.

Carl Pavano, Florida's starter, had given up six runs without retiring anyone and sat on the bench dazed afterward. Guillen said Pavano asked him what happened.

"I told him, 'You were horseshit,'" Guillen said. "Then I said I was happy I was here, and so should he be. We're never going to see that again. Three hits in an inning? I couldn't get three hits in a month."

Instead of crying, the Marlins laughed. Then they beat the Red Sox 10-9 the next day and kept winning, all the way to a World Series championship.

◆

Given the support he received from Reinsdorf, Williams remained as aggressive as any general manager in baseball. If there was a quality player available—even if it was a huge name like Alex Rodriguez or Randy Johnson—the White Sox were certain to be somewhere in the conversation, even if it appeared to be on the periphery.

Williams and his assistants—Rick Hahn, Dan Fabian and a staff of longtime scouts headed by Dave Yoakum, Bryan Little and Bill Scherrer—certainly knew the Seattle Mariners were considering trading Freddy Garcia at midseason 2004. Garcia, their ace and a fellow Venezuelan who was close to Guillen, was eligible for free agency at the end of the season, and the Mariners were off to a stumbling start. It appeared almost certain that he would be one of the most attractive players available at the July 31 deadline.

But Williams wasn't going to take a chance of not getting him. He made the Mariners an offer they couldn't turn down more than a month before the deadline, giving up catcher Miguel Olivo and two top prospects, center fielder Jeremy Reed and shortstop Michael Morse, for Garcia.

"Seattle made out very well in this deal," Williams said.

But Williams wouldn't give the Mariners everything they had wanted. The discussions began with Seattle asking for Olivo and Joe Crede, but Williams wouldn't give up two regulars, not with the Sox trying to run down Minnesota.

He preferred to borrow from the future by trading Reed, whom many considered the organization's top prospect. Williams was confident that there were better outfielders coming from the lower minors, including Brian Anderson, Ryan Sweeney and Chris Young.

When the Garcia deal was announced on June 27, after the Sox had just taken a series from the Cubs at U.S. Cellular Field, the Sox were only one game behind Minnesota in the Central. Williams said his motivation for the deal was simple, maybe even primal.

"Two words: nineteen-seventeen," Williams said, referring to the last year the Sox won the World Series. "How many more generations of fans are going to have to wait? I don't want to wait.... You've got to be able to dream and allow for hope."

Pitching coach Don Cooper was so happy to have Garcia on his staff that he immediately gave him the shirt off his back, switching from No. 34 to No. 21 so Garcia would have the number he had worn in Seattle.

"There's a lot of pressure on myself and Coop," Guillen said. "We've got to win."

Williams had asked Seattle to make the deal conditionally, giving the Sox 72 hours to sign Garcia to a contract extension. But when Seattle GM Bill Bavasi said no, this is it, take it or leave it, Williams took it.

"There is no doubt this is the guy who is most coveted on the market," Williams said. "I feel we have the opportunity to sign him to an extension more so than other teams, and I was willing to pay the price to do just that."

Williams felt he had an ace up his sleeve in the relationship between Guillen and Garcia, and he was quickly proved correct as Garcia signed a three-year extension for $27 million. Guillen said he might have to ask Williams for a raise because Garcia would spend a lot of time raiding his refrigerator.

Garcia was engaged to Guillen's second cousin, and they were married after the 2004 season. Guillen's wife, Ibis, had helped raise Garcia's fiancée, Glendys Bracho.

"It's a lift," Guillen said of the deal. "We gave up pretty good players to get him, but just because we brought Freddy in doesn't mean we are going to win. Freddy will help us once a week. The other four or five days, we have to play without him."

It turns out Garcia was no savior. The Sox followed that deal with another one destined to pay dividends, getting Jose Contreras from the Yankees for Esteban Loaiza at the deadline.

But they went 44-46 after the Garcia trade, playing most of the second half without Magglio Ordonez and Frank Thomas, who were injured, and finished nine games behind Minnesota.

Along the way, Guillen became convinced that his initial instincts were correct. If the Sox were going to win, they were going to have to do it by getting more pitching, improving defensively and becoming more versatile with their lineup.

It seemed unlikely they would re-sign Ordonez, who was a free agent after earning a club-record $14 million in 2004, and likely that at least one more of their right-handed-hitting cornerstones would have to go. That turned out to be Carlos Lee, who was traded to Milwaukee for Scott Podsednik, reliever Luis Vizcaino and the payroll flexibility for Williams to fill in the missing parts on the rebuilt team Guillen envisioned.

It was a telling time for a franchise that had been drifting for years. It would be the transition of a lifetime for Reinsdorf and his handpicked architects, Guillen and Williams.

"You have to give Kenny credit for sticking with his convictions on what he set out to do," Milwaukee GM Doug Melvin said later. "A lot of teams would not do what he did and make such difficult changes. You have to have a lot of guts to do this job sometimes, and he certainly does."

Valuable imports

**Newcomers provide an early spark,
led by a pair of Cuban pitchers**

When the White Sox assembled in Arizona to prepare for the 2005 season, Magglio Ordonez, a four-time All-Star whose departure was clouded by a mysterious knee injury, was gone. So were Carlos Lee and Jose Valentin.

Among them the threesome had given the Sox an average of 82 home runs and 271 RBIs per season since 2000. But they had also earned a combined $25.5 million in 2004, when the Sox's total payroll was $65 million. Ordonez, in the last year of a back-loaded contract he signed in 2001, had made $14 million by himself.

That represented 21.5 percent of the payroll at the start of the '04 season. No team had ever allocated more than 20 percent to one player and gone to the World Series, although the Houston Astros would soon change that, with Roger Clemens' $18-million salary accounting for 23 percent of their payroll in 2005.

Paul Konerko would be the highest-paid player on the roster this time around. His $8.75 million salary was less than 12 percent of the payroll, which Chairman Jerry Reinsdorf had increased to $75 million after adding Freddy Garcia and Jose Contreras in midseason deals the year before.

Spreading the Ordonez-Lee-Valentin money around, general manager Ken Williams had brought in seven newcomers with significant major-league experience. Orlando Hernandez, the Cuban legend who had won nine postseason games for the New York Yankees, and Jermaine Dye, who replaced Ordonez in right field, were the biggest names.

But just as important was the addition of catcher A.J. Pierzynski, outfielder Scott Podsednik, second baseman Tadahito Iguchi and relievers Dustin Hermanson and Luis Vizcaino. Hermanson would open the year 30-for-31 in save attempts.

Konerko and his longtime teammates weren't surprised by the change. They not only had seen it coming, they encouraged it.

◆

Like a modern-day Noah, Williams appeared in spring training to have grabbed two of everything. He had the Dominican Republic duo of Juan Uribe and Timo Perez, who hail from the same small town, and the Japanese duo of Iguchi (a four-time All-Star for Japan's Fukuoka Daiei Hawks) and Shingo Takatsu, who led the White Sox in saves in 2004. But Hernandez and Contreras, the two Cuban defectors, were the duo creating the most curiosity.

With their unusual style of training–throwing softballs and weighted baseballs, among other things–they livened up spring drills. They were generous with their time, perhaps because they so enjoyed each other's company.

Hernandez had left Cuba by boat with his wife and a few close friends. Contreras had sneaked away from Fidel Castro's team in Saltillo, Mexico, working his way north until he reached San Diego and political asylum.

Their styles are as unusual as their stories. Their presence on the White Sox guaranteed this would be a fascinating season, and possibly a successful one. If things could click for the two Cubans, if El Duque could stay healthy and Contreras could throw more strikes and avoid early-inning meltdowns, they figured to become a major story line in the American League.

Hernandez and Contreras had been hotly pursued when they made themselves available to major-league teams. The Yankees got them both, outbidding the Anaheim Angels for Hernandez and the Boston Red Sox for Conteras. The Red Sox had pursued Contreras with such vigor that his rejection prompted club President Larry Lucchino to term the Yankees baseball's "Evil Empire.'"

Easy lives had not come with the big contracts. Both pitchers had been torn apart emotionally by having to mourn the death of a father from afar, unable to return home and pay their last respects. El Duque did that in 2001, just before facing the Seattle Mariners in an ALCS game. Contreras did it after the 2004 season.

Things seemed to have taken a good turn for both of them. The White Sox signed Hernandez as a free agent, reuniting the two Cuban legends. They were working with a pitching coach, Don Cooper, who long ago forged a personal bond with the greatest Cuban pitcher of all time, Luis Tiant.

This was the first time Hernandez and Contreras had been together for an extended period. While they had spent most of their careers with the Yankees, they overlapped only for small parts of the 2004 season. Hernandez had been traded to Montreal just before Contreras' first spring with the Yankees. He re-signed with the Yankees for 2004 but spent the first half of the season recovering from shoulder surgery, which had caused him to miss the 2003 season. Hernandez didn't join the rotation until July 11 of '04, and Contreras was sent packing three weeks later. He had allowed 28 runs in 15 1/3 innings over five career starts against Boston, an unforgivable sin in George Steinbrenner's world.

Contreras had only recently been reunited with his wife in New York. He was confused by the trade and saddened that he would not have Hernandez as a teammate.

"I never expected that," Contreras said of his trade to the White Sox. "I was devastated because El Duque had just gotten there. I thought he was going to help me. He was sad about it too. I told him goodbye and we hugged each other. I told him, 'Don't worry about, we'll be together again soon.' "

Cooper loved being around the two of them. Their training habits and wry humor kept him entertained while he was helping them work out.

"Jose will back up behind the mound and throw all of his pitches with a softball, a Clincher, even his forkball," Cooper said. "It's really something to see. The first game he pitched for us was in Kansas City. He's out in the bullpen warming up and he starts with the softball. The first pitch he throws is a fastball that sails over the catcher, over the fence and goes almost all the way to shortstop. [Bullpen coach] Art Kusnyer starts yelling, 'Hey, we need that ball. We have to have that ball.' Guys were looking at him like he's crazy, but we only had one softball."

Cooper would come to call himself "the assistant pitching coach" for Contreras, insisting Hernandez had more influence with him. But he was a good match for both Cubans. His two favorite pitchers to watch as a teenager in New York were Tom Seaver, who was as technically sound as anyone, and Tiant, who won 229 games by being unconventional. Tiant was famous for twisting so much in his delivery that hitters could read the back of his jersey, yet he was precise with a vast assortment of pitches.

"I've always felt that Cuban pitchers, the ones who float up on shore, they can really pitch," Cooper said. "You know they've got heart and guts or they wouldn't take the trip in a raft. And they just know how to pitch. It seems like they all share a feel for pitching."

After warming up to start a game, Tiant had once tossed a ball into the seats to a 15-year-old Cooper, who years later would repay the favor by recommending Tiant for a job as a minor-league pitching coach with the White Sox.

Like Tiant, Hernandez is one of a kind. He starts his delivery by raising his left knee so high that he would bloody his nose if he ever lost his balance.

"That's classic," Cooper said of the leg kick. "It's the same thing as Tiant twisting, wheeling and throwing. They used to say Tiant had 1,000 different pitches from 1,000 different places. I'd say El Duque has 500 different pitches from 500 different places."

Several Cuban pitchers have made a big impact in the major leagues, most notably Tiant, Camilo Pascual, Hernandez and his half-brother, Livan Hernandez. But not since the Pascual-Pedro Ramos Senators of the late '50s had there been a major-league staff that had two Cubans working together. What would that mean?

Hernandez's face lit up when a reporter asked him that question.

"That's going to be for the end of the year," Hernandez answered, flashing his bright smile. "If we do what we can, you probably won't have to ask the question because you will see what it means. It will be a big year for both of us and for the team. We will enjoy each other and help the team win."

◆

Opening Day at U.S. Cellular Field might as well have been Turn Back the Clock Day. Mark Buehrle and Cleveland's Jake Westbrook re-enacted the pitchers' duel staged between the Sox's Eddie Smith and the Indians' Bob Feller in 1940, only this time it was Buehrle getting the 1-0 victory.

The game lasted only 1 hour 51 minutes, with the only run scoring when rookie shortstop Jhonny Peralta, who was replacing surehanded veteran Omar Vizquel, muffed a roller by Aaron Rowand in the seventh inning. The game would have almost certainly gone to the bottom of the ninth inning scoreless had the 22-year-old Peralta been able to make a play at the plate on Rowand's grounder. It was right at him, but it quickly became clear Peralta won his International League MVP award with his bat, not his glove.

Peralta and Cleveland manager Eric Wedge believed the lead-footed Konerko would have been out had the ball not bounded into the air off the heel of Peralta's glove. Third baseman Aaron Boone, playing in his first game since the 2003 World Series, sympathized with his teammate.

"With Konerko, who obviously doesn't run well, on third, he's one of the few exceptions where you're not all the way in [on the grass]," Boone said. "You're halfway, and Peralta had to come in on the ball. Bottom line, it's a tough play. It's do or die."

Buehrle, the sixth-year veteran who had long ago established himself as the anchor of the Sox's pitching staff, was as sharp as in any of his 140 career starts. He gave up only two hits before an admiring crowd of 38,141. There was nothing surprising about this. The lefty with the linebacker's number (56) long ago spoiled Sox fans with how easily he succeeds in a game so many others make complicated.

Before the opener, Ken Williams had joked about how little

attention Buehrle demands at the ballpark, saying he's often in and out of the clubhouse so quick that "maybe he's got another job he has to get to." Buehrle showed exactly what Williams was talking about, breezing through the Indians and then declining some postgame radio-TV appearances. "I've got to get out of here as quick as I can," Buehrle said, explaining he wanted to spend time with family members before they headed back to Missouri.

Between daylight-saving time and the pace established by Buehrle and Westbrook, those folks could have gone out with him for a quick bite on Taylor Street and still been to Springfield before dark.

There's no cooler score to win a ballgame by than 1-0. This wouldn't be the biggest game the Sox won by that margin, although no one knew it at the time.

◆

Buehrle set the tone, and his teammates followed. The Sox took two of three from Cleveland in the opening series, then went to Minnesota for the Twins' home opener.

Before a rollicking crowd of 48,764, Hernandez pitched a game that was just as big as the one by Buehrle in the season opener. His concentration level high because of the setting, El Duque treated the perennial Sox nemeses as if they were an international also-ran, say, Panama or even the Netherlands.

His leg kick was never higher, and he had one hitter after another off balance with his sneaky quick fastball and tantalizingly slow curveball. Hernandez pitched seven innings before leaving with a 5-1 lead in a game that would end with that score. He gave up six hits, struck out five and didn't walk anyone, retiring the last seven hitters he faced. "That's El Duque," Twins center fielder Torii Hunter said. "That's what he does."

That was exactly what Williams had envisioned when he

signed Hernandez to a two-year contract in January. He want-ed someone other than Buehrle who could win tough games and would give the Sox a 1-2 combination to match the Twins' Johan Santana and Brad Radke.

Konerko and Rowand hit home runs and Carl Everett, fill-ing in for the injured Frank Thomas as the designated hitter, had three hits, including two doubles. "So much for Ozzie's speed ball," Twins manager Ron Gardenhire said.

Losing pitcher Kyle Lohse envied the power he still saw in the Sox lineup. "You've still got some guys over there with pop," he said.

Only now the Sox believed they could win games on days when they didn't drive the ball out of the park.

"We're going to hit home runs, but we're not going to play the game relying on them," said Konerko, who was coming off a 41-homer, 117-RBI season. "We feel like even if we don't hit a ball into the outfield, we can win the game."

Nothing makes hitters more comfortable than playing be-hind quality pitching. Through four games, Buehrle, Garcia, Contreras and Hernandez had combined for a 1.33 ERA. But the biggest surprise wouldn't come until the fifth game.

Jon Garland, a first-round pick in the 1997 draft whom Ron Schueler stole from the Cubs in a deal for middle reliever Matt Karchner in '98, had been a big tease throughout his eight pro seasons. He got to the big leagues when he was only 20, using a 9-2 run at Triple-A Charlotte to get him 13 starts for the first-place White Sox in 2000.

His two-seam fastball had tremendous sinking action and hitters would pound it into the ground, but he was slow in de-veloping command of it and mastering a curveball or change-up to use as a complement to the hard sinker. He worked behind in the count too often. Garland had bounced between the rotation and the bullpen under Jerry Manuel before landing a permanent spot as a starter. He proved durable but predictably mediocre, going 36-36 over 98 starts in 2002-04, his earned-run average stuck between 4.51 and 4.89.

Give Williams credit for not giving up on Garland. He saw the potential, the experience he was piling up at a young age, and overlooked the fact that salary arbitration was enabling Garland's salary to grow while his performance was staying the same. He had cost the Sox only $375,000 in 2003, but that jumped to $2.3 million in '04 and to $3.4 million in '05. That's a lot of money to pay a fifth starter, which is all Garland figured to be in Ozzie Guillen's second season. No one could know he would pitch his way onto the American League All-Star team.

Though he had spent Friday night back at the team hotel trying to get over a case of the flu, Garland picked up where Hernandez had left off against Minnesota.

He held the Twins scoreless for four innings, working with a 3-0 lead, but then surrendered a three-run homer to Shannon Stewart in the fifth inning. Garland shook it off and retired the next two hitters, then escaped a bases-loaded mess in the sixth when Joe Crede started a double play on a grounder by Michael Cuddyer. That allowed him to be the pitcher of record when Timo Perez led off the seventh with a homer against Radke, and the Sox pushed the lead to 7-3 with three more runs off Radke and the relievers who followed him.

"You see the guys on your team going out, giving it their all and doing great, you just want to do that much better," Garland said. "I want to keep it going, keep it rolling. I want to keep these guys at the same intensity I was at."

Garland's win gave the Sox a 4-1 record, which didn't impress Radke. "They can get out and win as many games as they want," he said. "It's April."

But with Garland, Buehrle and their fellow starting pitchers leading the way and top-of-the-order hitters Podsednik and Iguchi making opponents uncomfortable, the Sox kept winning. They finished April 17-7, pushing their record to 24-7 with an eight-game winning streak against Detroit, Kansas City and Toronto. Sure, it was early, only May 8, but the Sox had built a lead of 4 ½ games over Minnesota and 9 ½ over everyone else in the Central.

Garland was 6-0 and wouldn't lose a game until May 23, when the Los Angeles Angels' Ervin Santana beat him, dropping him to 8-1. Along with Podsednik, he was giving the Sox more of a lift than even Guillen had imagined.

Podsednik was at his best in the first game of the year's interleague series with the Cubs, always a much bigger deal for the Sox. Jerry Reinsdorf loves the guaranteed sellouts he gets by hosting his city rivals for three games a year. But if it was up to Tribune Co., the Cubs would host the Sox only every other year, if that often. The bully on the block never has much to gain by having to meet his competition in a fair fight.

When Guillen's Sox traveled to Wrigley Field on May 20, they were 29-12 and fast becoming the talk of baseball. The Cubs, who had lost seven of their last nine to miss the playoffs in 2004, were off to a disappointing start. They had an 18-20 record and Greg Maddux on the mound for the first game of the City Series.

As always, the Sox players were excited by the chance to play in front of frenzied fans, the upper deck certain to be full, not sparsely populated, as often was the case at U.S. Cellular. "It's definitely a lot of fun playing in a series like this," Crede said. "There are a lot of fans and electricity. It's so much better."

Podsednik entered his first Cubs series hitting .283, with 24 steals in 30 tries, including two four-steal games. His confidence was rising and would soar once he unsettled a Hall of Famer.

Nothing bothers Maddux. Not taxes. Not car pools. Not bumpy greens. Not even having had to face steroid-fueled hitters for years with a fastball that wouldn't impress a college coach. But Podsednik got to him.

After stealing 137 bases in 2003-04, Podsednik had a reputation. Every team the Sox played would spend as much or more time talking about him as it did Konerko and Dye. But he had seldom received more attention from a pitcher than he got from Maddux in the Sox's 5-1 victory.

When Podsednik dropped a perfect bunt down the third-base line with one out and no one on base in the fifth inning, two batters after Crede's line-drive homer had given the Sox a lead, there was nothing the Cubs could do about it. Aramis Ramirez didn't even attempt to throw on what Billy Williams called "one of those Rod Carew bunts."

That's when the fun began. The surprise was that Maddux fell into the same trap as so many lesser pitchers. He had long been one of the easiest pitchers to steal bases against and had seldom allowed it to bother him. But this time he made just about every adjustment a pitcher can make, and before he knew it a one-run inning had turned into a three-run mess and a 4-0 hole that was a death sentence for a Cubs team struggling to score runs.

Dusty Baker got edgy before Maddux did. He ordered a pitchout on the first pitch to Iguchi, but Podsednik wasn't running. Maddux then threw over to first, trying to keep Podsednik close. His next pitch was delivered with a slide step, the abbreviated motion designed to get the ball to home quicker, and sailed high for ball two. Maddux threw another fastball, and Iguchi hit the 2-0 pitch into center for a single.

Podsednik advanced only to second base, but he stayed on

Maddux's mind. After Rowand took a first-pitch fastball for ball one, he flied out on the next fastball, leaving runners on first and second with two outs.

Here's where Maddux did something really unusual. Instead of putting all his focus on Konerko, he got caught up worrying about a double steal.

Konerko fouled the first pitch back. Before throwing the 0-1 pitch, Maddux wheeled toward second and bluffed a throw, forcing Podsednik back to the bag. Konerko fouled off another pitch, putting Maddux one strike away from escaping with a 2-0 deficit. But he couldn't put Konerko away. He pulled the 0-2 pitch between shortstop Neifi Perez and Ramirez for a single, scoring Podsednik.

Before Maddux could get out of the inning, he allowed another run-scoring single to Pierzynski. The only stats Podsednik got out of the inning were a single and a run scored, but he deserved assists on the hits by Iguchi and Konerko, if not also Pierzynski.

It was water torture, baseball-style.

Contreras, Konerko and Everett did the heavy lifting the next day. The Sox won 5-3 to give themselves a chance to sweep the Cubs in their home ballpark, either a temple or a giant public toilet, depending on whether it's being described by baseball's wordsmiths or by Guillen, who would love to take a wrecking ball to the place. While the Cubs would avoid a sweep on Sunday, with Mark Prior grinding out a 4-3 victory, it was possible to hear a changing of the guard in Chicago baseball.

All you had to do was close your eyes and listen. It sure didn't sound like the Cubs' year.

When Konerko lined a solo homer off Prior in the ninth inning on an afternoon when the weather was Ferris Bueller nice, it was impossible to tell the game was being played at Wrigley Field. Not only were Sox fans louder than their North Side counterparts, they also seemed to have more than their share of the good seats. A glance at the stands behind the plate showed more paying customers sporting Sox jerseys than ones in the Cubs' colors.

It sure looked like the fans who had so eagerly awaited Year 3 of the Prior/Wood/Zambrano/Maddux experience had already lost faith. And the faith of Sox fans was growing.

Why not? Their team had an unusually strong pitching staff and a pesky personality worthy of its manager.

Even though his team had won, Baker left Wrigley grumpy, steamed at Juan Uribe, the Sox shortstop who "deked" the Cubs' Derrek Lee into a base-running blunder in the first inning.

Lee was running from first when Jeromy Burnitz lined a ball down the right-field line, and Uribe told him the ball was foul as Lee pulled into second, causing him to stop for a few seconds before third-base coach Chris Speier waved him to third. He was stranded there when Podsednik caught Ramirez's wicked liner, keeping the Cubs from scoring a run they should have had.

"That's not proper etiquette," Baker complained afterward.

Maybe not, but you'd better believe Guillen liked it. Heck, he was probably the one who taught Uribe that trick.

Indians surge

Cleveland's charge fuels doubts about the Sox and tension in the clubhouse

By the All-Star break the White Sox were 57-29. They led Minnesota by nine games and third-place Cleveland by 11. They came out of the break with five straight wins, sweeping a four-game series from the Indians at Jacobs Field, including a 1-0 victory pitched by Jose Contreras and a 4-0 win pitched by Jon Garland. By Aug. 1 they had raised their record to 69-35. They led the Central by 15 games, with Cleveland having pased the Twins to move into second place.

Gravity being as much a factor in sports as in the rest of the universe, there was really only one way for Ozzie Guillen's team to go: down. The only question was how far it would fall.

The Sox were 12-16 in August. The lineup was slumping and Frank Thomas was lost for the season, if not forever, with another stress fracture in his left ankle, a duplicate of the injury that caused his 2004 season to end early. Cleveland, meanwhile, was showing why it had been the flavor of the month for ESPN's Peter Gammons and other analysts back in March.

On July 30 the Indians had been a pedestrian 54-51,

14½ games behind the Sox. But they found their stride in August, scoring 5.8 runs per game behind switch-hitting catcher Victor Martinez, designated hitter Travis Hafner, shortstop Jhonny Peralta and center fielder Grady Sizemore, whom Guillen would come to call the best player in the league. They went 21-8 to raise their record to 75-59 on Sept. 2, when they trailed the Sox by 7½ games.

No team in the history of the major leagues had ever led by 15 games and not gone to the playoffs. It still appeared the Sox were a lock to play in October, but the weight of the lead, and the strain of the season, began to slow down bats and cause pitchers to miss the location on their pitches.

While the White Sox weren't really collapsing, that verb (**collapse** [kə laps'] **1** to fall down down or inward suddenly; cave in; **2** to cease to function; to break down suddenly in health or strength; **3** to fold compactly) would quickly become part of Chicago's sporting conversation as Cleveland continued to apply pressure.

While the hardest-core Sox fans had come to distrust the Tribune—whitesoxinteractive.com maintains a standing stream on its discussion board called "Boycott the Tribune"—it was the Chicago Sun-Times that seemed to take the most pleasure in the Sox's growing discomfort. Columnist Jay Mariotti was practically gleeful in predicting doom. Ditto the Sun-Times' Greg Couch, whom Aaron Rowand tagged "mini-Mariotti."

Back in May, Mariotti had described the Sox as "the biggest overachievers in baseball," although he qualified his praise in June by writing, "I can safely say the Sox won't win a World Series as long as [Jerry Reinsdorf] owns them."

With the Sox coasting in first place, Mariotti didn't seem to know what to make of them.

"I could ... concur that the rotation is the best we've ever seen, point out that the White Sox are the 12th team since 1996 to take a winning percentage of .673 or better into June, further point out that 10 of the previous 11 made the playoffs … and then conclude, This is definitely is the year!" he wrote on June 14. "But that would be a lie. And I sure don't want to lie to anybody … Will [Ken] Williams recognize his Joe Crede problem and pursue Shea Hillenbrand?"

A week later, he wrote: "I will state for the record today, on the bosom of Hawk Harrelson, that the Sox are crashproof in this regular season. You may as well sit back and enjoy the next 3½ months. They are not going to miss the playoffs. Hear me? They aren't choking. Got that?"

By Aug. 21, Mariotti was making comparisons between the White Sox and the 1969 Cubs, who lost 11 of 12 in one stretch and fell behind the New York Mets in one of baseball's all-time fades. At the time the Sox's lead was still 8½ games.

What Mariotti didn't want to acknowledge was that the Sox's problem wasn't their play, it was the Indians' incredible surge, which showed no signs of abating. After back-to-back losses at Minnesota on Sept. 2-3, Cleveland reeled off a seven-game winning streak against Detroit and Minnesota. The Sox went 3-4 in that stretch, including a home sweep at the hands of the Angels, who loomed on the radar as a possible playoff opponent.

This assumed, of course, that Guillen would guide his team to the playoffs. The lead was down to 5½ games after the Angels' sweep.

After a loss to Oakland on Sept. 12, the Indians ran off five more wins against the Athletics and the Royals, bringing them to Chicago for a showdown against the Sox with 11 wins in their last 12 games and a 33-11 record since July 30.

The Sox had finally gone into something looking like

free fall. After the Angels' sweep at U.S. Cellular, they had dropped back-to-back games in Kansas City, where the woeful Royals (46-96) had been expected to be pushovers. The losses were especially galling: A 10-9 game in which Garcia had been working with a 9-4 lead and a 7-5 game in which the Sox scored only two runs in six innings of Zack Greinke, he of the 6.06 ERA.

After the loss on Sept. 15, Guillen couldn't take it anymore. He exploded with a tirade that loomed as a possible epitaph.

"We're playing lousy baseball on the bases, pitching, everything," Guillen said. "There's no doubt about it. We really flat-out stink. It's not the same team I've been watching all year. … If I named all that I was disappointed about, we might be here all day."

On Sept. 18, after the Twins' Johan Santana had beaten the Sox with a four-hitter in a performance that would have beaten any team in the majors, Mariotti called for a media blackout.

"If there is any sense of mercy, the White Sox will be blacked out the rest of the season so a terminally cursed city needn't witness The Mother of All Collapses," Mariotti wrote. "The next 14 days and nights will be hell for the Sox, their fans and a city sick of applying the Heimlich maneuver. Watch at your own risk."

When the Indians body-slammed the Sox in the series opener, winning 7-5 to get within 2½ games of the lead, the Sox had lost eight of 10. They would go on to lose 10 of 14 in the one stretch of the schedule that had threatened to become a collapse.

The Tribune, in one of those articles the whitesoxinteractive.com crowd would cite as evidence of a vast conspiracy to keep South Siders in their place, studied the worst stretch-run failures in history. The piece concluded that losing a 15-game lead would rank as the second-most embarrassing finish in history, behind only the 1964 Philadelphia Phillies.

That team would be the first item mentioned in many obits on its manager, Gene Mauch, who died in August 2005. It failed to hold a 6½-game lead with 15 games to play, going 1-12 in the games that mattered the most. If not for those Phillies, the distinction of worst collapse would belong to the 1995 California Angels, who had led by 12½ with 42 games to play, followed by the 1969 Cubs, 1951 Brooklyn Dodgers and 1978 Boston Red Sox.

"Didn't like your column," Rowand said to the writer on the afternoon of Sept. 21, when it appeared in the Tribune. "Didn't like it all. In fact, I think it sucked."

By then the Sox's clubhouse had taken on a different feel than it had for most of the season. There was tension that hadn't existed for most of the season, and it showed up in key at-bats as Konerko, Rowand and others seemed to be grinding their bats so tightly you expected to find sawdust in the batter's box.

But that didn't keep them from the occasional huge victory. They got one in the second game of the Cleveland series, beating the Indians 7-6 in a game that was saved by a superb defensive play from Uribe, the shortstop Williams had stolen from Colorado after the 2003 season. He sent the Rockies only second baseman Aaron Miles, whose lack of fielding skills had kept him from the big leagues. The win pushed the lead back to 3½ games.

In a series that had been tighter than the Kansas City Royals' budget, Uribe's unbelievable throw from shallow left in the eighth inning was a godsend for Guillen. It arrived in Konerko's mitt an eyelash ahead of the speedy Coco Crisp, who was denied a game-tying single.

With the Sox leading 6-5, Cleveland had two outs and runners on first and third. Uribe was shaded toward the middle and seemed to have no chance to make the play when Crisp hit a grounder to the left side. Reliever Cliff Politte remembered thinking, "Oh, man, get there.

"After that," he said, "it was, 'Wow, what a play!' "

Rowand called it the biggest play of the season, not just for the White Sox but in the majors.

"When he hit it, I knew Juan would get it," Rowand said. "I wasn't sure he'd get the out because [Crisp] can run, but somehow Juan put something on his throw. That's the toughest play, even with Paulie running. With Coco Crisp running ... it's got to be a candidate for the best play in the major leagues this year."

Mariotti wasn't impressed.

In his column, he wrote: "Other cities host the World Series. Chicago hosts Choke Job Theater.... Whether the Sox go on to finish the biggest regular-season fold in baseball history or somehow do a back-door slider into the playoffs, it should be obvious now that the rampaging Indians are a much better team and are worthier of the American League Central title."

A day later, as the Sox prepared for the third game against the Indians, Guillen seemed his usual chirpy self when he met with reporters. As the Sox took batting practice, he lingered between the dugout and the batting cage, doing an extended one-on-one interview with Mike Nadel, a baseball-savvy columnist from the Copley News Service, which provides content for several papers in the Chicago suburbs.

Guillen was talking as much with his hands as his mouth. Nadel had clearly asked a question that touched a nerve.

Stressed out by the stretch run and worn out from criticism, Guillen told Nadel he had been vomiting after games and that he felt unappreciated by the fans he was working hard to please. He even said he was considering retiring after two seasons on the job, but only if the Sox won the World Series.

"I've got [championship] rings already and I'm proud of them, but if I win here, if I help the White Sox do this, it will give me a chance to walk away if I want to," Guillen told Nadel. "I will think about it. I will think about it twice. The way I'm thinking right now, I will tell Kenny Williams to get another manager and I'll get out of here. I'll make more money signing autographs instead of dealing with this stuff."

Nadel asked Guillen repeatedly to clarify his comments. He said Guillen kept saying the same thing, his voice rising as he tried to make his point.

"I'm not kidding, not at all," Guillen said. "I want the fans to be able to say, 'Hey, we finally did it!' I want to make them proud. I want to win the World Series, and then maybe I'm gone. I'll even help Kenny look for someone else. I don't give a damn about the money; I've got all I need.

"The thing is, I'm stressed every day. Do I have the best job in the world? Yes, because I'm managing the team I love. I'm managing my team. But every time we lose, I feel sick. I [vomit] sometimes. I get mad. I throw things in my office. It makes me crazy. I went to the World Series as a player [with Atlanta] and won one as a coach [with Florida]. If I can do it as the manager here, I can say, 'Everything I want to do in baseball, I did it.' Then I'll make my decision."

Guillen had occasionally been booed by frustrated fans. He had criticized the fans not for booing him but for booing his players, but it was clear he was hurting too.

"It makes me sad when they boo me," he told Nadel. "Sometimes I think they don't appreciate me. They should, because I played my butt off for them, and now I'm managing my butt off for them. You know how many managers are dying for 91 wins right now? And we have that and they don't appreciate that? It makes me wonder what happens if I only have 71 wins, how are they going to treat me? I mean, they treat me like [dirt] when I'm winning 91.

"My kids are here at the ballpark and they ask me later why I'm getting booed. I say it's part of my job, but deep down inside, it hurts. If I was doing a terrible job, sure, go ahead and boo me, but I think I'm doing pretty good."

With Cleveland pulling closer by the day, it seemed like crazy talk. Who cared if Guillen said he would quit if the Sox won the World Series? Who thought they could win the World Series?

Before Guillen's interview with Nadel on Sept. 21, Konerko had stood in front of his locker for a long time talking to reporters. Mariotti, typically, was nowhere in sight.

"We've been playing our game, for the most part," Konerko said. "We just haven't been getting the big hits we got early in the year. Guys are sometimes swinging at bad pitches, getting themselves out. A pitcher makes a mistake and we pop up a pitch we should be driving. Believe me, it hasn't been any fun.

"But this is a team that wins with its pitching, wins with its fielding, and we're starting to get the kind of pitching we got all season. Once we get into the playoffs, once we clinch that spot in the playoffs, I think you're going to see us having fun again. We're a dangerous team when we're having fun and playing our game."

Turns out he knew what he was talking about.

◆

Cleveland would get within 1½ games on Sept. 22, with Santana doing another huge favor for the Indians, who had left Chicago and headed to Kansas City. But the Sox still held the upper hand.

"It will be interesting to see how we rally," said rookie right-hander Brandon McCarthy, who had matched Santana for eight innings in a game Minnesota would win in 11. "It's by no means over."

In the end, after all the angst, it was the Indians who flinched. While the Sox took the next three games of a four-game series with the Twins, then won two of four in Detroit, Cleveland could not finish off its amazing run. The Indians won the first three games of their four-game series at Kansas City, giving them 38 wins in their last 50 games, but unraveled after Sizemore—of all people—lost a ball in the Missouri sky to cost them a game they had just tied in the top of the ninth inning.

With one out and a runner on second, Sizemore drifted back to get under a high fly by Kansas City's Paul Phillips. He was camped under it but then couldn't see it. The ball hit him in the leg and he froze, as if dazed, while Angel Berroa scampered home from second base to score the winning run.

"I looked around and there it was," Sizemore said. "I kind of waited a little too long. Probably should have picked it up and thrown it in. But I was a little frustrated, you know?"

An Indian, frustrated? That quote must have brought smiles to the faces of Sox players the next morning. Their lead had grown back to 2½ games.

It would drop to two games when they opened the last week of the season by losing in Detroit, on a homer by rookie Curtis Granderson, a Chicago native and University of Illinois-Chicago product, as Cleveland didn't play.

"Do you honestly think this team can do the slightest damage in the playoffs, assuming the Sox don't squander what is now a two-game divisional lead and two-game lead for the wild card?" Mariotti asked in the Sun-Times. "Just why are the Sox playing for October when they clearly don't belong there?"

When the White Sox lost again to the Tigers the next night, the Indians failed to take advantage, losing to last-place Tampa Bay, as they would again on Wednesday. Jose Contreras beat Detroit, raising his record to 11-2 in 15 second-half starts and giving the Sox a three-game lead with four to play.

Cleveland's C.C. Sabathia was brilliant on Thursday night, throwing a five-hitter to beat the Devil Rays, but by then the Indians cared only about the wild-card race. With super-sized rookie Bobby Jenks nailing down a save and Konerko slugging his 40th homer, Garcia helped the Sox win their 96th game, and clinch the division title, earlier that day.

Math was on the White Sox's side. Even if Cleveland had won the rest of its games, including a weekend sweep of the Sox, both teams would have had enough wins to make the playoffs, and the Sox held the season-series edge, using nine one-run victories to take 14 of 19 from the Indians. Thus they would have gone into the playoffs as Central champs.

"It's a great feeling," Guillen said. "The first step is a big step.... People don't know how hard it is to just get to the playoffs."

◆

After making the Tampa Bay Devil Rays look like, well, the Tampa Bay Devil Rays, Sabathia looked like a conquering hero in front of his locker. It had been a disappointing season in a lot of ways for the giant left-hander, but he was looking forward to one more start.

If there was to be one, it would have to come either in the first round of the playoffs or, on three days' rest, in a Monday playoff to get the Indians into the postseason.

"It feels good," Sabathia said. "I'm preparing to hopefully pitch on Tuesday. I'll come in, work out tomorrow, do some scoreboard-watching and hopefully I will be taking the ball."

Chicago Tribune photo by Scott Strazzante

A roster gamble who paid off, catcher A.J. Pierzynski leaps in excitement after Joe Crede's 10th-inning walk-off home run against Cleveland in late September.

The American League-leading White Sox boasted four All-Stars—Paul Konerko, Jon Garland, Mark Buehrle and Scott Podsednik—for the July game at Comerica Park in Detroit. Buehrle started for the AL and was credited with the victory. It was the Sox's largest All-Star delegation since 1975.

With Jose Contreras finishing the year as perhaps the most dominant starter in the AL, the Sox closed out the regular season on a five-game winning streak.

Tadahito Iguchi follows through on a three-run homer off Boston's David Wells to cap a five-run fifth inning and put the Sox ahead for good in Game 2 of the division series.

American League Championship Series MVP Paul Konerko is fired up after driving in an insurance run in Game 5 as the Sox clinched a World Series berth.

Joe Crede heads for third after Tony Graffanino's error on a Juan Uribe grounder set the stage for Iguchi's dramatic blast.

After going the distance in Game 4 of the ALCS, Freddy Garcia whoops it up as he walks off the mound.

Mark Buehrle is happy to have escaped a seventh-inning jam against the Angels in Game 2 of the ALCS. That was the game that featured A.J. Pierzynski taking first base on Josh Paul's dropped third strike.

Jerry Reinsdorf hoists the American League championship trophy, his first since buying the White Sox in 1981.

Sabathia spoke before watching Boston rally from a 4-1 deficit to beat Toronto 5-4 on a David Ortiz single. That win kept the defending World Series champions tied with the Indians in the wild-card race. But the Red Sox weren't yet focusing on the wild card. They were only one game out of the AL East lead with the Yankees coming to Fenway Park for the final weekend of the season.

On Friday, Guillen essentially thumbed his nose at the Red Sox and Yankees, starting a junior varsity unit against the Indians. Podsednik and Crede were the only regulars in the lineup behind Buehrle. But still Cleveland couldn't halt the downward spiral that had begun when Sizemore lost the ball in the sun. The White Sox pulled out a 3-2 win in 13 innings, with Ross Gload driving in the game-winner, clinching home-field advantage throughout the playoffs.

In Boston, where civic sensibilities were at DEFCON 1 levels with the Yankees in town and neither team assured of a playoff spot, the Red Sox welcomed veteran lefty Mike Stanton, who had been acquired in a Thursday trade to add pitching depth for the Yankees series. It's never a good sign when it's Sept. 29 and your general manager is still trading for pitching.

The Red Sox won the Friday night game, tying the Yankees and moving one game ahead of Cleveland in the wild-card standings. Before the game, new Hall of Famer Wade Boggs was honored for his 11 seasons with the Red Sox (and 10,000 balls lined off the Green Monster).

Boggs said he'd never played in a Red Sox-Yankees game—on either side—with as much at stake as there was in that weekend's games. "These guys are trying to hang on by the skin of their teeth just to make the playoffs," Boggs said. "My God, what are the headlines going to look like Monday morning in New York if the Yankees don't make it? My God, a $200 million payroll doesn't win?"

Boggs was on the 1986 Boston team that had the World Series slip through its hands at New York's Shea Stadium. He could only imagine what it would have been like to celebrate a World Series victory, as the Red Sox did last year.

"It's a snowball going downhill, no question about it, with them winning last year," Boggs said. "Two-thousand-four took a lot of pressure off not only the organization but the fans, off New England in general. It took a lot of [trepidation] away that's been there for a long time. You can burn the scripts of choking in September and all you used to read about.

"Last year was so good for New England. It got the monkey off a lot of people's backs. Now the only one left to have the monkey on their back is the Cubs, and who knows when they'll get that one off?"

Hey, a Chicago reporter said to Boggs, what about the White Sox? They hadn't won the World Series since 1917.

"That's a good point," Boggs said. "I didn't realize that.… Maybe it's the whole city of Chicago that has the monkey."

Why not?

On Saturday, the Yankees clinched the AL East title when Randy Johnson beat knuckleballer Tim Wakefield, but the White Sox's victory over the fading Indians left the Red Sox still leading the wild-card race by one game. When Red Sox players left their clubhouse that night, the last thing they saw was a chalkboard with a simple order: "Tomorrow pack for a three-day trip."

It didn't specify Chicago as the destination, but it could have. If the Red Sox beat the Yankees or the White Sox beat the Indians on Sunday, the AL's two teams of Sox would meet in a first-round series, beginning Tuesday at U.S. Cellular.

If both Sox teams lost, Cleveland would have gone to Boston Monday for a 163rd game, with the defending World Series champions a loss away from extinction.

"We have been in worse situations than this one and we have come out of it," Red Sox slugger David Ortiz said. "We'll be fine."

With a playoff spot on the line, Boston would start Curt Schilling, a hero last October but an enigma in 2006. Had the Red Sox clinched earlier, they might have saved Schilling for Game 1 of a playoff series, but they didn't have that option.

If there was dread in the air Sunday at Fenway Park, it was quickly gone. The White Sox-Indians started an hour before Yankees-Red Sox, and the White Sox scored single runs in the first three innings. The way Cleveland was going, it was hard to imagine a rally against McCarthy.

In a stunningly anticlimactic ending to a previously electric weekend, the Red Sox were in the fifth inning of a 10-1 victory over the Yankees when the scoreboard registered the White Sox's latest win in Cleveland. The crowd of 34,534 cheered the Indians' elimination and immediately went back to a traditional New England mind-set:

No more rooting for the White Sox.

Instead the Red Sox would look ahead to a division series meeting with the White Sox, who last won a postseason series in 1917.

"The White Sox are tough—every team in the postseason is tough, even teams that aren't in," Red Sox center fielder Johnny Damon said. "If Cleveland had gotten in, they had as good a shot as anyone to win it. That's how great this league is this year. There's no favorite team. It's definitely special."

Schilling had held the Yankees to one run in six innings, but his fastball peaked at 92 m.p.h. and his split-finger fastball didn't have the sharp break it featured when he was a World Series hero for Arizona in 2001 and Boston in '04.

"I'm not where I want to be," Schilling said. "But it's a new season. Everybody starts 0-0 tomorrow."

The right Sox

**Boston gets rude awakening upon arrival
in Chicago for AL Division Series**

There's something about baseball in the Northeast that's cool if you're part of that scene and just about revolting if you're not. It's like chowder that has gone cold. That has never been truer than between 1996 and 2005, when the Yankees and Red Sox spent good money after bad, chasing each other and pretty much leaving everyone else in the dust.

The Yankees had won four World Series in this period, the Red Sox finally their first since 1918 in 2004. They had faced each other in the American League Championship Series in 1999, 2003 and '04 and were in line to do it again in '05.

But for that to happen, the Red Sox and Yankees would have to beat teams with better pitching and arguably more balance: the White Sox and the Los Angeles Angels. And they'd have to do it even though they had not wrapped up playoff spots until the last weekend, leaving managers Terry Francona and Joe Torre no time to arrange their starting rotations.

Still, this didn't rob those around the teams of their characteristic smugness. On the day before the Red Sox-White Sox series began, both teams worked out at U.S. Cellular Field, the sun bright and the air a little crisp.

Francona, the Red Sox's manager, was asked about the series being a matchup of Boston's hitting against the White Sox's pitching.

"I hope it's pitching versus pitching," Francona said. "We really love our lineup. Over 162 games, our lineup has been pretty special. But to win in the playoffs, we're going to need pitching. If you hear the White Sox talking about their pitching a week from now, I may not be sitting here smiling."

Francona was acknowledging a reality in the matchup. The White Sox, who finished the season with a 3.61 staff earned-run average, had an advantage of more than a run a game over the Red Sox, who finished with a 4.74 ERA.

But the difference between the teams wasn't immediately obvious to everyone, especially those who had grown accustomed to the Red Sox's success. On his way back to his Chicago hotel after the Monday workout, Chris Snow, an excellent young baseball writer for the Boston Globe, offered this prediction: "Red Sox in three."

Based on what? Well, based on pedigree more than anything else. These Red Sox had won the last eight postseason games they'd played, coming back from a 3-0 hole to beat the Yankees in a magical ALCS and then sweeping St. Louis in the 2004 World Series. The White Sox hadn't won a postseason series of any kind since Red Faber led the 1917 team to a World Series victory over the New York Giants, with the deciding Game 6 played at the Polo Grounds.

Heck, the White Sox had thrown a World Series since they'd last won a playoff series. Why would this year be different?

◆

Two pitches, one big play.

When Game 1 finally arrived, on an 85-degree afternoon, Frank Thomas was given the honor of throwing out the first pitch. Jose Contreras got the start despite a career record of 2-5 with a 10.20 ERA against Boston. Contreras started Johnny Damon with a high, 93-m.p.h. fastball for ball one. The next pitch was another fastball, this one also 93 and on the inside corner, and Damon smashed it toward right field. But first baseman Paul Konerko, who was a defensive liability no more, lunged to his right to intercept the line drive, cradling it for the first out.

Damon had been a dynamo for the Red Sox last October, playing with a verve that epitomized the desperation of a franchise intent only on winning. But a lot had changed since then in Boston.

The Red Sox's roster had changed, with management allowing Pedro Martinez, Derek Lowe and Orlando Cabrera to leave as free agents. The franchise's hunger had also changed. No matter how much players and club officials talked about wanting to win again, human nature always argues against an encore.

The last weekend of the regular season, the Boston Globe had published a feature that perfectly illustrated how the Red Sox players had morphed into being entertainers, not ballplayers. The story was about Michelle Mangan, the new wife of Damon, and offered an unusually candid look at life in the fishbowl.

In it, Mangan denied allegations about having broken up Damon's first marriage—"he was already out and dating," she said—and objected to a previous newspaper report that she had once worked as a stripper. "If it was true, I wouldn't care," she said. "I'd say it."

Mangan talked in indelicate terms about the possibility

of having Damon's baby. "I'm scared, but he's been telling the whole world he's planning on knocking me up in February—that's the term he uses," she told Globe reporter Bella English.

She talked about being the stepmother of Damon's 6-year-old twins, who live with their mother in Florida. She said she thought she and Damon's first wife, Angie, could be friends, adding, "It would help if she met someone." Ouch.

The story talked about the Damons' 7,500-square-foot home in Brookline, not far from Fenway Park, and their 47-foot powerboat. They kept that in Florida, where Damon has a lakefront home that features a depiction of Da Vinci's "The Last Supper" painting, with Damon in the role of Jesus and other players as the disciples.

So much for the Olde Towne Teame being a collection of regular guys.

◆

Boston's Game 1 starter was Matt Clement, familiar to Chicago fans from his three seasons with the Cubs. The White Sox had pursued him when he filed for free agency the previous winter, forced to the wayside because of the Cubs' commitment to Mark Prior, Kerry Wood, Carlos Zambrano and Greg Maddux.

Some with the Cubs had questioned Clement's competitiveness, but there could be no doubting it after he picked Boston over offers from at least seven other teams, some of which would have been happy with .500 finishes. He said he wanted to go to a team with a good catcher (Jason Varitek) and a good chance to win.

For half the season, Clement was Boston's best starter, earning a trip to Detroit for the All-Star Game. But the second half was a nightmare. He was hit in the right side of the head by a Carl Crawford line drive July 27 at Tampa Bay, knocked to the ground as the ball caromed out to left field in one of the scariest moments of anyone's season. He was carried off the field on a stretcher and spent 24 hours in the hospital. Clement got back on the mound on Aug. 4, beating Kansas City, but never really got his mojo back, going 3-4 with a 5.72 ERA in 14 second-half starts.

On Monday, in the interview room at U.S. Cellular Field, Clement sounded ready.

"I'm motivated just because I'm pitching in a big game," he said when asked about being back in Chicago. "The Chicago factor, with all due respect, doesn't faze me other than I know where I'm at. I'm in a comfortable spot as far as getting something to eat tonight."

But it took only 13 pitches for the White Sox to jump ahead of Clement. Plate umpire John Hirschbeck is known for having a large strike zone, which would help Contreras as the day went on, but there was nothing anybody could do about Clement's wildness. He hit the leadoff man, Scott Podsednik, and No. 3 hitter Jermaine Dye. Podsednik stole third and scored on Konerko's fielder's-choice grounder.

So much for jitters. And the White Sox were just getting started.

With two outs and men on first and second, Aaron Rowand delivered a single in front of Damon. It scored Konerko, who had advanced on Carl Everett's single, and put two men on for catcher A.J. Pierzynski, who had been a teammate of Damon's at Dr. Phillips High School in Orlando.

With first baseman Kevin Millar playing deep, Pierzynski tried to bunt the first pitch, but the ball went foul. Good thing, as the left-handed-hitting Pierzynski lined the next pitch from Clement over the wall in left-center for a three-run homer.

The White Sox had a 5-0 lead in the first inning and cruised to a 14-2 victory, their first in the postseason at home since Game 1 of the 1959 World Series.

"I was trying to take advantage of the situation," Pierzynski said of the bunt attempt. "The guy on third, two outs and Millar playing way back, I was trying to get a cheapie. It went foul and it worked out."

The White Sox pounded Red Sox pithers for five home runs before the game was over, including a second one from Pierzynski and one by Podsednik, his first in 524 at-bats.

◆

Contreras lived in the strike zone during $7^2/_3$ strong innings and didn't need much help. He held the Red Sox to two runs. They came in a fourth inning that could have been much worse.

Trot Nixon led off with a single, and Varitek hit a dribbler down the third-base line that Joe Crede kicked all the way into foul territory by the Red Sox dugout. Millar shot a two-run double into the right-field corner, cutting the White Sox's lead to 6-2. There were still no outs.

Bill Mueller hit a grounder to second baseman Tadahito Iguchi, which everyone (except Iguchi) figured would move Millar to third. Iguchi looked toward third, pumped once and threw to Crede. The throw beat a shocked Millar to the bag but was a tough play for Crede, who grabbed the one-hop throw and tagged Millar for the first out.

Iguchi's gamble paid off, but only after scaring his manager to death. Television replays showed Guillen reaching his hands behind his head in exasperation, if not shock, as Iguchi threw to third, and then wiping his brow and heaving a giant sigh.

"I went from saying, 'No, no, no,' to 'Attaboy, good job,' "

Guillen said afterward. "I didn't think it was the right play, but it worked out pretty good for us."

Millar went home shaking his head.

"I've gone second to third on that ground ball my whole life," he said. "Everybody in baseball goes second to third on that ball. I can't ever remember anybody making that throw. Billy hit the ball hard, and Iguchi made a big play. His throw had a chance to get away, but Crede made the tag. That was a big play."

◆

Coming back from deficits had been a popular theme in Boston since last year's ALCS. The third game of that series was a 19-8 Yankee win, almost as ugly as this one. So Francona naturally fielded a question about whether the Red Sox would be more comfortable down early to the White Sox because they had rallied to beat the Yankees a year ago.

"That was a long time ago," Francona said. "It's a little different team. ... You know, last year is a long time ago, different team, different scenario."

Francona got that right. When the Pinstripes had teed off on Bronson Arroyo in Game 3 in 2004, Francona came back with Derek Lowe in Game 4, Pedro Martinez in 5, Curt Schilling in 6 and then Lowe again, on short rest, in 7. Only Schilling was still with the Red Sox in 2005.

The rebuilt Red Sox had invested heavily in keeping Varitek and adding shortstop Edgar Renteria, leaving themselves thin on the pitching side. The two starters behind Clement in this series were David Wells, with a 4.45 ERA, and Tim Wakefield, with a 4.15 ERA. Schilling, whose ERA was a bloated 5.69, wasn't available until a possible Game 4.

While the 2004 ALCS illustrated the best possible Red Sox response to a blowout, you only had to go back to mid-September to see how quickly one bad thing could lead to another.

After Clement was knocked out in the second inning by Oakland on Sept. 18 at Fenway Park, Wells didn't make it through the third at Tampa Bay the next night. Schilling earned an important win for Boston on Sept. 20, but the Red Sox lost to the Devil Rays the following night, with Wakefield and Timlin giving up five eighth-inning runs.

That wasn't just a blueprint for the White Sox. It was a fresh blueprint.

Graffanino's gaffe

Error by ex-White Sox opens door for Iguchi's pivotal homer in Game 2

For the second day in a row, Chicago was blessed with both an Indian summer afternoon and playoff baseball. The Red Sox-White Sox games were all scheduled for late-afternoon starting times, as Fox had selected the Yankees-Angels series for prime time.

As the teams took batting practice under a bright blue sky, fans entered U.S. Cellular Field wearing short-sleeve shirts. Those who brought windbreakers carried them, as it was 81 degrees when Mark Buehrle threw the first pitch.

White Sox Chairman Jerry Reinsdorf, unusually visible these days, stood on the field watching batting practice. He did an interview with Scott Merkin, the White Sox correspondent for MLB.com, and then another with Fox Chicago's Corey McPherrin. He had put off the Tribune's Melissa Isaacson earlier, but she took another stab at him and hit the jackpot. This was the Reinsdorf the public should see more of, the one who not only has something to say but also expresses himself in an interesting way.

Reinsdorf was recalling the brutal days of late September, when the magical season was threatening to turn into a cruel joke, at his expense.

"I felt like, as the lead was dwindling from 15 games to 1½, that somebody had tied me to the railroad tracks and there was a train coming and he was trying to stop and all I could do was pray that he would stop before he ran over me, but there was nothing I could do about it," Reinsdorf said. "So once that happened, once the train stopped, it was nothing but relief. ... It's been a great year. No matter what happens, it has been a successful year, and everything from here on is great."

Isaacson, who had covered the Bulls during the Michael Jordan era, reminded the chairman of one of his most famous quotes. He had said—or at least he was reported to have said—that he would trade all of his NBA championship rings for just one World Series ring.

"The story from that is I was getting a lot of criticism from White Sox fans that I was paying too much attention to the Bulls, so I tried to defuse it," Reinsdorf said. "But it was a silly thing to say. You can't trade one for the other. ... They're just different. That was a phenomenal experience being associated with six world championships and with the greatest player ever to play the game. It was just different."

As a child in Brooklyn, Reinsdorf was devoted to the Dodgers. His love affair with baseball had survived the franchise's move to Los Angeles, as well as one disappointment after another during his involvement with the White Sox. All was right in his world now that he had one of eight horses still running in baseball's version of the Triple Crown.

"The fact is, baseball is baseball," Reinsdorf said. "It's bigger than all the other sports. If you said nobody can bet on football, half the people wouldn't watch it anymore. I've had conversations with people who say, 'I like football better than baseball,' and I say, 'What was the first football game you ever went to?' and they say, 'I don't remember.' But they all remember their first baseball game, who they went with, who was playing. Baseball is part of the fabric of America. As somebody once said, if you want to understand Americans, you have to understand baseball, and that's true."

◆

Boston fans turned out all over North America to watch the World Series champions play in 2005, but there seemed to be only a few Red Sox fans among the crowds for Games 1 and 2 at U.S. Cellular. Their absence was both noticeable and surprising—before the best-of-five division series began, a story in the Boston Globe had suggested it would be cheaper for Bostonians to buy plane tickets and pay for hotel rooms in Chicago than it would be to try to get into Fenway Park for Games 3 and 4 over the weekend.

Either tickets in Chicago weren't as easy to get as the Globe suggested—some fans paid up to $400 per ticket to sit in the upper deck at the Cell—or Red Sox Nation wasn't following the 2005 team as closely as one might have thought.

"I think they think the Red Sox are going to win this series," said Art Spohr, a 58-year-old White Sox season ticket-holder who had grown up in Boston. "They still feel they're going to make it to the ALCS to play the Yankees."

◆

Buehrle, starting a playoff game for the first time, did not come out throwing zeroes. Johnny Damon led off the first inning with a single that got past Joe Crede at third, and Edgar Renteria followed with a double into the left-field corner. They both scored on Manny Ramirez's single to left-center.

Boston scored two more runs in the third inning, the rally

again started by a Damon single. Like the White Sox's Paul Konerko, Damon was expected to be one of the top players available on the free-agent market during the winter, and here was his chance to showcase himself. After an 0-for-4, two-strike-out performance in Game 1, he had belatedly joined the fray.

But the baseball gods had not deigned this to be Damon's day. They spin and twist games, especially those in October, with no pattern and often little foreshadowing. Every player reports to the ballpark hoping to be today's hero but knowing that someone has to be the goat.

This day was to be all about the second basemen: the Red Sox's Tony Graffanino, a native New Yorker who had been with the White Sox when they last went to the playoffs, and the White Sox's Tadahito Iguchi, who had more playoff experience (albeit on the other side of the earth) than any of his teammates.

Back in December, when Iguchi was as well known in Chicago as most of his teammates on the Fukuoka Daiei Hawks, agent Richard Moss figured he had the perfect destination for him: Boston. He even got Iguchi a tryout with the defending World Series champs.

Good thing for the White Sox that didn't work out.

With Iguchi in the Chicago lineup and Graffanino filling a hole for Boston, second base was a win-win situation for the home team in Game 2. Iguchi delivered a three-run homer into the left-field bullpen in the fifth inning, turning a 4-2 deficit into a 5-4 White Sox lead. It came two batters after Graffanino, whom Reinsdorf had called his favorite player during his four-season stay in Chicago, had allowed a grounder to roll between his legs.

"Everybody who has played this game has made mistakes," the classy Graffanino said later. "Today was my day."

Iguchi had had his share of bad days too. But as much as anyone, the four-time Japanese Pacific League All-Star represented why this had been such a magical season for the White Sox.

Like catcher A.J. Pierzynski, leadoff man Scott Podsednik and reliever Dustin Hermanson, Iguchi was a great fit for a huge need. He was available and general manager Ken Williams went out and got him, although in Iguchi's case Williams needed the last ounce of his patience.

Moss believed Iguchi could follow the lead of Ichiro Suzuki and Hideki Matsui and get top dollar from a major-league club because he was such a proven talent. The Red Sox seemed a perfect fit more because they were a team in transition than because they had just won the World Series. The departure of Pedro Martinez, Derek Lowe, Orlando Cabrera and Nomar Garciaparra meant they had money to spend.

But Red Sox GM Theo Epstein didn't bite at Moss' asking price of $20 million. Williams expressed interest but didn't have much money to spend. Moss just kept waiting and waiting, hoping Boston or another big fish would bite. When no one did, Iguchi eventually signed with the White Sox for two years and an option, with $4.95 million guaranteed.

Like the dinner tab on a first date with your eventual spouse, that was money well spent.

Boston didn't pursue Iguchi harder because Epstein & Co. believed they would be all right with Mark Bellhorn, a 2004 World Series hero, as the regular and internal options like Ramon Vazquez and Kevin Youkilis as his backup. But Bellhorn went cold just as suddenly as he had gotten hot, the cycle he followed during a previous stint with the Cubs.

Epstein traded for Graffanino in July and released Bellhorn, then hitting .216, on Aug. 20. During the 2005 season, manager Terry Francona used seven players at second base. The Red Sox had played 15 there over three seasons, including the likes of Todd Walker, Lou Merloni, Damian Jackson, Pokey Reese and Alex Cora. They even moved first baseman Doug Mientkiewicz to second for one game in 2004.

Graffanino, 33, might have been a fill-in, but he was a good one, hitting .319 and barreling into the pivotman on double plays while making only three errors in 51 games. Reporters swarmed him on the last weekend of the season when Boston hosted the Yankees with playoff spots on the line because he spoke for his team as if he'd been there forever.

That's Graffanino: capable, gracious, unafraid.

He was trying to get an inning-ending double play on a grounder by Juan Uribe but came up without the ball. He said later that it "crushed" him to see Iguchi capitalize with a two-out, three-run homer that turned David Wells' two-run lead into a one-run deficit.

Ozzie Guillen, the old shortstop, tried to explain that even simple tasks aren't as simple as they look from the cheap seats.

"Graffanino's ground ball was not as easy as people think it was," Guillen said. "There was a lot of spin on it. I was explaining to one of my kids. He asked me what you do on that particular thing. I said you've got to stay back. It was a big break for us, [but] if people think it was an easy play to make, they're wrong."

Guillen had said repeatedly he considered Iguchi his most valuable player. How different things might have been had Iguchi showed the Red Sox a little something more at that December tryout in San Diego.

Winning at a high level, a relatively new experience for the White Sox, was old hat for Iguchi, whose teams were a combined 146 games over .500 the last seven seasons. Five of them—four with the Hawks in Japan—won division championships.

Iguchi was probably Guillen's steadiest player, hitting .278

with 15 homers and 71 runs batted in while bunting often, working counts and hitting the ball to the right side when Podsednik was on base. He had been a middle-of-the-order hitter playing for manager Sadaharu Oh but revamped his game completely to fit the role Guillen gave him. Before Game 2, he lacked only one thing: a signature moment.

That's what he got when he sent an 0-1 curveball from Wells flying into the White Sox's bullpen. If Buehrle and the bullpen could make it hold up, it would leave the Sox only one victory away from their first October celebration in 88 years. Someone would have to explain to Iguchi why winning is such a big deal in Chicago.

◆

With a 5-4 lead in the top of the eighth inning, Guillen called down to the bullpen to bring in his closer, Bobby-gulp-Jenks.

A big kid with an arm that could make Bob Gibson envious, Jenks had quietly been acquired for $20,000 the previous winter when the Los Angeles Angels put him on waivers. He had been made available after first having a permanent screw placed in his elbow, which was threatening to implode, and then, according to some reports, cold-cocking a minor-league teammate.

In seven-plus months in the Sox organization, the 24-year-old Jenks had been nothing but a model student. He embraced a move to the bullpen when it was proposed during spring camp and then went to Double-A Birmingham-a possible step back in his development-to learn to relieve. He was a natural for the closer's role, maintaining his composure and throwing more strikes with his high-90s fastball and snapdragon curveball than anyone expected. Jenks was leading the Southern League in saves when Williams summoned him to Chicago in July.

Guillen eased him in gradually, letting him get his feet on the ground in the middle innings before giving him more significant situations. But with Dustin Hermanson losing velocity and sometimes unavailable because of lower-back problems, Guillen turned to Jenks as his closer down the stretch. He was untouchable at times and did not get down on himself when he failed to come through, including back-to-back blown saves against Cleveland Sept. 19-20.

As Jenks took the mound at U.S. Cellular, there was a huge roar and then chants of "Bobby! Bobby!" from the crowd of 40,799. But as Manny Ramirez walked toward the plate, an uneasy quiet followed. A question hung in the air: Could the kid handle the big stage?

"I was more nervous in the sixth and seventh innings after Iguchi hit that bomb," Jenks said later. "Then I started to think about it and got goose bumps and that gut-wrenching feeling."

Jenks started Ramirez with a 97-m.p.h. fastball, which the slugger took for a strike. Jenks then missed with a curve and a fastball, taking the count to 2-1. He fired a 98-m.p.h. fastball past Ramirez, then hit 100 m.p.h. on the ballpark radar gun with the next one. Ramirez caught it on the nose but didn't elevate it, as a hitter would say. Instead he drove a liner right at Rowand in center field.

Jenks went on to get five more outs, preserving the 5-4 victory. Graffanino, hoping for redemption, had doubled with one out in the ninth. But Jenks got Damon on a foul pop to A.J. Pierzynski and Renteria on a grounder to Juan Uribe. Konerko walked to the mound and handed him the game ball. "It's going on top of the mantel," Jenks said.

◆

On their way home, whether on the "L" or by car, the most observant Sox fans could discuss a possible omen. Iguchi's game-winning homer had sailed almost directly over a sign Major League Baseball had placed on the outfield wall. It read "8 Teams, 1 Champion."

Money players

Konerko's homer, Hernandez's high-wire act help finish off Red Sox

Playoff baseball always brings its special rewards. The White Sox wound up with one of the best ones a team can have, getting storied Fenway Park to themselves for an afternoon workout the day before Game 3 of the division series.

With the Green Monster and all its nooks and crannies, the Pesky Pole in right field and the left-field pole that allowed Carlton Fisk's home run to pass by safely in the 1975 World Series, there's no park in the major leagues like Fenway. It was Ted Williams' home throughout his career, and before that it had seen Babe Ruth pitch a World Series shutout.

When Fenway Park is quiet, with Yawkey Way missing the vendors that bring the neighborhood to life when the Red Sox are playing, it is as close to church as you get in baseball. Watching a team work out there must be like sitting in the back row at Carnegie Hall for a sound check.

Given their 2-0 lead in the series, it's safe to say the White Sox players were in high spirits as they dressed in the tiny visitors' clubhouse.

Paul Konerko, a Rhode Island native, knew all about Red Sox Nation. It was a way of life for his family in Cranston, R.I., about 60 miles from Fenway. His father Hank had moved his family to Connecticut when Paul was 6 and then on to Scottsdale, Ariz., when he was 11, but their roots were firmly in New England soil.

Konerko would have many family members at Game 3.

"They're still Red Sox fans, but I think they're going to pull for me," Konerko said. "The fact that Boston won the World Series last year takes some heat off. If they hadn't won last year, they'd probably still be pulling against me."

In truth, it's hard to pull against Konerko. He's a working-class player who fit well on the team from the working-class part of Chicago.

In a front-page profile in the Chicago Tribune on the day of Game 1, David Haugh captured the essence of Konerko, a fixture in the White Sox's lineup since 1999, when he was acquired from Cincinnati in a trade for center fielder Mike Cameron.

"The way Konerko goes about his business, his black Sox cap might as well be a hard hat and his spikes a pair of steel-toed boots," Haugh wrote. "He is a foreman wearing a first baseman's glove, a snug fit in a city full of Polish-Americans who identify with his last name and working stiffs who relate to his love for labor."

Throughout his career, Konerko's coaches had lamented that he was a high-maintenance player. He always studied and tweaked his swing, rarely letting himself relax. His ritual in the on-deck circle, first bending at the waist and twisting his body around, sometimes resembled someone trying to crank-start a 1920 Ford.

Konerko was notoriously tough on himself when he made

outs, often fretting his way into prolonged slumps. He had never taken a dollar of Jerry Reinsdorf's money without giving him $1.50 in sweat.

While his season totals were remarkably consistent—he averaged 28 home runs and 95 RBIs for the White Sox in the last seven seasons—he often he piled up production numbers while he was hot, squirreling them away for the cold stretches sure to follow. He never stopped working at trying to be more consistent.

"My grandpa always told us that just having a job is honorable, so treat it with respect no matter what it is," said Peter Konerko, Paul's older brother, a photographer in New York. "Paul's attitude came from learning at a young age that whether it's hitting a 90-m.p.h. fastball or digging a hole, your job requires integrity. I think Paul works harder now than he did when he was in A-ball."

Konerko would get his work in on this day, just as he would any other. But his first item of business was dealing with the waves of reporters who visited his locker, which was tucked behind a pole around the corner from the spartan room that passed for a lounge.

While the White Sox had scored 19 runs in the first two games, Konerko said Jose Contreras and Mark Buehrle were the reason they had jumped ahead of Boston. Pitching had been the key to a 13-6 run that started with a 2-1 win at Minnesota on Sept. 16.

Shutting down the Red Sox was never easy. They not only had the big boppers in the middle of the lineup, they had disciplined, on-base-machine type hitters from the top to the bottom.

Consider this comparison: Boston had eight hitters who drew 50-plus walks during the regular season, while the White Sox had only one (Konerko, with 81). Yet through the first two games in the series, White Sox hitters had drawn three walks to the Red Sox's two. Contreras and Buehrle had combined to throw 140 strikes out of 195 pitches. That's 72 percent, even better than the 70-percent standard pitching coach Don Cooper preaches.

"Our pitching is the reason we're even in the playoffs," Konerko said. "It doesn't surprise me that these guys have brought their 'A' games. That's what I've seen all year. I look at it from a hitter's standpoint, and these guys pitch the way you're supposed to pitch. They attack people. They're fearless."

This season, and in many before it, Konerko had been the last player White Sox fans had to worry about. But because he would be eligible for free agency after the season, he was about to become the organization's biggest question mark.

Winning in the playoffs would make it easier to fit a fat Konerko contract into the 2006 payroll. According to major-league sources, teams earned only about $2 million from ticket sales in the first round, but that number could increase to $3 million to $4 million in the championship series and $4 million to $5 million in the World Series, depending on the length of the series. With additional revenue from parking and concessions, World Series teams could make $15 million to $17 million, according to one estimate.

Ozzie Guillen long ago had made it clear he wanted Konerko back. "I will do everything in my power to keep him, but my power doesn't include money," Guillen said at the workout. "It's up to Jerry Reinsdorf. Paul knows for a fact we want him back. Kenny [Williams] wants him back. It's up to him what he wants to do."

Konerko talked about how the White Sox had to execute with runners on base because they didn't have any players as good as Boston's Manny Ramirez and David Ortiz. He didn't mention that only five major-league players had hit 40 or more homers the last two seasons, and that he was one of them, along with Ortiz, Ramirez, Albert Pujols and Adam Dunn.

Konerko had 97 or more RBIs in five of his last six seasons. There were only nine others who had done that: Jeff Kent, Carlos Delgado, Jim Thome, Miguel Tejada, Alex Rodriguez, Vladimir Guerrero, Gary Sheffield, Pujols and Ramirez. But Konerko wouldn't put himself in that group.

"You guys look at it from numbers," Konerko said. "I look at situations."

Konerko said he didn't believe he belonged in that group of elite hitters, at least not yet.

"I'm not as good as those guys," he said, referring to Ortiz and Ramirez. "I know I can drive in runs and I can hit the ball out of the park, but there's different tiers of hitters in my mind. I don't think I'm quite on the same level as those guys. Part of it is they've done it in the World Series and in the post-season a number of times. That's a different game, and you need to do that if you want to become one of the really good hitters, if you want to take it to another level. That's where I want to take it."

◆

Few cities, probably none, get a better feeling on the day of a big game than Boston. Whether it's at the Prudential Center downtown or across the Charles River in Cambridge, there's a delicious air of anticipation when the Red Sox are in the thick of the action.

There was no mistaking that the Yankees had been in town the last weekend of the season. With a division title at stake and neither team assured of a playoff spot when the series began, Red Sox Nation was on high alert. But with the home team trailing two games to none and forced to count on knuckleballer Tim Wakefield to get the division series in Curt Schilling's hands, the city was most notable for its quiet.

It felt nothing like it had a year ago, when baseball's most loyal fans practically willed their Red Sawx back into their historic American League Championship Series with the Yankees. Even the Boston Globe, a newspaper whose sportswriters combine passion with insight and excellent writing, didn't seem into this one, not anymore. On the morning of Game 3, the Red Sox didn't have a prominent presence on Page 1, and the featured photo in the paper was an overhead shot of elephants crossing a bridge, announcing that the circus was in town.

Forever, it seemed, the biggest circus in Boston had been at Fenway Park. But success had changed that.

"After 2004, every game the Red Sox play the rest of my life will be an exhibition game," said Bill Ballou, a New Englander who had covered the Red Sox for the Worcester, Mass., Telegram and Gazette since the days of Bill Lee and Jim Rice.

◆

Freddy Garcia's control wasn't sharp in Game 3. He walked Johnny Damon in the first inning and Ramirez and John Olerud in the second inning. Yet the Red Sox couldn't capitalize to take an early lead.

In the bottom of the first inning, Guillen's overshift on Ortiz-the result of work by the White Sox's advance scouts-resulted in one of the strangest (luckiest?) double plays you could ever see.

With Damon on first base and one out, the White Sox stationed second baseman Tadahito Iguchi on the edge of the outfield grass toward first base. Shortstop Juan Uribe slid over to the first-base side of the bag, playing deep, like a second baseman shading a hitter up the middle. Third baseman Joe Crede moved over within 20 feet of second base, leaving the third-base line and left field wide open.

Ortiz, known for his monstrous power to right field, didn't seem tempted by the openings. He took a 1-1 fastball that was just outside, an ideal pitch to go to the opposite field. He then swung through an inside fastball, evening the count, and took a ball, getting to a full count. Damon was running on the 3-2 pitch, the first of which Ortiz pulled foul.

On the next one, Crede-not Uribe-was breaking to cover second base, and Ortiz lined the ball up the middle. Crede barely had to move to catch it. He then tagged Damon for an unassisted double play, possibly the first one ever by a third baseman with a runner on first. "When you're hot, you're hot," Chris Berman said on ESPN's telecast.

The White Sox took a 2-0 lead with a two-out rally against Wakefield in the third inning. Uribe and Scott Podsednik delivered back-to-back doubles, Podsednik slashing a knuckleball into the left-field corner. Iguchi and Jermaine Dye followed with singles before Wakefield escaped the inning on another hard-hit ball, Konerko's liner to right fielder Trot Nixon.

But Garcia did not have his best stuff. Ortiz and Ramirez hit back-to-back homers in a stretch of five pitches in the fourth inning, tying the score 2-2.

Konerko untied it in the sixth.

After Dye walked to start the inning, Konerko mashed a high floater, driving it high and onto Landsdowne Street, near the Cask 'n Flagon, one of the city's best known bars. The White Sox had a 4-2 lead.

Ramirez re-energized the Fenway Park crowd of 35,496 by blasting a leadoff homer to center field in the sixth inning, making it 4-3. Garcia departed in favor of Damaso Marte, Guillen putting his trust in the enigmatic reliever from the Dominican Republic whom he had temporarily kicked off the team in

September when Marte angered him by arriving late for batting practice. Many fans and some reporters had argued against Marte being on the playoff roster, saying the spot should have gone to rookie Brandon McCarthy. But Guillen wanted a left-hander to use early in games, allowing him to save the electrifying Neal Cotts for late-inning situations.

Marte just about took the White Sox out of the game. The first hitter he faced, Nixon, singled to right. Marte walked the next two, Bill Mueller and Olerud. Plate umpire Mark Wegner was not giving Marte much of a strike zone, prompting Guillen to scream at him from the dugout between pitches.

Bases loaded with no outs for Jason Varitek, who was pinch-hitting for Doug Mirabelli. Gulp.

The fans at Fenway did a double take when Guillen went to the mound and signaled for the bullpen. He wanted the White Sox's "Señor Citizen," Orlando Hernandez. El Duque had built a 9-3 postseason record while pitching for the Yankees, but he'd done so poorly in August and September that McCarthy took his spot in the rotation. Even though Guillen used El Duque twice out of the bullpen the last weekend of the season in Cleveland, he had seemed an unlikely choice for the playoff roster. The biggest benefit to him being on the roster, it seemed, was his ability to soothe Contreras, who could start twice if the division series went its full five games.

But Guillen was looking for more than emotional support from Hernandez. He was looking for him to use his big-game experience to throw strikes and get outs when lesser men would be gasping for air.

"I went to him because he's the only guy with experience," Guillen said later. "He's had a lot of success against the Red Sox, he's known Varitek a long time, and I know this kid is going to show up with cold blood."

Varitek was 3-for-28 in his career against Hernandez. El Duque started him with a big curveball, just missing the inside corner. There was more screaming from the White Sox dugout, this time Guillen flinging a towel to the dugout floor and storming to the top step. Wegner took off his mask and told Guillen to calm down. Hernandez came back with a high fastball at the edge of the strike zone but again didn't get the call from Wegner.

Two-and-oh, bases still loaded, still no one out.

Hernandez, unlike Guillen, kept his cool. He threw a 91-m.p.h. fastball past Varitek for his first strike, then got Varitek to chase a fastball at the letters. He swung underneath it, hitting a high pop that Konerko caught in foul territory.

Up came Tony Graffanino, the Game 2 goat. Hernandez started him with a fastball over the middle of the plate, and Graffanino fouled it off. He missed with a curve, then got ahead in the count when Graffanino fouled off a high curve. He missed outside with a curve, Graffanino not fishing, and then came with a high fastball, which Graffanino fouled back. Hernandez came back with another curve aimed on the outside corner, which Graffanino took to work the count full.

One ball and it would be a tie game. Hernandez threw a strike, which Graffanino fouled off. He missed the outside corner with a fastball, but Graffanino couldn't lay off it, fouling it off. The next pitch was further outside the zone, high and away, but Graffanino didn't want to take a called third strike, so he fouled it off.

Before the fourth 3-2 pitch, A.J. Pierzynski went to the mound to talk to Hernandez. The catcher, who had been criticized in San Francisco for not working well with pitchers, listened as Hernandez told him he had Graffanino set up for a curveball. The old warhorse wanted to throw that pitch, and

Pierzynski told him to trust it. He snapped one off low in the strike zone, and Graffanino popped it up in the infield. Pierzynski pumped his fist as Uribe was making the catch, then exchanged a high-five with Hernandez.

Now it was Damon's turn. Bases still loaded, now two outs.

Hernandez started Damon with a slow breaking ball for a called strike. But Damon, like Graffanino before him, was patient enough to get the count to 3-2. With the runners starting on the pitch, Hernandez zipped a 91-m.p.h. fastball in on Damon's hands. He fouled it back, forcing Hernandez to throw his sixth 3-2 pitch in a span of two batters.

Again, Pierzynski went to the mound to talk to Hernandez. He threw his curveball, this time low and inside. It should have been ball four, forcing in Nixon with the tying run, but Damon was too geared up to make something happen. His fast-twitch muscles got him as he started to swing and couldn't stop. Pierzynski, who had gone down in the dirt to catch the ball, came up with it and tagged Damon. Wegner called it strike three on the checked swing.

Hernandez worked two more scoreless innings, yielding just one hit, and the Sox squeezed home an insurance run in the top of the ninth for a 5-3 lead. Although it was up to Bobby Jenks to protect that lead, the game and the series were effectively over when Damon went down swinging.

"The right pitch at the right time," Damon said later.

The Globe's Dan Shaughnessy wrote that Hernandez's pitches were "moving like Allen Iverson in traffic." Nice description.

Hernandez had never thrown a better inning under more pressure.

"I saw the situation, and the first thing was getting the key out," Hernandez said. "Once I got Varitek out, I knew I had a chance with the next batter. Graffanino had a great at-bat. He battled and I had to resort to my experience, and it's kind of a gutsy call. I called that pitch inside. My catcher was surprised, but I thought that's the only way I could get him out."

After Edgar Renteria hit a grounder to Iguchi for the 27th out, White Sox players rolled out of the tiny dugout to celebrate the clinching victory on this baseball holy ground. Hernandez and trainer Herm Schneider held an embrace for a long time. It hadn't been easy to keep the fragile, sometimes finicky Hernandez on the mound, but Hernandez worked hard on the schedule he and Schneider put together. It was all worth it on this one afternoon.

"We got a lot out of him this year, 10 wins," Schneider said during the celebration. "I don't know if anybody else could have gotten that out of him."

◆

These days, no one was getting more out of his team than Guillen. Maybe Guillen really should walk away if the White Sox won it all, because it was impossible to imagine he would ever be hotter than he was at the moment.

The fiery little shortstop who couldn't get the White Sox to the World Series during 13 roller-coaster seasons as a player stood four victories away from becoming the first manager since Al Lopez to take the South Side team-or any Chicago team-to the major leagues' promised land. He was not exactly riding anyone's coattails either.

Calling on Hernandez-and overlooking his 5.12 earned-run average during the 99-win season-to protect a one-run lead with the bases loaded and no outs in the sixth inning was one of many winning moves by Guillen in the White Sox's first-round sweep.

"No one believes this, but the success we have had, a lot of it is due to Ozzie," Hernandez said later, with a proud Ozzie

Guillen Jr. serving as his translator. "When he makes a move, none of us complain."

Given Guillen's willingness to say and do almost anything, it was no surprise he was slamming a towel around in the dugout when Wegner wouldn't give Hernandez or Marte the benefit of the doubt, risking a playoff ejection. But underneath the volatile, entertaining exterior, it was becoming more clear by the day just how smart Guillen was and how much he had learned from some of the best in baseball, including Tony La Russa and Bobby Cox. He was sweating the small stuff just like Buck Showalter and the control freaks.

"Ozzie, the coaching staff-these guys prepare," Konerko said. "I know Ozzie gets the reputation for the other stuff and all that, but our guys are organized, and they study the game while it's going on."

While the White Sox won three in a row against the defending World Series champs, outhomering them 7-3, they very easily could have found themselves having to beat Schilling in Game 4 on Saturday to force a Game 5 back in Chicago on Sunday.

The 5-4 victory in Game 2 and the 5-3 win in Game 3 were decided by Guillen's risk-taking with his bullpen and a series of incredibly small plays that all seemed to go in the White Sox's favor.

One universally overlooked example from Game 2: Immediately after Iguchi's home run had given Buehrle a lead, Varitek led off for Boston. As Varitek stepped into the box, Guillen frantically waved toward left field, capturing Podsednik's attention.

Guillen motioned for Podsednik to move back, and Podsednik retreated five or six steps. Varitek immediately lined a 1-0 pitch toward the left-field line, and it took a quick burst by

Podsednik to cut the ball off, holding Varitek to a single and turning down the heat on Buehrle. The Red Sox would have had the tying run on second with no outs if the ball had gone to the wall.

As a rule, Guillen doesn't like to go to the top step of the dugout and move his outfielders around. But this time he felt he had no choice.

"I thought he was playing too close, especially with the way the wind was blowing," Guillen said. "Who knows? Maybe if I don't move him back he would have caught it [on the fly]. … I don't like to do that. You move a guy over, everybody in the ballpark sees you, and the ball goes right to where he was standing. It makes you look like an ass."

Fair to say Jenks could have made Guillen look silly when he was handed one of the toughest save situations imaginable in Game 2: one-run lead, six outs to go and Manny Ramirez at the plate. But it worked.

Hernandez could have made Guillen look silly in Game 3. But instead he made him look brilliant.

Hernandez fell behind 2-0 to the first hitter he faced, Varitek, and then went to three-ball counts on Graffanino and Damon. He retired all three, getting Graffanino and Damon after they had forced him to throw a total of six pitches with 3-2 counts.

"I was nervous in left field," Podsednik said. "I was thinking, 'If I'm this nervous, how does El Duque feel? What does it feel like to stand on the mound?' … But that's what he's all about. He's a money pitcher."

Guillen had done a marvelous job using players in situations where they can succeed. He did that in the top of the ninth in Game 3, ordering Uribe, a terrific bunter despite his free-swinging nature, to suicide-squeeze on a 2-1 pitch from Mike Timlin, scoring Pierzynski with an instant insurance run.

Guillen's fielding alignments—suggested by scouts Dave Yoakum, Bryan Little, Bill Scherrer, Doug Laumann, Gary Pellant and others who followed Boston in September—also clicked against the Red Sox.

The White Sox got four outs from the exaggerated shift they used on Ortiz, including two groundouts Iguchi handled from right field and the unusual unassisted double play in the first inning of Game 3.

Guillen's only real misstep was taking a reporter's bait and talking about his pitching and roster considerations for the league championship series before the game in Boston, and the baseball gods gave him a pass on that one.

As easy as the three-game sweep might seem in retrospect, it could have turned on many plays, including that Varitek single in the sixth inning of Game 2. What if Guillen hadn't moved Podsednik back?

"I've got no idea," Podsednik said, his victory cigar blazing as he stood near where third base had been almost an hour earlier. "It's tough to talk about the what-ifs. Maybe I would have got a good jump. Maybe I would have got a bad jump. Who knows? This game gives us a lot of questions that we never know the answer to."

Guillen had all the answers.

◆

While reporters were working on their Game 3 stories in the press box high atop Fenway Park, the Globe's Shaughnessy approached a reporter from the Chicago Tribune. "Tag," Shaughnessy said. "You're it.'"

The ride was picking up speed.

Another break

Weather and travel test Angels and Yankees as Sox rest and wait

How hot were the White Sox?

A day after wrapping up a division series sweep of the defending World Series champions, their first victory in a postseason series of any kind since the 1917 World Series, all they did was travel home from Boston to Chicago. Yet they still gained an advantage.

The Los Angeles Angels led the Yankees two games to one in the other AL Division Series, but Game 4 at Yankee Stadium was rained out, putting the Sox's next opponent behind schedule.

And the advantage would be even bigger if the Yankees could win Game 4, forcing the teams to fly across America to play a deciding Game 5 at Angel Stadium on Monday night, the eve of the scheduled AL Championship Series opener at U.S. Cellular Field.

While the Yankees had the bigger reputation, this year's Angels had the better team, largely because of a deeper pitching staff. The best-case scenario for the Sox appeared to be the Yankees winning the next two.

The Sox had an advantage against Boston because the Red Sox didn't clinch a playoff spot until the last day of the regular season, only two days before the first-round series began. Matt Clement, who had gone 3-4 with a 5.72 ERA in the second half, started Game 1, which turned into a 14-2 win for the White Sox. They were headed toward a similar advantage in the championship series.

◆

In the rain-delayed Game 4, the Angels were forced to start their Game 2 starter, John Lackey, on short rest because left-hander Jarrod Washburn was sick at the team's Manhattan hotel with strep throat. Manager Mike Scioscia could have used his ace, Bartolo Colon, but he had sent him home early to Anaheim so he could get treatment for a sore back before starting Game 5, if it was necessary.

Of course, the Angels hoped to avoid Game 5, which would free up Colon to start the ALCS opener against the White Sox. They figured to have a decent chance as the Yankees were starting Shawn Chacon, an unknown quantity acquired from Colorado in a midseason move to prop up a collapsing starting rotation.

But Chacon was money. He blanked the Angels in the first five innings, not allowing a runner until the fourth, and eventually held Los Angeles to two runs and four hits in 6⅓ innings, leaving with the Angels ahead 2-1 on back-to-back doubles by Chone Figgins and Orlando Cabrera.

But Lackey and Scioscia's deep bullpen couldn't protect the lead. The Yankees rallied for a 3-2 victory, with Derek Jeter driving in the go-ahead run on a two-hopper down the third-base line off Scot Shields in the seventh inning.

You won't find that fielder's choice on Jeter's career highlight reel, but it was a big play for the 2005 Yankees and maybe even a bigger one for the Sox, who were comfortably watching the game on the plasma screens in their Chicago homes.

Jeter fought off a nasty two-strike pitch from Shields, reaching down and sending a topspin slapper toward Figgins, the third baseman. He had one choice: Make a perfect play or allow the go-ahead run to score.

Figgins' shot at the perfect play was probably lost when the ball spun sharply to his right, forcing him to move his glove maybe 18 inches. That was just enough to complicate the snap throw he had to make to catcher Bengie Molina. The throw was toward the first-base side of the plate, and Molina's tag on Jorge Posada was a nanosecond late.

Yankees 3, Angels 2. Mariano Rivera warming in the bullpen. The series was going to a fifth game, a 2,800-mile flight away.

Scioscia acknowledged Sunday that he had learned Washburn could be unavailable before Colon had left for the airport. But Scioscia decided not to use Colon in Game 4, going for the jugular. The manager's feelings about his ace couldn't have been a confidence-builder for the Angels.

"Bart needs the time," Scioscia said.

Colon, the supersized right-hander who pitched for the Sox in 2003, had won 21 games and the Cy Young Award during the regular season. But his back had been a problem late in the season and might have contributed to his loss to Mike Mussina in the division series opener.

◆

This being baseball, off-the-field intrigue was part of the picture.

The Yankees wanted to play Sunday's Game 4 in the late afternoon, which would have made it a little easier on them if they won and had to go to Anaheim for Game 5. But Fox television was scheduled to carry the NFL during the afternoon. It wanted the game in its prime-time window and had the right to schedule the game at night, which it did.

The New York Daily News created a stir by reporting that the players union had signed off on an evening game only after being assured that the ALCS would be pushed back a day if the division series went five games, meaning the Sox might have to wait until Wednesday to get back on the field.

It was a bogus report. The union did not have the power to demand such an arrangement, and Commissioner Bud Selig said he had not been contacted by union officials.

The ALCS, Selig said, would start Tuesday unless the Yankees and Angels experienced more weather problems, which was highly unlikely with Game 5 set for California. Executives from the Angels and the Yankees had called MLB officials to see if the ALCS could be delayed, giving their teams time to recover from the extended first round. But there was no precedent for such a change, and Selig wasn't looking to create one.

◆

Game 5 began with Colon allowing a leadoff single to Jeter. He would face only five hitters before turning the game over to rookie Ervin Santana.

Colon winced in pain after a 1-1 pitch to Hideki Matsui in the first inning. Scioscia, who had been watching him closely, immediately went to the mound for a visit. The Angels' ace would stay in the game to strike out Matsui on a 95-m.p.h. fastball but struggled just walking back to the dugout.

When the second inning began, Santana was on the mound. Colon was out with an injury termed an inflamed shoulder, not just for the rest of the game but the rest of the postseason.

Suddenly it didn't really seem to matter who won this series. The Sox's pitching figured to be in much better shape than either the Angels' or the Yankees'.

Chicago romantics would have preferred a Game 5 victory by the Pinstripes, setting up a scenario in which the upstart Sox could roll through two of baseball's traditional power-houses before possibly meeting another one, the St. Louis Cardinals, in the World Series. What could be sweeter?

But October baseball in California is a sweet thing, too, especially with rain forecast in New York for another week as an offshoot of Hurricane Wilma, which had sliced across South Florida. Consider this a win-win for the Sox, who had earned an edge in preparation by wrapping up the Boston series three days earlier.

Mussina, rarely a bulldog, had remained in California with one of the Yankees' bullpen catchers after Game 2. The idea was that since he wasn't going to pitch in New York, he might as well remain as comfortable as possible.

Not that it mattered. The Angels' emergency alternative, Santana, far outclassed Mussina, who was making $17 million from George Steinbrenner in the fifth year of a six-year contract. A solo homer by Garret Anderson and a two-run triple by Adam Kennedy, both in the second inning, put the Angels in control.

After Joe Torre pulled Mussina in the third inning, Randy Johnson hung up zeroes for 4⅓ innings to keep the Yankees close, but in the end the Angels won 5-3, putting the game away on a great play by first baseman Darin Erstad, who robbed Matsui.

"Right now [Scioscia's] got a blend of the blue-collar guys and these young upstarts who don't know if they should be nervous or not," said Torre, who was a gentleman in defeat, as always. "It's a very impressive club. Plus he's got that pitching, and that combination is pretty tough."

But it didn't look as if the Angels would have Colon, and Washburn had already been ruled out of a possible Game 1 start because of his illness. What would the Angels do?

Scioscia honestly didn't know, and for a little while longer didn't want to care. The manager who had guided the Angels to a World Series title in 2002 wanted to savor this victory for an hour or two, which was all the time he had before hopping back on an airplane for the 2,000-mile trip to Chicago.

He knew he faced a chore in improvising a rotation for the best-of-seven series against the Sox. The first decision: Go with Paul Byrd on three days' rest in Game 1, give a start to somebody out of the bullpen, such as Kevin Gregg, or try a sneak attack with someone who hadn't been on the first-round roster, perhaps rookie lefty Joe Saunders.

"We've got a three-hour plane flight to try to figure that out," Scioscia said. He also was worried about a bullpen that wouldn't get a day off after working 16 innings in four days.

Torre had seen enough of the White Sox to know his conquerors would have their hands full.

"You have to be impressed with the job Ozzie Guillen did, and I think probably the best thing that happened to them this year is the fact that they were challenged at the end," Torre said before Game 5. "Sometimes when you have a big lead and you're not challenged the whole time, when you do get challenged, you're not up to it. But they had to work hard to get here, and certainly they came in playing well."

Torre admitted he was surprised that the White Sox eliminated Boston, which had matched the Yankees' total of 95 victories.

"I thought Boston was going to beat them," he said. "Does

that mean I didn't think the White Sox were a good team? No. But Boston is ferocious, and the White Sox were impressive. … Sure, they don't have the explosiveness of a Red Sox type of club, but you control the game with defense and pitching, and they got the momentum going and they used it."

Cold start

Sox struggle in Game 1 of ALCS, making mistakes on bases and at plate

Give Arte Moreno and Bill Stoneman credit for chutzpah, if nothing else. As the Los Angeles Angels prepared to play the New York Yankees in Game 5 of their division series on Monday night, their owner and general manager were busy working the telephone with Commissioner Bud Selig and other Major League Baseball officials.

They did not think it was fair they would have to start the American League Championship Series without even one day off, while the White Sox had been idle for three days. Ozzie Guillen had again lined up his second-half assassin, Jose Contreras, to work the opener and had used the time off to rest Orlando Hernandez, Bobby Jenks and their bullpen mates while scheduling a simulated game for Jon Garland, the 18-game winner and All-Star who had been lined up for Game 4 against Boston.

Like little kids, Moreno and Stoneman kicked and screamed. Selig would not give them their way.

MLB sources said the commissioner's office did go so far as

to call St. Louis' Tony La Russa and Houston's Phil Garner to see what the National League managers thought about starting the National League Championship Series on Tuesday, a day earlier than scheduled, so the Angels could get their day off. La Russa, according to the source, blew a gasket at the idea, saying many of his players had headed to their homes after the first-round clincher in San Diego and would not be returning to St. Louis in time.

It's hard to imagine any team being audacious enough to think three others should be inconvenienced for their sake, but that was the Angels.

As late as Tuesday afternoon, when he sat in the interview room at U.S. Cellular Field's splendid Conference and Learning Center, Angels manager Mike Scioscia acted as if he'd rather be catching up on his sleep.

The Angels had not arrived at their Michigan Avenue hotel until 6:30 that morning, only about 12 hours before the scheduled first pitch from Contreras.

"Well, we're going on adrenaline, just like we did in last night's ballgame," Scioscia said. "I'm trying to get a little calendar going, a body calendar. But we're fine. We probably … got about as much playoff sleep as you get anyway. So we're ready to go."

A reporter asked: "Pushing this game back to tomorrow had been discussed or considered, raising the issue of fairness on the cross-country travel. Do you have any thoughts on that? Should it have been pushed back?"

Replied Scioscia: "Well, our feeling is this: I know the guys in our clubhouse, if they scheduled a game for 1 in the morning, we're going to show up and play. They're very professional. They know what it's about. We have a tough schedule, but we're still playing baseball, and we're getting to do something we enjoy."

He should have stopped there, but he didn't.

"Should the game have been pushed back?" Scioscia asked rhetorically. "Absolutely. But that's not our call. We're going to play by whatever schedule is handed to us, and that's just the luck of the draw."

Scioscia took the safest option open to him for a Game 1 starter, using Paul Byrd on three days' rest even though Byrd had been knocked out in the fourth inning of his Game 3 start against the Yankees. The good news for Scioscia was that Jarrod Washburn had recovered sufficiently from his strep throat to be listed as the Game 2 starter. The bad news, which he must have expected, was that Bartolo Colon was still having too much pain in his shoulder to be included in the ALCS plans.

Guillen was asked how much of a relief it was to not have to face Colon.

"It's great," Guillen said, honest as always.

◆

Guillen's pregame session in the interview room ended abruptly, with Guillen rapping his knuckles on the table in front of him, then marching off, speechless for once.

He had been asked about Chico Carrasquel, who had been first in the White Sox's line of Venezuelan shortstops that included Hall of Famer Luis Aparicio and Guillen himself. What would Carrasquel have thought about Guillen getting his team this far in the playoffs?

"You're going to make me cry here," Guillen said. "Chico was one of my best friends in Chicago. I think I know where he is right now. He would be proud."

Then Guillen exited, stage left.

Friends until the end, Guillen had spent as much time as he could with Carrasquel, who was getting dialysis treatments three times a week and battling diabetes before dying of a heart attack in May.

"The thing I feel bad about is that he never had the opportunity to see this," Guillen said later. "He never had the chance to enjoy this. I know where he is right now. He wishes he was here at this moment. In the meantime, he wishes us to be the best we can be.

"That's why I was kind of sensitive about it. I always think about how bad he wanted this for the city of Chicago, for himself, for a lot of people. He was truly a baseball fan. When I was asked about it, the first thing that came to my mind was that he was so disappointed that it might be the last year he might get to see it. All of a sudden, a lot of people were going to enjoy this instead of him."

Carrasquel was the White Sox's shortstop from 1950 through '55, leaving before Al Lopez took the '59 team to the World Series. He was representing the Sox in 1951 when he became the first Latin player to start in an All-Star Game.

Even in his last years, Carrasquel was bothered by the fact that his teams had not gone to the World Series. He and Guillen would sit and talk for long stretches in Guillen's office before games, always getting around to how great it would be for the South Side to host another World Series.

"He wanted me to have success," Guillen said. "He never was a selfish guy. He never was jealous about anything. He was just happy with what he had. The way the White Sox helped him and the way he felt proud to be a Sox ... Sometimes you feel guilty about winning before somebody else does. That's how I feel about Chico."

There had been a memorable scene at U.S. Cellular Field in April 2004, when Guillen managed his first home game for the Sox. He asked to have Aparicio and Carrasquel share in the moment with him, and the three threw out ceremonial first pitches.

Carrasquel was wheelchair-bound by then, and Guillen had tried to help him up.

"He said, 'Don't hold me. I will get up,' " Guillen remembered in an interview with the Chicago Tribune's Rick Morrissey. "It was amazing. He had just come from physical therapy, and I know he was in bad shape on that particular day. But just to have him there was great."

Carrasquel had been an inspiration for Guillen. It was clear that Guillen planned to carry on the chain, inspiring others as he had been inspired.

◆

Despite everything the Sox seemed to have going for them in Game 1, they were frustrated by the Angels' Byrd, who did more with a mid-80s fastball and a collection of breaking pitches than anyone would have figured he could.

On a beautiful 61-degree evening, the Sox seemed to be trying to force the action. That played right into the hands of Byrd and his teammates. The game that had appeared to set up so well for Guillen & Co. turned into their first loss in two weeks. They had won eight in a row since a Sept. 27 loss in Detroit.

The questions this night: Which team was playing its third game in three nights in three time zones? Which one got into town at 6:30 in the morning? Which one was using its ace, and which one was using a surgically repaired gamer on three days' rest?

It turns out teams using starters on short rest against rested starters don't lose every time in the postseason, just two out of every three times. This was the one that keeps guys like Bobby Cox from ever pitching his Horacio Ramirezes.

Byrd, who had lasted just 3 $^2/_3$ innings against the Yankees the previous Friday in New York, and reliever Scot Shields turned the Sox's aggressiveness against them to raise the record of teams using starters on short rest against rested starters to 15-29 since the third tier of the playoffs began in 1995. The difference in the game was the two runs Los Angeles scored on a slow roller to Joe Crede and a one-hopper to Contreras, who tried to start a double play instead of taking an out at home plate.

Those small plays made a huge difference in a 3-2 game. Ditto the two outs the Sox lost on the bases, when Scott Podsednik (off a well-timed pitchout called by Scioscia) and A.J. Pierzynski were caught stealing. Pierzynski had apparently thought third-base coach Joey Cora had put on a hit-and-run, and he was dead meat at second base in the seventh inning.

The recap of mistakes didn't end there either. Podsednik and Aaron Rowand failed to get bunts down in the eighth and ninth innings. Even Jermaine Dye, shocking the world, popped up a bunt to give away an at-bat. The Angels were extremely beatable, but you're not going to beat a good team when you have seven hits and almost as many mistakes.

The Angels were 4-2 in the postseason and still didn't seem to have hit their stride.

◆

At least Guillen kept himself entertained. When he went to the mound to visit Contreras in the eighth inning, with Vladimir Guerrero at the plate, he flung something toward home plate that almost hit the umpire, Jerry Crawford.

He said later that it was a wad of gum and that it had been aimed at Guerrero, the reigning American League MVP. They had become good friends in 2001, when Guillen was a coach on the Montreal Expos.

"People will say, 'Look at him. He doesn't have respect for

the game. He's talking to people on the other team,'." Guillen said later. "Believe me, I'm hugging Vlad right now, but if we had to hit him, that's the first one I'm going to pick. If something happened on the field, I'm going to pick Vlad…. That's the way I am."

Catching flak

Dropped 3rd strike leaves
Angels' Paul the victim in Game 2

The first thing you need to know about Josh Paul is that he's a really nice guy, a kid from Buffalo Grove who went to Vanderbilt University to learn about life and to prepare himself for the world outside of sports as much as to play baseball. He learned about tragedy the hard way on Sept. 11, 2001, when one of his Vanderbilt teammates was killed in the collapse of the twin towers of the World Trade Center.

A quirk of fate found the White Sox in New York on the day terrorists hijacked jets that crashed into those buildings. Paul immediately began calling Mark Hindy's cell phone but didn't get an answer. He called for days before learning Hindy had not made it out of the building.

Paul, a journalism major, wrote about his friend in a moving piece he posted on ChicagoSports.com, the Web site that publishes content from the Chicago Tribune's sports department. It was an extremely well-written piece, at least as polished as most written by newspaper professionals.

Paul is gifted athletically, but not more so than most in his world, so he's had to separate himself from the competition with hard work and a great attitude.

Those two things, as well as his innate intelligence, are why he entered the 2005 playoffs having played parts of seven seasons in the major leagues, five with the White Sox (and three games with the Cubs) and the last two with the Los Angeles Angels.

It was a huge thrill when the Sox picked him in the second round of the 1996 draft, as he had grown up idolizing Carlton Fisk during the era he caught pitchers from Tom Seaver through Jack McDowell. Paul would be the top player from that draft, as first-round pick Bobby Seay didn't sign with the Sox.

A versatile player his whole life, Paul played mostly outfield and third base at Vanderbilt, but the White Sox's minor-league staff converted him to catcher. The switch came in part because he had broken the hamate bone in his right wrist, slowing his development as a hitter. He adjusted well to catching, becoming an above-average receiver, but versatility remained his calling card.

That's what entered into Ron Schueler's thinking when he made a surprising decision on the day the Sox's first-round playoff series against Seattle began in 2000.

Schueler, then the Sox's GM, dropped backup catcher Mark Johnson from the playoff roster, even though Johnson had been in uniform for all 162 games that season, to add Paul, whom he pictured being able to use as a pinch-runner and bench player. The thinking was that Mark Johnson, a good-field, no-hit player, would never get in a game with Charles Johnson doing all the catching, so Paul could be more useful.

The decision shocked the Sox's pitchers, who liked working with Johnson, and it devastated Johnson, who left the ballpark without comment at a time when he should have been getting ready for a playoff game. It left Paul in an awkward spot, which only got more awkward when manager Jerry Manuel decided to pinch-run for Charles Johnson in Game 1. That put the inexperienced Paul, who had been in only 42 big-league games, behind the plate in extra innings. He wound up catching Keith Foulke for maybe the fourth time that year, and the Mariners scored three runs in the 10th inning to start toward a sweep.

For Paul, it was a case of wrong place, wrong time. It wasn't his fault that Seattle beat the Sox, but it was a natural second guess to wonder what would have happened if Foulke had been pitching to Mark Johnson, a longtime teammate at that point.

Paul spent parts of the next three seasons with the Sox before being released on June 25, 2003, two days after he had thrown out the speedy Tom Goodwin in the ninth inning to help the Sox hold on to a one-run lead against the Cubs at Wrigley Field.

Paul ended 2003 with the Cubs, who did not put him on their playoff roster, and then signed with the Angels for 2004. He had evolved into the third wheel in a catching situation dominated by the Molina brothers, Bengie and Jose. His presence allowed manager Mike Scioscia to use Bengie as a designated hitter or pinch-hitter occasionally, without having to worry about running out of catchers, but playing time was scarce, as always. Paul got into 46 regular-season games in 2004 and only 34 in '05. He had been behind the plate only 216 times in his big-league career, barely 30 a season.

Infrequent playing time had taken a toll on Paul's hitting, as he batted only .189 in his second season with the Angels. Yet Scioscia and general manager Bill Stoneman included him on the postseason roster, and Paul was thrilled to get another chance in the playoffs.

During the first-round series, Paul had arrived in the visitors' clubhouse at Yankee Stadium accompanied by one of the team's media-relations staffers.

"Could you please interview Josh?" the staffer asked a Los Angeles reporter, citing the lack of attention being paid to the No. 3 catcher.

Paul laughed at the joke. "I'm having the time of my life," he said. "I love this team."

◆

The weather cooperated for Game 2 of the ALCS, as it had for Game 1. It was 61 degrees when Mark Buehrle threw the first pitch, after Billy Sawilchik, the lead guitarist of the Chicago band Lovehammers, had whipped through his version of Jimi Hendrix's national anthem.

You'd figure a Jerry Reinsdorf team more for Michael Buble or another Tony Bennett sort of singer, but Sawilchik was a perfect choice for the assignment. Fiercely independent and only moderately successful, the Lovehammers were to the Chicago music scene what Paul Konerko had been to the sporting scene: bigger on integrity than notoriety.

Like singer-songwriter Michael Glabicki, who had played a short set while Roger Bossard's grounds crew was putting the final touches on the Cell's playing surface, Sawilchik came with a name that fit these White Sox. Names like Konerko, Pierzynski, Podsednik, Hermanson, Garcia and Iguchi fit perfectly in a city that is at the same time a melting pot and evidence that segregation isn't dead.

From the start, this looked like it might be an easy night for the Sox.

Jarrod Washburn, scratched from possible starts in the Angels' last three games because of an untimely case of strep throat, fielded a Podsednik grounder in the first inning but heaved it far over the head of first baseman Darin Erstad. Podsednik gave the Sox a 1-0 lead after an Iguchi sacrifice and a grounder to shortstop by Jermaine Dye, whose father was conspicuous behind home plate in his "Dye" jersey, just as he had been during his son's three playoff runs with the Oakland Athletics.

But third-base coach Joey Cora probably cost the Sox an easy run in the bottom of the second. He got swept up in the moment when Aaron Rowand led off with a double that turned into more when Vladimir Guerrero had trouble coming up with the ball in the right-field corner, then overthrew the cutoff man. Rowand, who had gone into second standing up, chugged to third as the ball rolled in the grass behind shortstop and third base. Rowand didn't know where the ball was, however, so he dove headfirst into third, expecting a play that didn't come.

Cora was wildly waving him home, thinking the ball was going to roll to the wall. But this had not been one of Guerrero's strongest throws, and the ball was dying. That allowed third baseman Robb Quinlan (a good lineup decision by Scioscia) to make a sliding pickup. By then Rowand had picked himself up and was heading home, but he stumbled and couldn't regain the head of steam he'd carried into third. Quinlan's off-balance throw was toward the inside of the plate, but Jose Molina grabbed it and made a swipe tag, which just beat Rowand to the plate.

Rowand later insisted he was safe, but replays did not confirm that position. The real question was why Cora sent Rowand home in the first place, given that there were no outs and the Sox had Pierzynski, Joe Crede and Juan Uribe coming to the plate.

The failure to get that run home played a huge role in the game.

Quinlan, a right-handed batter who had hit Buehrle hard

throughout his career, drove a 1-0 pitch over the left-field fence leading off the fifth inning, tying the score 1-1. And Washburn and the Angels' bullpen shut down the Sox, keeping the score tied entering the ninth inning. That's when one of the craziest games anyone had ever seen broke out.

◆

Paul, who had caught only two innings that mattered for the Angels since Aug. 7, entered the game in the bottom of the eighth inning. Scioscia had pinch-run for Molina after a lead-off single in the eighth inning, but Jeff DaVanon was stranded on third base, leaving the score stuck at 1-1.

You can argue about much of what would follow that decision, but it's hard to defend running for your starting catcher in a tie game, especially with the other regular catcher, Bengie Molina, in the lineup as the designated hitter.

If it's a tied playoff game or even a close playoff game, your best catcher should be handling your pitcher. But just as Manuel took a horrible risk in Game 1 of the division series in 2000, pulling Charles Johnson for a pinch-runner who would prove insignificant, Scioscia had fallen into the same trap. It was Paul's misfortune to be the available catcher both times.

What are the odds of that?

The Sox's eighth was uneventful, as Kelvim Escobar struck out the side around a Dye single. Escobar then got the first two outs in the ninth, retiring Carl Everett on a grounder and then striking out Rowand, who went down with the weakest of hacks. That brought Pierzynski to the plate.

The Sox catcher worked Escobar to a full count but then swung through a split-finger fastball that was biting hard, headed for the dirt. Paul shifted his body and his mitt toward the ground to receive the pitch. He did not roll his wrist, which would have put the web of the mitt below the ball. Instead he caught it from the top down, essentially smothering it, either at ground level or just above it. The important thing, at least in Paul's mind, was that he had caught the ball cleanly.

Behind Paul, umpire Doug Eddings, at 37 a seven-year veteran, made a fist with his right hand and punched it emphatically in the air. The inning was over, or so thought Paul.

He rolled the ball toward the mound as Escobar headed off the field, along with most of the Angels. Pierzynski flipped his bat and took one step toward the third-base dugout. Then he broke for first base, reaching without a throw as the Angels looked on in confusion.

Eddings ruled that Escobar's pitch had hit the dirt before Paul got it in his glove, which meant Pierzynski was not out until he was either tagged or the ball was thrown to first base ahead of him. It's the most obscure way a better could reach first base, but Pierzynski remembered it happening to him a year earlier.

While he was with the San Francisco Giants, he had failed to tag Boston pitcher Bronson Arroyo in an interleague game at SBC Park. The Red Sox pitcher walked all the way to the top of the dugout before someone put the idea into his head to run to first. Pierzynski, who was at the mound talking to the pitcher, could do nothing to stop him at that point.

"It happened to me last year in San Francisco," Pierzynski said afterward. "I was the catcher and I did that. The pitcher tried to bunt and he didn't get it down…. [Arroyo] ran halfway to the dugout and then ran to first and they called him safe. That popped in the back of my head, just to run, and if he calls me out, he calls me out."

To the great shock of the Angels, especially Paul, Eddings did not call Pierzynski out, and the other umpires did not overturn the call. Scioscia charged out of the first-base dugout to argue. He stayed on the field a long time, twice starting back toward the dugout before turning around, but he could not persuade the umpires that Pierzynski was out.

Scioscia's basic argument was that when Eddings had pumped his fist, he had called Pierzynski out, ending the play. But Eddings told him that was his "called-strike mechanic," saying it meant only a strike, not an out. The Angels looking in to the plate, including Escobar and Erstad, were clearly thrown off by the gesture, but Eddings insisted it was a live ball because it was a third strike that hit the dirt and that he had never called Pierzynski out.

"I caught the ball," the bearded Paul said calmly in the Angels' clubhouse afterward. "When you catch the ball, you just walk off the field.… I'm a little confused because I thought I caught the ball."

Paul said he had never seen a similar play, calling it "a one-in-a-million situation." But Erstad, the first baseman, said he knew the Angels were in trouble before the final ruling. The ball was rolling toward the mound, Pierzynski was running up the first-base line and Eddings was paying way too much attention to all this action.

"Once I watched Josh roll the ball to the mound, I'm ready to go," Erstad said. "Doug was still watching the play. He didn't take his helmet off. A.J. was still running. That's when I knew something wasn't the way it was supposed to be.… People, when they say they've seen it all, they haven't seen it all."

What a break for the home team.

But no matter how loudly Angels fans complained about it later, the call did not cost Los Angeles the game. After all, the game was still tied 1-1, and now there were two outs in the ninth with only a man on first base.

It proved fatal for Los Angeles only because Escobar and

Paul could not stop Pablo Ozuna, who was pinch-running for Pierzynski in a tie game–this time with Ozzie Guillen taking the bad risk–from stealing second base as Paul could not get the ball out of his mitt. Escobar then hung an 0-2 split-finger fastball to Crede on the next pitch after Ozuna stole second. Crede seized the moment, driving the fat pitch on a line off the left-field wall. Ozuna was met at home plate by a wave of celebrating teammates as U.S. Cellular's traditional fireworks were launched.

In the upper deck, Naperville cartographer Chris "Spike'" Devane could not believe the scene around him. The crowd of 41,013 was beyond jubilant.

"Man, what a thing, what a scene," Devane said. "I'm 45 years old and been going to games at Comiskey and the new Comiskey my whole life. It was the loudest I've ever seen it. It was the first time I've seen the fireworks and not been able to hear them."

◆

After the game, Major League Baseball brought a three-man crew of officials to the interview room to discuss the Pierzynski call. It comprised Eddings, crew chief Jerry Crawford and umpires supervisor Rich Reiker.

Eddings said he had seen replays and stood by his call.

"We saw a couple of different angles, and if you watch it, the ball changes direction," Eddings said. "I don't see how you guys can say it's clearly a caught ball."

Reiker said Eddings' ruling was that Paul had "trapped" the ball against the ground. While there were no replay angles that showed the ball hitting the dirt, it was only millimeters above it when it disappeared behind Paul's glove in the most telling angle. But from there, it was impossible to say if it had hit the dirt or bounded upward only after getting into the webbing of the mitt.

"We've looked at it in the [television production] truck," Reiker said. "We've blown it up. I'm sure some of you have seen that angle. We have some technology, and Jerry Crawford saw it also, the whole crew, and there was definitely a change in direction there. At this point I would say at best it's inconclusive. I wouldn't totally agree that the ball was caught, but there was a change in direction that we saw and the replay is available to us."

Scioscia, a catcher throughout his 13 seasons with the Los Angeles Dodgers, defended his catcher.

"[Eddings] called him out, and that's what is disappointing," Scioscia said. "When an umpire calls a guy out and you're the catcher, and I've caught my share of them, he's out."

◆

Paul insisted then, and days later, that he had done nothing wrong.

He said most plate umpires usually say something like "no catch, no catch" if the ball is in the dirt. He assumed the play was over because he heard nothing. But Eddings said he never says that, and every elementary school kid has been taught what happens when you assume something.

Paul could have saved everyone, especially Eddings, a lot of trouble by simply tagging Pierzynski when he had the chance. It happens in just about every game: A catcher grabs a borderline pitch at ground level for the third strike and reflexively slaps a tag on the batter, making sure of the out.

Isn't that a routine move?

"Yes," Eddings said in the interview room. "That's why I'm pretty shocked about what took place. That was what I was talking to Scioscia about."

There was a split even among former catchers as to who was to blame, Paul or Eddings.

Jim Sundberg, who won six Gold Gloves, said early in his career he was involved in a play similar to Paul's and learned to complete the play and not rely on the umpire saying "no catch."

"From that point forward, in any situation like that, I would hold the ball up high to sell it as much as I could and go through with the play," Sundberg said. "You have to anticipate and think in advance of situations and take away as much of the doubt as you can. It was a horrible way to lose a game. In the catcher's mind, it was a full catch. Most umpires, if the catcher throws it out to the mound, they go by that. But the hitter, who's a catcher, sold it better. Take the doubt out of it. Don't assume anything."

But another longtime catcher, Ted Simmons, said Paul had done nothing wrong. He put the responsibility on Eddings.

"In my judgment the catcher has absolutely no issues here," Simmons said. "The catcher at this point almost is incidental, inconsequential because he didn't do anything out of the ordinary, extraordinary, unusual or anything. He did what any catcher in those circumstances would have done. He caught the ball on a swing-and-miss strike three, in his mind unequivocally. No questions, no uncertainty, no doubt. So under those circumstances, I would have, any catcher would have, flipped the ball to the mound with enthusiasm and run to the bench.

"What happened subsequent to that really doesn't involve that catcher anymore in my judgment."

◆

Who can imagine the feelings swirling through Bill Paul, Josh's father?

"Josh knew he caught it," Bill Paul said. "If he had short-hopped it, he would have tagged Pierzynski on the butt. I was proud of the way he played ball. To say he made a mistake is wrong."

Paul said he wasn't worried about his son. "He's very tough," Bill Paul said. "He'll be fine."

He wasn't as sure about Josh's mother Linda. "She wanted to kill six umpires," he said.

The Pauls have an ally in Simmons.

"He didn't do anything out of the ordinary," Simmons said. "He did everything that anybody in their right mind would have done. He caught the ball. He flipped the ball out and he was excited. He got out of the inning without giving up a run."

What a way to lose a game.

"I know I haven't seen it all, and I never will," Erstad said. "That's the beauty of baseball, even if it sometimes stinks."

California cool

Pierzynski shrugs off taunts, Garland, Konerko shine as ALCS shifts to Anaheim

It figured that Anthony John Pierzynski would be in the spotlight during the playoffs. He had always played his game with a transparent cockiness that rubbed players, even some on his own team, the wrong way.

Aaron Rowand acknowledged that he and his White Sox teammates did not know what to think about Pierzynski when general manager Ken Williams signed him. They had always regarded him as a troublemaker when he played with the rival Minnesota Twins.

"A.J. was always doing stuff to get under your skin," Rowand said. "You'd make an out, and he'd step on your bat. No catcher does that stuff, but A.J. does."

Pierzynski was having quite the autumn. He had accounted for nine runs in the three-game division series sweep of Boston, going 4-for-9 with two home runs and four RBIs while scoring five runs. He had only one hit in the first two games against the Los Angeles Angels but managed to make the biggest play while striking out.

When Pierzynski was announced with the rest of the Sox before Game 3 on a warm evening in Anaheim, the crowd of 44,725 let him have it. Pierzynski smirked-he is a starter on the all-smirking team-and then touched the brim of his cap, prompting fans to boo him even more loudly.

Pierzynski, as a catcher should be, is into every pitch of every game. He said there was a time earlier in Game 2 when one of plate umpire Doug Eddings' calls surprised him. That, as well as the play with Boston pitcher Boston Arroyo a year earlier, put it in Pierzynski's mind to run to first.

"It was the same situation when Garret Anderson was up earlier in the game," Pierzynski said. "I thought we caught him, I threw it around and the umpire said it hit the ground. It was a foul tip. I thought I caught that one. I watched the replay and couldn't tell if that one hit the ground either. It was a tough situation, and I ran. I was like, 'Well, if he calls me out, we'll try and shut them down in another inning,' and luckily Joe [Crede] hit one to win the game."

Running to first wasn't Pierzynski's first instinct. He took a step toward the dugout, stepping across the plate from the batter's box for left-handed hitters. It would prompt some to suggest Pierzynski was shrewd enough to fake out Josh Paul, the Angels' catcher.

"I didn't fake them out," Pierzynski said. "I was off balance. I took one step to the dugout and realized he didn't tag me, so I ran. There's no faking. It's not like I took my helmet off and put my gear on and then ran to first. It just happened, and I always seem to be in the middle of it."

Ron Gardenhire could not have been surprised. He was with Pierzynski for six seasons with the Minnesota Twins, managing him on playoff teams in 2002 and '03. While some pitchers would say they were happy to see Pierzynski gone—they believed his running commentary upset umpires and cost them borderline strikes—the trade to San Francisco after the '03 season was more a matter of circumstances than an indictment of his style.

With tight-fisted owner Carl Pohlad, the payroll always seemed to be an issue in Minnesota. And the Twins believed they had a better, and less expensive, option in a guy billed as the next Johnny Bench, Joe Mauer.

Gardenhire wasn't happy to see Pierzynski return to the American League Central after only one year in San Francisco. The Giants had non-tendered him because of concerns about his meshing with their pitching staff as well as his salary.

"I had as many wars with the guy as anybody, but I have the utmost respect for him," Gardenhire said. "When he stepped between the lines, the kid played the game. And played it the right way. He is a gamer. We all know he is a different breed, he can irritate people. But over here we had a lot of fun with that. It just takes a little bit of getting used to."

When Pierzynski is irritated with a pitcher for shaking off his signs or falling behind in the count too often, he will fire the ball back to the mound. If he thinks a pitcher has lost it, he will glare into the dugout, practically screaming at his manager to get the guy out of the game. Those things sometimes don't sit well with pitchers.

Pierzynski did both those things during Damaso Marte's wild sixth inning in Game 3 of the first-round series with Boston. It was as if he couldn't wait for Ozzie Guillen to get Marte out of the game.

"You're not going to please everybody," said Chris Widger, Pierzynski's backup. "And to be honest, A.J. really doesn't care about anybody outside the guys in this clubhouse, and that's why nobody here has had a problem with him. They know when he goes out there, he gives everything he has for this team. He's always in the middle of any controversy, so it couldn't happen to a better guy because A.J. is used to it. He can handle it better than anyone."

Geoff Blum, traded to the Sox from San Diego at the July 31 trade deadline, said he initially eyed Pierzynski warily.

"You heard things, and everyone has reputations, and they might have rubbed some people the wrong way," Blum said. "Everyone has their quirks, but you want to play with a guy who's competitive and will do what it takes to win games. He's definitely one of those guys."

Blum saw that side of Pierzynski during a 5-0 loss to the New York Yankees on Aug. 20. Shawn Chacon, the Yankees' pitcher, came over to tag him after an eighth-inning nubber rather than toss the ball to first base. Pierzynski raised his elbow in an unsuccessful attempt to jar ball out of Chacon's glove. The two jawed at each other afterward.

"You don't want to do it dirty, but you have to do it in a way to win games," Sox reliever Cliff Politte said. "There are people who slide into second hard and break up a double play, which is dirty, but it's the right play. You have to break up that play to get the guy on first. If you're running and your elbow flies out, it's part of it.... There are a lot of people who give A.J. a bad rap for the way he goes about the game. But he plays hard, and he's doing the little things right and always is thinking ahead.

"Like last night," Politte continued. "I don't know how many guys would think about running down to first base. A.J. had his mind in the game, and as a hitter with the ball down on strike three, you're assuming the ball is in the dirt and you have to run."

◆

Pierzynski shared the spotlight with Eddings before Game 3.

Eddings had the misfortune to fly from Chicago to John Wayne Airport in Santa Ana., Calif., on a flight carrying many media members. They cornered him at the baggage-claim carousel.

"The whole argument in the beginning was not whether it bounced or not, it was about mechanics," Eddings said, referring to his strike-three fist pump. "I think I'm going to change my mechanics a little bit now.... The only thing I'm down on myself is, I should have sold it either way. I should have said, 'No catch,' or if I did have a catch, that he was out. But I never said he was out. A.J. realized I never said he was out."

Eddings said he was sure he made the right call, however.

"I still feel that way," he said. "I want everything to go smoothly. That's why they pay me to do this job. In tough situations you're going to have to step up and handle it.... I love my job, and I still do. You feel bad. I'm human. You want to do your best job, and I know I did my best job last night."

The rotation that umpires use in the postseason had Eddings moving from home plate to the right-field line. That put him close to hundreds of red-clad Angels fans, who let him have it during Gam3 at Angel Stadium. One showed up carrying a sign that read, "Forget the players; drug test the umpires!" Another listed the price of several items in the ballpark before concluding, like the credit-card commercial, "Not Having Eddings Behind the Plate ... Priceless."

Fans yelled insults at Eddings when he took his position on the field. One season ticket-holder, Ryan Dickey, said fans from the seats along the right-field line met before the game to coordinate their chants.

A few hours before the game, Eddings had taken a phone call from former umpire Don Denkinger, whose blown call had played a major role in the 1985 World Series, leaving him reviled in St. Louis 20 years later.

"I just informed Doug of what he could expect and told him to keep his head up," Denkinger told a reporter later. "I think he has his mind on straight and was doing as well as could be expected. I think he also knows he's partly to blame because he did not [call strike three] audibly. But I told him that he's a good umpire or else he wouldn't be there."

Back at Eddings' family home, in Las Cruces, N.M., his parents, Russ and Betty, were watching the game with more than a little trepidation.

"There are always idiots out there, and you never know what they're capable of," Russ Eddings said. "I know my wife worries about that, and I have it in the back of my mind too."

◆

Pierzynski said the Sox weren't lucky to win Game 2.

"Did [the Angels] feel lucky when they won?" he asked. "No, we feel like it can go either way. This is two really good teams battling each other, and every pitch counts."

Sox fans knew their team was fortunate to have the series tied when Game 3 began. The Sox were starting Jon Garland, who hadn't been on the mound since Oct. 1 in Cleveland. He was left in the on-deck circle when the Sox swept the Red Sox, reduced to throwing a simulated game during the three-day break between series.

Garland had won 18 games during the regular season, but would he be the same guy? That was the Game 3 question.

There was little concern about Los Angeles starter John Lackey, who had been the Angels' star in Game 7 of the 2002 World Series. He had a reputation as a big-game pitcher and had added to it by pitching well against the Yankees on three days' rest in his last start, when Jarrod Washburn was scratched because of strep throat.

But using a starter on short rest in the playoffs is always a huge risk, and there is almost always a price that must be paid for it. The Angels would pay that price in Game 3. Lackey was not nearly as sharp as normal, most likely because he was fatigued from burning so much adrenaline at Yankee Stadium.

Lackey opened the game with 91- and 92-m.p.h. fastballs for strikes to Scott Podsednik but was unable to back up the praise of Fox's Tim McCarver, who told viewers they would see "one of the best curveballs in baseball." Lackey threw an 0-2 curve to Podsednik, but it didn't have its usual sharp break, and Podsednik lined it into right field for a single.

Tadahito Iguchi bunted Podsednik to second, and Jermaine Dye followed by smashing a 1-0 fastball into the gap in right-center for a run-scoring double. The pitch was an 88-m.p.h., two-seam fastball that stayed up in the strike zone, over the middle of the plate.

Lackey needed to gather himself, and Paul Konerko presented a huge challenge. Lackey hung a 1-1 curveball to the Sox first baseman, and Konerko ripped it down the left-field line, just foul. The count ran full, and Lackey didn't seem to think he had a good enough fastball to throw Konerko. He went to a curveball and once again hung it. Konerko offered no forgiveness. He smashed the Frisbee up in the strike zone, over the inside part of the plate, into the left-field bleachers, giving the Sox a sudden 3-0 lead.

It was Konerko's third homer in six postseason games, and it would not be his last. With Dye on second and first base open, he was surprised Lackey had not pitched around him.

"He's got a base open," Konerko said. "I don't know—you're trying to get a read on whether he's coming after you or not coming after you, and you have to kind of … well, I was trying to resist the urge to think he was going to walk me and start with the next guy because when you do that, you usually let a good one go. I was trying to stay in there but not try to do too much. It didn't really feel all that great. Home runs happen when you least expect it, and that was definitely the case there."

◆

Garland's belated playoff debut began alarmingly. He got the Angels' leadoff hitter, Chone Figgins, to an 0-2 count but allowed Figgins to work him for a walk—the first by a Sox pitcher in the series and only the ninth in six playoff games.

But with fans beating their white ThunderStix together, Garland put on a clinic against the next hitter, Orlando Cabrera. He painted the corner with a 93-m.p.h. fastball for strike one, got him to foul off a hard breaking ball and then threw a 93-m.p.h. fastball past him for a confidence-building strikeout. That brought Vladimir Guerrero to the plate.

The Angels' go-to guy had been hitless in Chicago, raising some question about the condition of his left shoulder, which he had been icing in the clubhouse, and also his knees. Lou Piniella, working the Fox telecast, said Guerrero had appeared stiff at U.S. Cellular Field but should be looser with a game-time temperature of 89 degrees.

Garland, who was a first-round draft pick of the Cubs after playing at Kennedy High School in nearby Valencia, Calif., showed his focus facing Guerrero. His fielders looked locked in too.

Garland started the impatient Guerrero with a ball, sandwiching throws to first base around the pitch, but came back with a 93-m.p.h. sinker at the bottom of the strike zone that Guerrero-maybe as good a low-ball hitter as has ever played the game-chased. He hit only the top of the ball, driving a hard hopper off the plate that bounced over Garland's head. Iguchi stepped on second base at the same instant he caught the ball, then threw to Konerko for an inning-ending double play.

With his rhythm remarkably smooth after the layoff, Garland didn't need a lot of help. But he got some in the bottom of the second, when Erstad's impatience showed.

Normally as heady as anybody in the majors, Erstad suffered momentary insanity after lining a pitch from Garland into the right-field corner with two outs and nobody on base. Erstad should have stopped at second, which would have given Juan Rivera a chance to drive him in, but he wanted a triple. He was a dead duck on Iguchi's relay throw from Dye to Crede.

Garland wound up doing as Mark Buehrle had done in Game 2, earning a complete-game victory. "We didn't know how Garland was going to show up after the long layoff," manager Ozzie Guillen conceded. "I was concerned and worried."

Pitching coach Don Cooper said Garland also had been worried. But you couldn't tell it by his performance. He held the Angels to five hits, Cabrera's two-run homer in the sixth inning the only damaging one, in a 5-2 victory built around Konerko's three-hit night.

Afterward Konerko wanted to talk about Garland, not himself.

"All four of our starters have been aces at some point during the year," Konerko said. "I don't know how many teams can say that."

Starting pitchers were carrying the Sox, as they had after the AL Central lead had fallen beneath five games. They had worked 45 ⅓ innings in the six playoff games, allowing 13 runs.

"It's something we've done all year long," Garland said. "We've gone out and given our team a chance to win most of the time we've stepped on the mound. I think any manager in the major leagues will take that. If you're going out there and giving your team a chance to win, keeping them in striking distance, I mean, who wouldn't want that?"

Big outs are often the difference between a pitcher winning and losing. During the playoffs, Garland and his fellow starting pitchers had given up just five hits in the 27 at-bats opponents had with men on second or third base.

Guerrero, Anderson, Manny Ramirez, David Ortiz and Johnny Damon were a combined 2-for-12 in those situations. The Sox's starters seemed to be constantly elevating their game.

"Our guys have short memories, which is good when you're going bad and good when you're going good as well," Konerko said. "I think a lot of it has to do with Ozzie. He preaches coming to the park every day ready to play the game regardless of what happened the day before, and that also means good things. When you have good games, you've got to forget about them because when you're playing a good team like the Angels, those guys will be ready to play.

"Ozzie told us at the beginning of the playoffs, every time you win a game in the playoffs, the next game will be the toughest game to win because the team you're playing is good and they're going to dig down even harder to win that game because now they have to."

◆

Pierzynski went 1-for-4 with a harmless single in Game 3, and he and Eddings avoided the spotlight. Eddings had no tough calls to make, although fans razzed him every time he made an obvious fair-foul call on the right-field line, and Pierzynski earned his keep by calling an excellent game for Garland, who threw more four-seam (maximum velocity) fastballs and fewer two-seam sinkers than normal. It was a winning recipe, shifting the burden onto the Angels, as it had been on the Sox in Game 2.

Rocking Santana

Konerko, Pierzynski batter rookie as Garcia goes the distance

Hawk Harrelson, the broadcaster/cheerleader who was forced to follow the White Sox on television with network announcers working the postseason telecasts, always says it's not what you hit, it's when you hit. Sometimes baseball is also about whom you face.

Had Bartolo Colon been able to finish his scheduled start in the rain-delayed Game 5 of the division series, which had been played on Monday night at Angel Stadium, he would have been on the mound for Game 4 of the American League Championship Series, held the following Saturday. But Colon had left in the second inning with pain in his shoulder, and it didn't feel better a day later when rosters were set for the ALCS. So the Angels' Mike Scioscia would be the only manager in the playoffs to need a fifth starter.

He called on Ervin Santana, a 22-year-old rookie from the Dominican Republic who had shut out the Sox in May for his first major-league win. Santana also had come out of the bullpen to get the win in the Angels' Game 5 victory, holding the

Yankees to a manageable three runs in 5 ⅓ innings.

It was an impressive outing-on the surface, anyway. But to the Sox's team of advance scouts following the series, Santana had been as lucky as he had been good. He had not been in a game in 12 days and was all over the plate with his pitches.

Santana had walked the first two hitters he faced, needing 30 pitches to get through the second inning before hitting his stride. The story of that night was written in the fifth inning, when Santana retired Gary Sheffield, Hideki Matsui and Robinson Cano with two on and no outs.

As the Sox prepared for Game 4, hitters watched video from that game and others late in the season, not the five-hit shutout Santana pitched May 23. Hitting coach Greg Walker preached three things: patience, patience and more patience. And the players were listening.

◆

Scott Podsednik, who had been on base at least twice in each of the first four games, perfectly executed the approach that Walker had emphasized.

Santana's first pitch was a 94-m.p.h. fastball, which Podsednik looked at for a called strike, with Ron Kulpa making the call. The next was a 95-m.p.h. heater, up and in, and Podsednik fouled it back. The crowd of 44,857 was jazzed. It looked like the kid had his good stuff. But that would prove misleading.

Podsednik laid off the next two pitches, getting the count to 2-2. He fouled off the next two, then had to dance out of the way of a fastball for ball three. Now the pressure was on Santana, and he wilted. The eighth pitch in the sequence was another fastball well inside, which Podsednik looked at for ball four.

The game was on.

Tadahito Iguchi had been a master at advancing Podsednik with a bunt, a strategy Ozzie Guillen employed a lot in August and early September, when Podsednik was caught stealing more often than he succeeded. But Iguchi didn't need to give himself up here.

Scioscia called for a pitchout, but Podsednik wasn't running. Santana, put in a hole by the pitchout, hit Iguchi in the left elbow with his next pitch. Two on, no outs for Jermaine Dye, who flied out to center. Both runners took advantage of the Angels' Steve Finley, moving up a base. It was a gamble by Iguchi, but he slid in easily at second base as Finley's throw tailed away.

Up came Paul Konerko, who had hit a two-run homer on a 3-2 pitch from John Lackey in the first inning the night before.

Konerko took a good slider for strike one but then worked the count to 3-2. The 2-2 pitch, a slider in the dirt, had come close to getting Konerko, but he was locked in enough to check his swing. Catcher Bengie Molina appealed to the first-base umpire, Ed Rapuano, who confirmed that Konerko had held up. Scioscia started barking from the dugout, and Molina went out to talk to the rookie starter.

Santana unbuckled his belt and started tucking his jersey into his pants, trying to get comfortable in an uncomfortable situation. Like Lackey, he would wish he had just put Konerko on base.

The 3-2 pitch was a nothing slider at the knees, and Konerko went down to get it. He drove it out toward the fake rocks in left-center field for his fourth homer of the postseason, which broke Ted Kluszewski's White Sox record of three, set in the 1959 World Series. Freddy Garcia had a 3-0 lead to take to the mound.

The Sox had led in every inning since pinch-runner Pablo Ozuna had scored in A.J. Pierzynski's place in the ninth inning of Game 2.

◆

A decade earlier, Scioscia had been fresh off his career as a catcher with the Dodgers. He stayed in the organization as a minor-league catching instructor, and one of his first assignments was working with Konerko, who had been selected in the first round of the 1994 draft as a catcher.

"We worked very closely with Paulie," Scioscia recalled. "He was signed as a catcher, and I was doing catching instruction at that time. You could see from a very young age what kind of hitter he was going to be. And you could see from a very young age what kind of catcher he wasn't going to be."

◆

Scioscia's comments were later relayed to Konerko.

"I was going to say it was my catching instructor's fault," he said. "But, no, I think Mike was one of the guys who moved me. I caught about a year and a half in the minor leagues … and I think a couple of people, [Scioscia] included, put their heads together and decided it would be best if I moved.

"They told me if I really loved catching I could go back to A-ball, but if I wanted to move I could be the starting first baseman in Double A, and I said, 'That's all I need to hear. Give me the first baseman's glove.'."

In his first season playing first base, Konerko would hit .304 with 30 homers and 88 RBIs between Double A and Triple A.

"Once the decision was made to move him out from behind the plate to first base, he relaxed," Scioscia said. "You could see that offensive talent take hold."

Konerko got to the big leagues in 1997, but he couldn't stay there, at least not with the Dodgers. He hit .215 in 49 games in '98, moving among first base, third base and left field, and was traded to Cincinnati in a deal for closer Jeff Shaw in July. He did no better there, batting .219 in 26 games for Jack McKeon's Reds, again moving among first, third and left. The Reds traded him to the Sox for center fielder Mike Cameron after the season.

"You know, he really didn't get a great look with the Dodgers," Scioscia said. "But once he settled in with the White Sox, he established himself as one of the top run producers in the game."

Scioscia was asked if he wished he had urged Konerko to continue catching.

"Yeah, I'm kind of kicking myself," Scioscia said. "If we had kept him at catcher, he'd probably be in Triple A right now instead of swinging the bat like he is against us."

◆

Garcia, historically better on the road than at home, was working on three days' rest after the birth of his daughter. He had left U.S. Cellular Field during Game 2 to go to a Chicago hospital to be there for the delivery, which came shortly after the goofy Pierzynski play that led to a series-turning victory.

When a pitcher is given a lead, he is supposed to shut down the opposition immediately. Garcia did that in the first inning, setting down the Angels on seven pitches. Leadoff man Chone Figgins, who was having a bad postseason, showed his frustration after swinging through a low pitch for strike three, slamming his helment into the rack. Orlando Cabrera grounded out on the first pitch, and Vladimir Guerrero took only one pitch before also grounding out.

But Garcia got himself into a little trouble in the second inning. With one out, he walked Darin Erstad on four pitches, then threw wildly to first base after making a bare-handed pickup of a Casey Kotchman nubber up the third-base line. His throw sailed over Konerko's head, allowing Erstad to go from first to third while Kotchman hustled to second. Molina followed with a single to center, scoring Erstad and moving Kotchman to third.

Steve Finley, a speedy 40-year-old whose homer total had dropped from 23 in 2004 to 12, came up next. He took a pitch for a strike, then went after a low fastball. He sent a seemingly routine grounder to Iguchi, who moved to his left and made a snap throw to Juan Uribe, starting an inning-ending double play, with the relay beating Finley by an eyelash.

It wasn't the kind of hard-hit grounder that typically produces a double play. But Finley had been a step or two slow down the line.

It turns out he had a reason to be slow. As he was swinging at the Garcia fastball, Pierzynski reached to catch it. His mitt moved slightly farther forward than normal, and Finley's black bat hit the top of it. Finley broke toward first base but slowed to point toward Pierzynski with his left hand, telling Kulpa, the umpire, that it was a case of catcher's interference. That break in stride gave Iguchi and Uribe time to get the critical double play.

Finley again pointed back toward the plate after Rapuano called him out at first base. Scioscia did not come out to argue this call, but it was a critical one for the Angels.

Had Kulpa spotted the catcher's interference, which was clear on the instant replay, viewed during the game by Angels hitting coach Mickey Hatcher and others, Los Angeles would have had the bases loaded and one out for No. 9 hitter Adam Kennedy. But another break had gone the Sox's way, and again Pierzynski was in the middle of the action.

◆

Give Pierzynski credit for his honesty.

Asked afterward about the Finley play, he admitted that he got any with one.

"Yeah, I felt it, but I couldn't really hear it," Pierzynski said. "The only two people who knew it hit me were me and Steve.

You know, we got a break. I mean, he hit it right at the guy and they turned a double play. It was a lucky break. What can you say?"

The Sox got their first lucky break involving Pierzynski on Dec. 20, 2004, when San Francisco didn't tender him a contract. His one-year stay with the Giants had been troubled almost from the start, but general manager Ken Williams did his homework, calling Dustin Hermanson and others in a background check that included 10 hours of phone calls.

Even though Williams had defended the 2004 tandem of Ben Davis and Jamie Burke, he knew he needed help behind the plate. In the previous decade, Tampa Bay had been the only American League team to get so little production from its catchers.

The trend of light-hitting Sox catchers started when age caught up to Ron Karkovice and continued with a run of primary catchers that included Jorge Fabregas, Chad Kreuter, Brook Fordyce, Mark Johnson, Sandy Alomar Jr., Miguel Olivo and Davis. Only once in the last 10 years had the Sox's top catcher had an OPS (on-base percentage plus slugging percentage) of at least .700. That was Fordyce, in 1999.

During that decade, 54 of 80 major-league playoff teams had catchers who were quality hitters (.700-plus OPS). Thirty-one of those had a catcher whose OPS was over .800. The Sox hadn't had one since they played at the original Comiskey Park.

Pierzynski led National League catchers with 77 RBIs in 2004. He led American League catchers with a .312 average in 2003. As a contact hitter (19 walks, 27 strikeouts in 508 plate appearances last year), Pierzynski would fit Guillen's plan to manufacture runs. His left-handed bat could be used to break up the right-handed hitters who figured to form the middle of the lineup: Frank Thomas (once healthy), Konerko, Dye and Uribe.

After running his own investigation, Williams decided to offer Pierzynski a one-year contract. Now he said he had been "everything we hoped for"—quite a change from his unhappy season with the Giants.

In a San Francisco Chronicle story, an anonymous pitcher called Pierzynski a "cancer" after Felipe Alou's team got off to a bad start. He and the pitching staff patched things up well enough to win 91 games, but Pierzynski knew there was no getting away from the tag.

"If you get labeled what someone called me in the paper, it follows you around your whole career," he said.

Brett Tomko, a journeyman pitcher who was with his fifth team in six years, was believed to be the player who had smeared Pierzynski. When the Sox played San Francisco in spring training, Pierzynski offered any of his new teammates $100 for a home run off Tomko. Joe Borchard delivered one and afterward found a $100 bill tucked into the pocket of his pants.

Anyone would be sensitive about being called a "cancer," but the term carried extra weight for Pierzynski.

With his team possibly headed toward the World Series, Pierzynski found his thoughts turning to Scott Muhlhan, a lifelong friend who had been a teammate at Dr. Phillips High in Orlando. Muhlhan was 23 when he died of cancer.

Pierzynski served as a pallbearer at the funeral in 1998. There he reconnected with an old friend, who would become his wife.

"I knew him for so long that you always look back on that stuff, especially now, and wish he was here or could be here," Pierzynski said. "He was one of my best friends, and his brother was best man at my wedding. It was tough.... We were so close, and you don't ever want to see someone young die like that."

This wasn't the only time Pierzynski had been close to a

young person afflicted with cancer. Brittani Allie, the daughter of his high school coach, Danny Allie, was diagnosed with leukemia. Pierzynski would visit Brittani while she underwent treatment and had stayed in touch with her after she was in remission.

"I love the guy," Allie said. "He's really grown up a lot."

◆

Allie says the Pierzynski traits that would get under others' skin were there long before he got to the big leagues. He remembered him offending an opposing coach by flipping his bat and standing at the plate to admire a game-winning home run in the high school playoffs. He also heard about the reaction of fans at the University of Tennessee when Pierzynski, who was on the sidelines for a football game during a recruiting trip, cheered wildly when the scoreboard showed Florida, his favorite school, beating Kentucky.

"People were always complaining about something with A.J.," Allie said. "But he could walk the walk, and he worked hard. All the stuff you hear about him … I know the real A.J."

Because he was always in the middle of things, and because he was unafraid to speak his mind, some compared him with Bill Laimbeer, the enforcer/center on the Detroit Pistons' ultra-physical team in the late 1980s.

"I don't know why I'm becoming a villain," Pierzynski said. "I don't go out and get technical fouls. You guys are going to say what you're going to say, and sometimes I think it's b.s. But what am I going to do?"

Fair to say he wasn't losing sleep about anyone who thought he had crossed some invisible line by running to first on a strikeout or clipping Finley's bat with his glove, which only a fool would accuse a catcher of doing purposely.

"They say you only get what you can handle," Pierzynski

said. "I've been through a lot worse than this. The best part is I didn't do anything wrong. You read stuff and see stuff, people saying I was trying to cheat. That's ridiculous."

◆

With the Sox leading 4-1, Pierzynski came up to face Santana in the top of the fourth inning. He crushed an inside fastball, sending it on a line all the way to the blue tarp covering seats in center field at Angel Stadium.

"There's no controversy there," Lou Piniella said on the telecast.

There were other calls in the game that went against the Angels. Scot Shields had Podsednik picked off first base in the fifth inning, but Rapuano missed the call. Podsednik was out stealing second in the seventh, but umpire Randy Marsh gave Podsednik the benefit of the doubt on a bang-bang play.

But after Garcia escaped a second-inning mess on Finley's Pierzynski-assisted double play, the Angels could not generate enough of a threat to give themselves room to complain too loudly about those calls. Garcia went the distance in a six-hitter as the Sox won 8-2, moving within one win of the World Series.

"There's always going to be calls that go your way and calls that go against you," Scioscia said. "I don't think umpiring in these games is why we're behind 3-1."

Pennant payoff

Crede, Contreras send Sox to 1st World Series since 1959

Paul Konerko woke up on a sunny Sunday morning in Southern California only one victory away from realizing his childhood dream of playing in a World Series.

To his own great surprise, he didn't feel a whole lot different from when he woke up to get ready to face the Los Angeles Angels in September.

"Surprisingly, no," he said. "If you had asked me at the beginning of the season, I would have said, geez, everybody would be amped up, it would be a different feeling. But everybody in the clubhouse is talking about fantasy football like a normal Sunday. I think it really starts with our coaching staff and Ozzie.

"When it comes to this team's attitude … everybody as individuals has their own way they go about their business, but as far as the team and the way it comes to the field every day, or at least an hour before the game, how we get ready, it's really the staff and it's Ozzie and how we prepare every day. We could be on a seven- or eight-game losing streak, which we have been, and it's really not much different than when we were on eight-game winning streaks or now.

"You might not believe it, but it's the case. Anybody who's followed our team all year or been in the clubhouse knows what I'm talking about. It's what Ozzie said from Day 1 of spring training—'You come to play every day. Whatever it is you do, do it the same way every day. I don't care what you did the day before, good or bad, or what the team did the day before, good or bad. You do the same every day.' Guys latched on to it, and it's worked."

◆

As commanding a lead as the White Sox held in the ALCS, their stranglehold on the Angels was even stronger than it seemed. They had their second-half ace, Jose Contreras, on the mound for Game 5 against Paul Byrd, a finesse pitcher who wouldn't benefit from facing a team twice in five days.

Contreras' loss to Byrd in Game 1 had been only the third in his last 18 starts, dating to a July 6 win over Tampa Bay. He had seemed to gain confidence in just about every start since, going 13-3 with a 2.94 earned-run average.

The key to his success had been a willingness to challenge hitters and get ahead in the count. He entered the season having averaged 4.3 walks per nine innings as a big-leaguer but had essentially cut that total in half (2.2) during the run that made him the No. 1 starter on a staff that included Freddy Garcia and All-Stars Mark Buehrle and Jon Garland.

While Contreras had been the premier pitcher in Cuba, dominating the Baltimore Orioles for the Cuban national team in 1999 in the start that made him such a hotly pursued commodity once he defected, he said he had never been hotter than he was now.

"This is hands down the best part of my career," Contreras

said before Game 5. "I've gotten the most wins since I've been here. You can't compare Major League Baseball to baseball in Cuba. This is the best run I've had, and I hope there's more of it to come."

Contreras told anyone who asked that he had found himself in an ideal situation, playing for a manager he loved, a pitching coach who communicated well with him and alongside the pitcher he respected more than any other in the world.

With Ozzie Guillen Jr. handling the interpretation, Contreras offered thoughts on Orlando Hernandez, Don Cooper and Guillen Sr.

On Hernandez: "It's been an honor to be his teammate and his friend. Everyone knows the success El Duque has had in Cuba and in major-league baseball. El Duque helps out the whole team, not only me. He brings so much knowledge to the table that I think every pitcher has got a little something from him, and just having him as a teammate, such a great competitor, it's been an honor."

On Cooper: "My success is a lot due to Cooper and the patience he's had with me since last year and through the first half and now. Our pitchers get along with Coop. Coop understands us, lets us do what we think is best, and we feed off each other very well. He's been a great part of our success."

On Guillen: "I respect him as a manager and as my friend. We fed off each other when we first met. I knew him from before, but I had never really gotten to know him. He's a funny guy, and he's easy to get along with. I think that's why we've had the success we've had. It's a friendship on and off the field."

◆

While Guillen played the same lineup for the eighth consecutive game, Mike Scioscia shook up his lineup for Game 5. He moved Garret Anderson from left field to center, which allowed him to get Juan Rivera in the lineup instead of Steve Finley, who had gone 3-for-20 in the playoffs.

With light rain falling in Anaheim, Byrd pitched around some trouble to get through the first inning scoreless. Konerko had come to bat with the Sox already in their Three Run Formation, but Byrd got lucky. Konerko hit the ball on the nose but lined it directly at right fielder Vladimir Guerrero.

In the bottom of the first, Contreras got the first two outs on a fly ball by Chone Figgins and a popped-up bunt by Orlando Cabrera, the latter on a Contreras fastball that hit 94 on the stadium's radar gun. Anderson followed with an opposite-field single, bringing the slumping Guerrero to the plate.

Having gone 1-for-16 in the previous four games, Guerrero might have figured to look at a few pitches to get more comfortable. But this is a man of action. Guerrero, who'd had his best batting practice in a week, according to hitting coach Mickey Hatcher, swung at the first pitch from Contreras, a forkball that lacked its usual sharp break, and popped it up to second baseman Tadahito Iguchi.

At least the Angels weren't behind. For the first time in 19 innings, they were tied.

That changed in the top of the second, however. A leadoff double by Aaron Rowand that hit near the right-field line and skipped into the seats produced a vintage Sox run. A.J. Pierzynski bunted Rowand to third, and he scored on Joe Crede's sacrifice fly.

The Angels tied the game in the third, when Contreras did well to escape with a 1-1 tie. He gave up a quick run on a leadoff double by Rivera and a single by Adam Kennedy, and the Angels pushed the go-ahead run into scoring position with one out on a Figgins sacrifice.

But Contreras remained in control. Cabrera hit a grounder

to Juan Uribe on the first pitch, giving Kennedy no chance to advance. The 1-0 pitch to Anderson got past Pierzynski, allowing Kennedy to move to third, and Contreras walked Anderson on four pitches, bringing Guerrero to the plate.

Was Contreras eager to face Guerrero? That would be hard to believe, as Guerrero had hit over .300 every year of his career and had hit 32 home runs in the 2005 regular season. But he was clearly not himself.

He had seen only 37 pitches in his 17 previous plate appearances in the ALCS, including the ridiculous total of six when he went against Mr. Express Lane, Mark Buehrle, in Game 2. He had swung at the first pitch less than half the time but then almost always went after the second one.

Guerrero hadn't been to a three-ball count in almost a week, since facing the Yankees' Mike Mussina in the Monday night Game 5 of the first-round series, and against the Sox he'd been to a two-ball count only once, against Garland in Game 3.

With runners on first and third and two outs, this would have been the ideal time for Guerrero to get himself going. But he couldn't lay off a first-pitch forkball from Contreras, fouling it back for strike one. Guerrero dug back in for the next pitch, wiggling his bat menacingly as he stared at Contreras. The Cuban ran a 93-m.p.h. fastball in on the hands of the Dominican. Guerrero could hit only a routine grounder to Uribe, the 12th time in 18 at-bats he had been retired on a ground ball.

The Angels had tied the score, but they had hardly broken the Sox's mojo.

◆

Doubles by Uribe and Jermaine Dye gave Contreras a 2-1 lead in the fifth, but he couldn't hold it. The Angels scored two runs in their half of that inning to take a 3-2 lead, the first time they had led since winning Game 1.

Scioscia lifted Byrd in the top of the fifth, bringing in Scot Shields. He turned the 3-2 lead over to Kelvim Escobar to start the seventh. The Venezuelan heavyweight, listed at 6 feet 1 inch and 230 pounds but weighing much more than that, had been a go-to guy in October. He was making his sixth playoff appearance and had been scored on only when Scioscia left him on the mound to work a third inning in Game 2.

Crede had followed the non-strikeout of Pierzynski with a double off the top of the left-field wall at U.S. Cellular, finishing a 2-1 win that kept the Sox from falling into a 2-0 hole in the series. Crede would be the first hitter Escobar faced this time.

Scioscia might want to rethink that matchup.

On the second pitch from Escobar, Crede jumped on a fastball just as he had the hanging split-finger fastball four nights earlier. This time he got some elevation on the ball, driving it just over the left-field fence for a game-tying home run. It was Crede's sixth hit, and sixth RBI, of the ALCS.

"Good-looking young player," Lou Piniella said on the telecast. "Getting better and better."

◆

Crede had come to the Sox in the traditional way, as a fifth-round pick in the 1996 draft from Westphalia, Mo. He had caught the eye of Ron Schueler and Jerry Manuel early in his minor-league career and got his first big-league whacks in 2000, when he was only 22. He wouldn't be up to stay until 2002, but he looked ready.

Crede had hit .312 with 24 home runs at Triple-A Charlotte to earn a midseason promotion, then kept hitting. He wound up batting .285 with 12 homers and 35 RBIs in 53 games for the Sox that season, creating huge expectations.

They were not immediately fulfilled. He took a step backward in 2003, then another in 2004. Fans clamored for the Sox to look to upgrade at third base when Crede got to the All-Star break in '05 hitting only .242, but Ken Williams had never wavered in his support, largely because Crede was such a natural at third base. He had been the team's lone defensive standout during the Manuel era and now fit perfectly with Guillen's rebuilt team.

As a person, Crede was about as complicated as a game of checkers. What you saw was what you got, which was why he wore so well with his teammates.

Crede was an Air Force brat, and baseball had been the common denominator as he followed his father around the world. He was a first-generation pro but at least a second-generation seamhead, as baseball had also been his dad's passion.

"He played baseball wherever he was stationed," Crede said. "Germany, wherever else. Baseball is his love too. He had a couple of tryouts. The Dodgers. Didn't make the team, but at least he gave it a shot. Now he's living his dream through me. He watched every game on TV. Whenever I was struggling this year, my mom called me and said, 'You need to talk to him.' He wants me to do so well, he's so worried. I had a bad year last year and I'd tell people, 'I don't know who had a worse year, me or my dad.' "

Like Buehrle, Crede had grown up in St. Louis Cardinals country. He once brought Rowand, his teammate since 2000, when they played together in Birmingham, Ala., to his hometown of Westphalia, which he says is home to only about 300 people.

"No stoplights," Crede said. "I brought Rowand and we counted the stop signs. I think there were four."

Crede had made it to Busch Stadium for Game 4 of the 2004 World Series, when the Boston Red Sox ended their 86-year wait for a Series championship.

"I just had goose bumps the whole time," Crede said. "It was like, 'Wow, I can only imagine if this was us out there playing the Cardinals and clinching in the stadium where I saw my first big-league game.' "

With the Cardinals trailing Houston 3-1 in the National League Championship Series after an agonizing 2-1 loss in Game 4 that ended with Tony La Russa and Jim Edmonds ejected, that did not appear likely. But with his homer off Escobar, Crede had left the Sox needing only one more run to win the American League pennant.

◆

Escobar, peering in at hitters from behind sunglasses, kept Podsednik on second base after a one-out walk and a stolen base on a pitchout following the Crede home run. He struck out Iguchi and Dye, keeping the score 3-3. But Contreras was gaining steam, not losing it. He retired the Angels in order in the bottom of the seventh, putting Escobar right back on the mound for the eighth.

Escobar appeared to be in control, starting the inning by striking out Konerko on a 3-2 splitter and Carl Everett on a 2-2 splitter. But Rowand worked a walk, bringing Pierzynski to the plate with two outs and the go-ahead run on first.

The human lightning rod took a pitch for ball one, then hit a rocket back up the middle. The ball deflected off Escobar's rump and rolled toward first base, where Escobar picked it up.

That should have been the inning, but Escobar got careless. Instead of flipping the ball to first baseman Darin Erstad, he decided to tag Pierzynski himself. He did so, slapping his glove against Pierzynski's left shoulder, and then heaved the ball toward a stunned Erstad.

One problem. The ball was in his bare hand, not the glove.

First-base umpire Randy Marsh, who had been screened off the play, initially signaled Pierzynski was out, and the Angels headed for their third-base dugout. Ozzie Guillen, meanwhile, shot out of the first-base dugout, telling Marsh that Escobar hadn't tagged Pierzynski with the ball. Marsh conferred with plate umpire Ed Rapuano, and Escobar was waved back to the mound.

It was another shot into the collective stomach for the Angels, and they could take no more.

Scioscia went to his closer, Francisco Rodriguez, who had not pitched since Game 1. Crede had another chance to be a hero, and he took the same patient, swing-only-when-spoken-to-by-a-fat-pitch approach that had served the Sox so well in the playoffs.

Crede fell into a 1-2 hole but worked his way back to a full count. He swung defensively at the 3-2 pitch, hitting a one-hopper that went just behind Rodriguez, who had slipped throwing the slider, and appeared headed up the middle. Kennedy, the second baseman, dove to cut off the ball. He fielded it cleanly behind second but was on his right knee when he made a desperate throw home. Rowand, who had been running on the 3-2 pitch, never slowed around third base and easily beat the weak throw, which tailed up the third-base line.

Make it 4-3 White Sox, and they'd score two more in the ninth off Rodriguez. Contreras was the ultimate executioner, retiring the last 15 Angels he faced in yet another complete-game victory by a Sox starter.

Guerrero got his final chance with two outs and no one on in the eighth inning. He went down swinging, of course, but instead of his trademark full hack—a swing as forceful as any in the major leagues—it was a defensive half-swing at an inside fastball. The ball went on a hop to Iguchi, and just like that a 1-for-20 ALCS was in Vlad's permanent record.

When Contreras sandwiched two more groundouts around a flyout in the ninth, it was time to break out the champagne and cigars. The White Sox had won the pennant for the first time since Sept. 22, 1959, a span of 16,825 days.

◆

Amazing.

Guillen had overwhelmed the second-strongest team in the American League using only a Gang of 15. He had used only one pinch-runner, Pablo Ozuna, who scored the winning run in Game 2, and one relief pitcher, Neal Cotts, who got the last two outs in Game 1, in addition to his regular lineup and his four starting pitchers.

Beginning with Buehrle's victory in Game 2, the Sox got four consecutive complete-game victories from their starters. No team had managed four consecutive complete games in the postseason since the Yankees in 1956. The Sox hadn't had four in a row at any time since 1974.

"With the experience I've had in the playoffs, whether I was managing or playing, I've never seen four horses like that come out of the gate and [pitch] so well," Scioscia said. "You might have to go back to Sandy Koufax, Don Drysdale, that group with the Dodgers or the group Baltimore had in 1966. These guys pitched tremendous baseball."

Konerko was named the ALCS Most Valuable Player, but he said he'd like to split the award into four pieces and give it to the starting pitchers.

"Those guys were the horses, and I was just along for the ride," Konerko said. "Really, we all were."

In the stars

Astros' GM reaches Series to meet the team he grew up rooting for

Tim Purpura wasn't much different from most kids growing up in Oak Lawn in the 1960s and '70s. He followed Chicago sports, baseball in particular. The White Sox were his team, even when their players were wearing shorts.

"Those," Purpura recalled, "were pretty bad."

Before Purpura and his friends could drive, he went with his family to Comiskey Park 10 or 15 times a year, with doubleheaders a special treat. That included the summer of 1969, when he remembers feeling lonely because so many of his friends had deserted the Sox to give their hearts to the Cubs, who would break them. He stood firm with his loyalties, and when he and his running buddy, Bob Dodge, got their driver's licenses, they raised the ante, going to the old ballpark at 35th and Shields 30 or 40 times a year.

With its exploding scoreboard, upper deck, heavenly smell of cooking bratwurst and Polish sausage and the greenest grass on the South Side, if not in Chicago—is there a better sight than the first view of a baseball field after a long winter?—Purpura was terminally hooked by the charm of the original Comiskey.

In 2004, Purpura became general manager of the Houston Astros. He says he hadn't even started grade school when he knew he wanted to find some kind of job in baseball.

"I've wanted to do something like this since I went to Comiskey Park when I was 4 or 5 years old. I saw the big green carpet out there, the green seats...."

Purpura, 47, was at Comiskey for the infamous Disco Demolition Night in 1979, when disc jockey Steve Dahl's promotion spawned an on-field riot that caused the Sox to forfeit the second game of a doubleheader against Detroit. All the action wasn't in the park either.

"Afterward, when we were leaving, there was this one guy going up and down the street with a bat, hitting everything in sight," Purpura said. "He put a dent in the car we were in."

Purpura eventually left Chicago, moving with his family to San Diego, where he encountered former Sox general manager Roland Hemond at a game at Jack Murphy Stadium. Purpura told Hemond that he would love to work in baseball, and as easy as that he had himself a mentor.

Hemond's first piece of advice to Purpura was to go to law school. Lawyers, he said, "are going to run baseball one day." Purpura did exactly that, getting his law degree after picking up a bachelor's degree from Loyola.

"I was scared to death that I'd have to become a lawyer," Purpura said. "I was frighteningly close to being a lawyer. Then Mike Port hired me in the Arizona Fall League."

Purpura's first check from baseball was for $100. It came as a thank-you from Tim Mead, the California Angels' public relations director, after Purpura and a couple of his law school friends worked as interns at the 1989 All-Star Game in

Anaheim. Port, a longtime executive who most recently was a Boston Red Sox assistant when they won the World Series in 2004, hired Purpura to help get the Arizona Fall League off the ground. He remembers being hired in August and having to lease ballparks, design uniforms and buy enough bats and balls for the six-team league, a combination showcase and finishing school for top prospects, before play began in October.

After two years in that post, Purpura went to work for Bob Watson, then the Houston Astros' general manager, as an assistant farm director in 1984. It's safe to say he wasn't taking home the same starting salary as others in his graduating class from Thomas Jefferson Law School in San Diego. But few of them probably had as much fun.

After apprenticing under Watson and Gerry Hunsicker, Purpura was handed the keys to owner Drayton McLane's operation in November 2004. Hunsicker, who had pulled off the trade for Carlos Beltran that helped Houston get to Game 7 of the National League Championship Series in 2004, got tired of having McLane looking over his shoulder.

The Astros had not been expected to do much in 2005, Purpura's first season in charge. They had re-signed Roger Clemens, but at $18 million, up from the coming-home bargain price of $5 million in '04. While McLane allowed Purpura to play poker with agent Scott Boras in the Beltran sweepstakes, the club's tight finances prompted the decision to allow second baseman Jeff Kent to leave.

When Beltran signed with the New York Mets, accepting a $120-million deal rather than a barely thinkable $100-million package from the Astros, Purpura's fallback position was to trust a group of young players he had overseen in the farm system, including outfielder Jason Lane and second baseman-outfielder Chris Burke. The loss of Beltran and Kent, who had played a role in producing more than half the team's runs during its 2004 postseason run, appeared too much to overcome when the Astros got off to a 16-31 start. Yet here were the Astros and their rookie GM still standing in mid-October.

Following a come-to-Jesus talk by manager Phil Garner after an especially bad loss in Milwaukee on May 27, Houston won 73 of its last 115 games, outlasting Philadelphia to capture the National League wild card on the final day of the season. The Astros knocked off Atlanta in the division series, winning an 18-inning marathon in Game 4 when Clemens, the Astros' last available pitcher, worked three shutout innings of relief on two days' rest after a Game 2 start.

In the National League Championship Series, the Astros jumped ahead of St. Louis three games to one, winning Game 4 on Sunday, Oct. 16, and avoiding extra innings when defensive replacement Eric Bruntlett (another of Purpura's kids) started an unlikely double play to seal the 2-1 victory. Afterward, Purpura sought out a television to watch Game 5 of the American League series in Anaheim.

This wasn't about scouting. The Astros had a highly experienced staff following the Sox and Angels. No, this was about watching the old hometown team, remembering the likes of Wilbur Wood, Dick Allen, Walt "No Neck" Williams, a polished Jim Kaat and a raw Goose Gossage, and remembering again why he had wanted to work in baseball in the first place.

As Purpura watched the Sox clinch the pennant, beating the Los Angeles Angels 6-3 behind Jose Contreras, he practically got light-headed.

In his first year as a general manager, having achieved a career goal that would have been impossible without the help of Hemond, Port, Watson and many others, the team he was running was one victory away from meeting the team he had followed as a kid in what would be Chicago's first World Series in 46 years.

How cool was this?

"It's kind of surreal," Purpura said. "I grew up listening to my dad talk about the '59 World Series with the White Sox. I still have a program from that Series that he gave me, so this feels very strange. To have grown up a White Sox fan, and to have a chance to not only go to the World Series in my first year as a general manager but to possibly play them ... it's pretty amazing."

Like his late father Jim, who had been an Oak Lawn real estate broker, Purpura had posed for photos wearing a White Sox cap on his wedding day. He could barely believe his eyes watching the team he had loved celebrate.

"It was emotional to see [Jerry] Reinsdorf, the players and just that old Sox logo," Purpura said. "The block-letter Sox logo ... how great is that? Watching them celebrate brought back a lot of enjoyment from my childhood, although we didn't have much to celebrate about. I felt emotional for them, emotional for the city. I was wondering what it was like to be in the city. I'd think it has to feel a lot like Boston did last year."

◆

Purpura was speaking alongside the infield at Minute Maid Park during batting practice before the Astros played St. Louis in Game 5 of the NLCS. One more win and the Astros would be in.

This would be a good thing for the Sox, because even though Reinsdorf and Ozzie Guillen were rooting for Tony La Russa, the former Sox manager, the Cardinals were the National League team that engendered the most fear. It was trendy to talk about Houston's starting pitching—the trio of Clemens, Andy Pettitte and Roy Oswalt was the most decorated in the playoffs—but St. Louis had the league's most dangerous hitter, Albert Pujols, and was the best team, even if All-Star third baseman Scott Rolen was out for the season with shoulder problems. The Cardinals had won 100 games during the regular season, and 205 over the last two seasons, finishing a combined 24 games ahead of Houston, the repeat wild-card winner they had faced both years in the NLCS.

Somebody had to knock them off. Boston had done it in the 2004 World Series, using a chance to open at Fenway Park to start a four-game sweep. The Cardinals had begun the Series with a day's less rest than the Red Sox because Houston had made them go the full seven games in the NLCS, which had started a day after the ALCS. And they were without injured ace Chris Carpenter.

If La Russa could get them back to the World Series, he would certainly have them in full complete-the-mission mode. You'd rather take your chances against the Astros, who had never been to the World Series and might just relax and enjoy the view.

Having seen the Red Sox and Angels softened up by the battles they faced before meeting Guillen's team, the smart White Sox fan wanted to see Houston win, but not in five. The ideal scenario would have the Cardinals coming back to extend the Astros to seven games, then step aside.

But that scenario didn't look very likely when Houston's Lance Berkman hit an opposite-field three-run homer off Carpenter into the cute but ridiculous Crawford Boxes at Minute Maid Park, a ballpark that had been born under a bad sign as Enron Field. The seventh-inning homer gave the Astros a 4-2 lead, leaving them only six outs away from the pennant.

When relievers Mike Gallo and Dan Wheeler combined for a perfect eighth inning, it seemed like the retractable roof was about to be blown off the stadium.

While George and Barbara Bush enjoyed the moment near-by, Astros owner McLane turned from his seat behind home plate to look around at a sea of joyous Texans. McLane is a second-generation trucking magnate who made his money by getting the contract to deliver Wal-Mart products from the warehouse to the thousands of stores across America. Before he sat down, he took the white towel he was holding as part of a stadium promotion and whipped it over his head.

The Cardinals looked like toast when Houston closer Brad Lidge came in. A Notre Dame product, Lidge combined the resolve of a Third World missionary with baseball's filthiest slider. With the Yankees' Mariano Rivera in semi-decline, Lidge was the last guy hitters wanted to see on the mound in the ninth inning. He had piled up 369 strikeouts in 259 career innings in the regular season and converted 42 of 46 save chances in 2005, including 24 in a row before an unlikely rally by the Cubs on Sept. 30.

Lidge blew away pinch-hitters for the first two outs of the ninth, leaving the Astros one out from the pennant. But baseball, as the Astros had learned in their eight previous forays into the postseason, can be the cruelest game.

Down to his last strike, David Eckstein slapped a single between third baseman Morgan Ensberg and shortstop Adam Everett. Then, after Eckstein had taken second while Lidge was busy trying to get the 27th out, Jim Edmonds trotted down to first base with a walk. That meant Pujols, second to the Cubs' Derrek Lee with a .330 batting average and third in the NL with 41 home runs, would get a crack.

"The mistake we made was walking Edmonds," manager Phil Garner said later. "You have to let Edmonds hit the ball in the next count. You can't walk him, and Brad knows that."

Lidge started Pujols with a slider for a strike. He came back with another slider, and Pujols was ready for it. The powerful Cardinal smashed it high and far. Had the roof not been closed, it would have exited the stadium. Instead it banged off the glass far above the limestone wall in left field. The ball seemed to be rising still when it struck the barrier.

Pujols was beside himself as he circled the bases.

"I just couldn't believe I did it," he said. "But it's just one win."

When Pujols got back to the dugout, La Russa grabbed him. "He just told me, 'The Great Pujols,'." Pujols recounted. "They're going to be ready in St. Louis. We just need to win two before we lose one."

Garner was subdued when he met with reporters.

"Well, it's terrible," he said. "You're high as a kite one minute … Of course, we were feeling pretty good, but you have to play every out. We failed to play every out tonight. We just didn't do it."

Berkman called the shocking loss "devastating," but it wasn't really. The Astros still led 3-2, even if the next two games were scheduled for Busch Stadium, which had a date with a wrecking ball after the postseason. Give Lidge credit for having the proper perspective.

"This is a bump in the road, but there is no way this is going to get anybody down," he told the reporters who encircled his locker. "This will sting a lot tonight, but when I wake up tomorrow I'll be ready to go."

The White Sox were the one certain winner on the Pujols home run. It meant the Astros would have to play a Game 6 and start Oswalt, who had moved past a tiring Clemens to become the team's true ace in the second half of the season. And with Oswalt starting Wednesday, only three days before the scheduled start of the World Series, he probably wouldn't be available until Game 3 of the World Series.

◆

Lidge proved prescient.

Because of Oswalt, Pujols' dramatic home run was only a detour, not a roadblock, on the road to the first World Series in Texas. A 28-year-old from the tiny town of Weir, Miss., Oswalt was not going to be denied in Game 6. He got Lidge off the hook with the kind of forgiveness that baseball rarely offers in October.

Throughout history, has the bigger failing been the dramatic misplay or the routine failing that has usually followed? Many of the moments that are burned into the minds of baseball fans could have been turned into footnotes-but weren't.

Was the big problem at Wrigley Field in 2003 Steve Bartman getting in Moises Alou's way or Alex Gonzalez and Mark Prior turning to mush? And was Dave Henderson's homer off the late Donnie Moore the thing that beat Anaheim in 1986, or was it the failure of Angels starters Kirk McCaskill and John Candelaria to get the job done the next two games?

Don't you think Leon Durham wishes Rick Sutcliffe had been able to get an out or two against Alan Wiggins, Tony Gwynn and Steve Garvey after the grounder went between his legs in 1984 at Jack Murphy Stadium? Or that Bill Buckner would give anything for Bruce Hurst to have gone out in Game 7 and beaten the New York Mets?

But bad had almost always begotten worse in postseason baseball. That's why Oswalt's dominating performance in the Astros' 5-1 victory over the Cardinals in Game 6 of the NLCS was so stunning.

"There's a reason our clubhouse was loose today," Garner said after the 51st and final postseason game at Busch. "When

Roy's going to the mound, you feel pretty good about your chances. The way he went about his business tonight gave us confidence. That's a powerful ballclub, powerful top to bottom, and Roy didn't back down."

Oswalt set the tone by blowing away Pujols after he had walked Edmonds in the first inning. He started Pujols with a 97-m.p.h. fastball for strike one. He threw back-to-back curveballs, one for a ball and another for a called strike, and then absolutely obliterated the best hitter in the game with a 95-m.p.h. fastball in Pujols' kitchen. His hands tied up, Pujols waved helplessly.

It was the start of a 0-for-4 night for the Game 5 hero and just about the end of realistic hopes for an I-55 World Series. Oswalt, Chad Qualls and Wheeler worked a combined four-hitter, wrapping up the National League pennant two days after Lidge had failed to secure it.

"The big thing for me was when we got the early lead I knew I could go at them with fastballs," Oswalt said. "I didn't have to throw too many breaking pitches."

The Cardinals needed great pitching to match Oswalt but didn't get it from Mark Mulder, a south suburbanite from Thornwood High School who missed a chance to pitch in a World Series in the park where he once bought tickets to watch Frank Thomas, Robin Ventura and Jack McDowell.

This was the third win in three playoff starts for Oswalt this October and fourth in six starts the last two postseasons. He was a smooth 44-22 overall the last two years, with his work against Atlanta and St. Louis in the playoffs giving him 23 wins this year.

Garner pulled Oswalt after seven innings because he had thrown 118 pitches. He probably could have got another inning out of him, but he knew he might have to get two World

Series starts from him, in Game 3 at Minute Maid Park and then (gulp) in Game 7 at U.S. Cellular.

For the White Sox, that would be motivation to make sure it didn't go further than Game 6.

◆

Even La Russa, a historically bad loser, saw a silver lining to this loss. It meant Houston's Craig Biggio and Jeff Bagwell would finally get to ride a season to its ultimate conclusion.

"Those two guys' impact, that's top-shelf," La Russa said. "They're great examples of competing, toughness, respect, playing the game right. They're as good as they come. Reluctantly, I'm really pleased for both those guys."

Oswalt's victory meant there would be no Game 7, giving the Astros two days off before Game 1 of the World Series on Saturday. They had time to settle into their Chicago hotel rooms rather than hang around St. Louis to see if the steady rain in Thursday's forecast would delay Game 7 to Friday, the eve of the World Series.

Well, they would have had time had Garner and McLane not done something really stupid. Rather than let the players celebrate Wednesday night in St. Louis, then use Thursday to get comfortable in Chicago, the Astros' decision-makers apparently overlooked the fact that Busch Stadium is only about 300 miles from U.S. Cellular Field. They ordered the team airplane home so the players could attend a Friday morning pep rally in downtown Houston and then, with wives and a bigger traveling party in tow, make the trip to Chicago on Friday afternoon.

Most players didn't get to their houses until after 4 a.m. Thursday and had to be back on an airplane a little more than 30 hours later.

"I wanted to go home," Garner said at a Friday workout in

Chicago. "I wanted to see what was going on in Houston. Our players generally are homebound guys. ... We had a big pep rally this morning when we left Houston. And that's exciting."

Let's hope the rally was really inspiring. When you get a break in the grinding postseason schedule, as the Astros did by having to play only six games, you don't throw it away.

"We got home very early [Thursday] morning after wrapping it up in St. Louis," Clemens, who had been listed as the Game 1 starter, said Friday. "But tonight guys will sleep, will be able to catch up if they missed out an any sleep during the celebration part of it."

La Russa still believes his Cardinals were at a disadvantage against Boston in the 2004 World Series because Game 7 of the NLCS was played on Thursday, a day after the Red Sox had played their Game 7. The Cardinals didn't have any choice but to scramble; the Astros flew about 1,600 unnecessary miles so they could dig themselves in front of the home fans. Bad move.

If you're in the World Series for the first time ever, shouldn't you be in a hurry to get there?

World stage

From veterans to rookies to fans, emotions run high on Series eve

When Thursday morning arrived in St. Louis, with rain pounding on windows and the National League champions in their Houston homes, having crawled under the covers only hours before, a contingent of White Sox advance scouts met over coffee and snacks in a lounge at the Renaissance Grand Hotel.

Dave Yoakum, Bryan Little, Bill Scherrer, Doug Laumann and Gary Pellant sat around a long conference table at the end of the room. In the week—and, in some cases, three weeks—before, they had studied the Astros, analyzing strengths and weaknesses and searching for tendencies that could give Ozzie Guillen's team an edge in the World Series. Now all they were figuring out was who was going to ride with whom on the five-hour drive back to Chicago.

A Chicago reporter stopped by to make small talk.

"What are they going to do with the DH spot?" one of the scouts asked. "Who are they going to use in Chicago?"

"From what Phil Garner was saying last night, it sounds like

[Jeff] Bagwell," the reporter said.

"No, they can't do that," the scout insisted. "They're not going to do that."

"Well, he didn't say for sure, but it sounded like that was the way he was leaning," the reporter said.

"I hope that's what they do, but I don't think it will be," another scout said. "There's no way they can play Bagwell, not with the way he's looking. He's changed his swing altogether because of the bad shoulder, and he's got no bad speed at all. He can barely get the bat through the zone against a good fastball."

Another scout chimed in.

"[Chris] Burke is a good player," he said. "He's swinging the bat well. He's got young legs. They've got to play him. Their best lineup is the one they used last night, the one with [Lance] Berkman at first and Burke in left. They can use the DH to get Mike Lamb in the lineup. He's swinging the bat real good too. That's what they've got to do.

"I know Bagwell has been a great player, big character guy, big career, huge hero, nice story to have him in the World Series. But right now they're doing you a favor to put him in the lineup and sit Lamb or Burke. Forget that sentimental stuff—this is the World Series. You get here, you play the guys who are going to help you win. Period."

The reporter shuffled over to the coffee pot.

"Hey," he said, "I'm just telling you what Garner said. I think they're playing Bagwell."

◆

Major League Baseball had put a limited supply of World Series tickets at U.S. Cellular Field on sale over the Internet two days after Jose Contreras wrapped up the pennant. For 18 minutes, everyone had a shot. But based on the action on stubhub.com, it appears the people with the most powerful computers were often those who obtained the tickets with the intention of reselling them at a huge profit.

Stubhub.com spokesman Sean Pate said there were 12 times as many tickets available through online brokers as there had been in 2004, when Boston played in the World Series for the first time since 1986.

Pate estimated that about 10,000 tickets per game had gone into what amounted to an online lottery. It was as easy for people who had no interest in actually going to claim tickets as it was for White Sox fans who had been waiting a lifetime for the chance.

"You're not just competing with White Sox fans, you're competing with scalpers and opportunists," said Brian Miller, a marketing assistant for a Chicago Internet company. "That's why Ticketmaster should quiz people, ask like, 'Who was the second baseman for the '59 White Sox?' That would work."

Unable to get tickets directly, Miller paid $720 apiece for $125 tickets in the upper deck in right field. Pate said stub-hub.com sold two tickets behind home plate for $7,500 the first day tickets were made available. The least expensive seat on the site was $515, a markup of more than 300 percent from face value.

Thomas Smith, an economics professor at the University of Chicago, lamented that there was no perfect system to get tickets at face value to the fans who valued them the most.

"They've got to put them on sale some way, but whatever way you do it, you're going to end up with some goofy outcome," Smith said. "There's probably other ways to sell tickets that might be more equitable, but you're always sort of slanting tickets to people with more and more resources."

The Sox had engaged in their own form of opportunism, offering World Series tickets to anyone who would also buy

2006 season tickets. They sold more than 1,000 season tickets that way on the day after the clincher against the Angels.

But the most extreme ticket offer was found by the Chicago Tribune in a posting on Craigslist.org, an online classified service in the San Francisco area. One person offered a healthy kidney—you choose left or right—for "two Sox tickets in the outfield." So while fans were not literally giving up arms or legs for tickets, body parts were in play.

◆

In the tiny farming village of Las Martinez, near the western tip of Cuba, Humberto Contreras and other baseball fans had their attention, if not necessarily their eyes or ears, turned toward Chicago.

Jose Contreras, the youngest of nine Contreras children who had been raised in a shack with a thatched roof and no electricity or running water, was going to be a Game 1 starter in the World Series. It was a proud moment for people in the region, many of whom had known the Contreras family for years and all of whom now seemed to be rooting for the Sox as passionately as lifelong South Siders.

"We are very happy," said Roberto Bordado, a 47-year-old farmer. "They are going to win the championship because we have confidence in Jose Contreras."

Humberto Contreras, one of Jose's older brothers, did not own a television or radio that would pick up the game, which was officially a non-event to Fidel Castro and Cuba's communist government. Humberto planned to hop on a horse 30 minutes before the first pitch and ride to the wooden shack of a friend lucky enough to own a reliable short-wave radio.

There, with a cigar in his mouth and a bottle of rum nearby, Humberto planned to listen to the game. He would close his eyes and try to picture Jose, whom he had last seen before he left for a tournament in Mexico with the Cuban national team in 2002. He would rely on the broadcast to describe the battle between Contreras and Houston Astros hitters well enough for him to remember every pitch for a lifetime.

"I'm always nervous, but I'm sure he's going to do well," Humberto said. "It's tough that his family, his brother, can't watch the game."

Before Contreras' defection, he had been one of Castro's personal favorites. His two-hit, eight-shutout-inning performance against the Baltimore Orioles in a 1999 exhibition game had been the stuff of legend. Castro even took to calling Contreras "el Titan de Bronze," the Bronze Titan.

But with their decisions to seek riches in North America, Contreras and his Sox teammate, Orlando Hernandez, became non-entities in the eyes of the Cuban government and Castro loyalists. Newspapers treated them as invisible men, ignoring their accomplishments, and when their images were shown on state television or referred to by Castro and other Cuban leaders, it was only out of scorn.

"In the case of Contreras, the thinking of Cuban authorities is: Why show and promote an athlete who was given privileged treatment and then abandoned the country illegally?" said Miguel Hernandez, a sports reporter for Granma, the official newspaper of the Cuban Communist Party.

On the day after Contreras pitched the Sox's pennant-clinching victory over the Los Angeles Angels, Granma's sports section led with a story about a local basketball club earning a bronze medal in a tournament in Russia. The White Sox might as well have been the Chicago Blackhawks, for all the attention they received.

Baseball had been huge in Cuba, especially in the 1950s, when Americans traveled from Miami to Havana as they now do to the Bahamas or Jamaica. There were dozens of Cuban major-leaguers in that era, including Orestes "Minnie" Minoso, who played 17 seasons in the big leagues, including 12 with the White Sox.

Minoso is more deserving of Hall of Fame status than some who have been enshrined, but he has been denied admittance into baseball's most exclusive fraternity. Yet Bill Veeck made sure he had his own place in history, giving Minoso the chance to be a big-leaguer in five decade by bringing him back at age 57 for two pinch-hit appearances for the Sox in 1980. Jerry Reinsdorf wanted to let Minoso become a six-decade player in 1990, but Carlton Fisk and other players complained about the gimmick.

When Minoso began his major-league career in 1949, World Series games had been televised in Cuba. But the Cuban-American baseball connection was broken after Castro took power in 1959 and abolished professional sports. In 2005, the top players in Cuba might have been considered "privileged," but they rarely made more than $20 a month.

Of course, that was almost twice as much as most Cubans earned. That's why it was so tough for the beisbol fanaticos to follow the World Series.

In Havana and along the northern coast, some fans could watch the games by turning makeshift antennas north to pick up signals from Florida. Others watched on pirated satellite television, risking a $300 fine, about twice the average annual income.

In Havana, a few hotels and bars carried the Series for a price. At El Conejito, an upscale Havana restaurant, fans were hit with a $1 cover charge and a minimum of two beers apiece, at $1 per, to watch the game. Yet a doorman said the place was always packed when the Sox played.

"Cubans love baseball, but now it's even more so because of

Contreras," Roberto Blanco said. "It's pride. People identify with him."

Outside Havana, fans learn results a day or two later, often by word of mouth. A few had radios that were strong enough to catch Radio Marti, the U.S.-government-funded station that was broadcasting playoff games, but Cuban authorities tried to jam the station's signal.

For Humberto, it would be a cruel twist to have his brother in the World Series and not even be able to hear the games. His brother's success had already cost him, as he had been forced out of his job as a captain in Cuba's Interior Ministry because he would not agree to cut off telephone communications with Jose.

"They told me I had to choose between my work and my brother," Humberto said.

◆

While Humberto Contreras and other Cubans just hoped to follow the World Series, Brandon McCarthy had just about driven himself crazy trying to figure out how he could play in it.

These opportunities can be once-in-a-lifetime things. Players, even players as young as McCarthy, understand that.

The 22-year-old Sox starter had taken Hernandez's spot as the fifth starter in September, and he felt crushing disappointment when he was told the 25-man playoff roster wasn't being adjusted for the World Series. He would travel with the team and hang out in the clubhouse before and after games, but he would not be eligible to pitch.

McCarthy had never been under serious consideration—the playoff staff wasn't broken, so why fix it?—but had kept coming up with scenarios in which Ozzie Guillen and Ken Williams might decide they needed a 12th pitcher. It was a silly thought given that six of the seven relievers had been idle in the championship series, but McCarthy literally became ill when the fantasy was taken away.

"You try to convince yourself that you're going to be part of it, and it's hard when you aren't," McCarthy said on the eve of Game 1. "Yesterday, when I realized I wasn't going to be on the roster, it was kind of a sick feeling. When I went home, I started dry heaving. I just had that release. I can't even explain it."

McCarthy earned his postseason share by going 3-1 down the stretch, including five strong innings on Oct. 2, when the Sox knocked the Cleveland Indians out of playoff consideration.

"Growing up as a White Sox fan, it's nice to know you knocked the Indians out," McCarthy said.

McCarthy was raised in Colorado, but he adopted the Sox as his team because of his admiration for Frank Thomas.

"Growing up, I always hated the Indians because they were knocking the White Sox out. It was nice to pitch in Cleveland and have a good game. That makes up for this a little bit."

◆

As Guillen prepared to face the Astros, his mind often wandered back to the late Chico Carrasquel, who had been his inspiration. When Carrasquel died, Venezuelan President Hugo Chavez called for two days of national mourning. Guillen's personal mourning had continued much longer.

"In Venezuela, some people like me and some people hate me," Guillen said. "Same thing with Luis [Aparicio]. Same thing with Davey Concepcion. Same with everybody from Venezuela who played. But you don't see anybody who hates Chico. Nobody."

Guillen's lone regret on the eve of the World Series was that Carrasquel had not lived long enough to share the moment. "You know, I have two pictures of Chico hanging in my office," Guillen said. "I don't have a picture of my parents."

At a news conference on the workout day before the Series opener, Guillen was asked about a statement he'd made in September that he just might walk away if the Sox won a championship. He said he might do exactly that.

"It's still in my mind because ... well, I would like to win first and think about it," Guillen said. "It's not because I want to quit. It's because I do something I always wanted to do-win with this ballclub. The main thing to me is winning here, and I will make up my mind. But I don't know if I can handle my family for the rest of my life without baseball. I'm already tired seeing them, and we had three days off between one game and another. It's not fun. I like to be around people. That's why I make my mind."

◆

Poor Bagwell.

He had waited 15 big-league seasons to get into a World Series. He tortured himself playing through pain from a 2001 operation on his arthritic right shoulder that just didn't heal and then worked like a madman to get back from a second surgery in May, which was supposed to keep him out until 2006, if not forever.

He couldn't throw the ball, so playing first base was out. He was a good soldier for the Houston Astros' first 10 playoff games, understanding the best he could hope for was a pinch-hitting assignment in a key situation. But now, with the rules having changed to include a designated hitter in games at the American League park, a lineup spot was back on Bagwell's radar.

And one of the first things he had done after the champagne stopped flowing in St. Louis was to seek out Garner. He told him that he was good to go. "The adrenaline is enough as it is," Bagwell said. "I can play DH."

Sure, he could. So could Gary Gaetti, the Astros' hitting coach. But neither Bagwell nor Gaetti was the bat that Houston needed in the lineup—not against Contreras in Game 1 and probably not against lefty Mark Buehrle in Game 2.

The truth was this: Bagwell found himself with an incredibly emotional dilemma. He was a player who had always done things the right way, and the right thing now for his team was the wrong thing for him.

Bagwell needed to go to Garner and tell his manager that he had given it a lot of thought and the right thing was to play someone else, most likely the dangerous Lamb, who had hit four homers in 12 career playoff games.

If Garner started this version of Bagwell, one held together by grit and anti-inflammatory medicine, he would be giving the Sox a break. But Garner would have a hard time dealing with the repercussions if Bagwell wanted to start and he didn't start him.

Frank Thomas, born on May 27, 1968, the same day as Bagwell, could relate. He was also a Hall of Fame candidate whose body was failing him.

Thomas thought it unrealistic to expect a competitor to scratch himself from this situation. Thomas had hurried to come back from a stress fracture in his left ankle by June, with the idea of jumping in on a first-place team and riding the deep pitching staff to the playoffs, but he lasted only until July 20, when a new fracture was discovered in the ankle.

The walking boot he still wore took away any motivation Thomas might have felt to push himself onto the field when he was a shell of his former self. But Thomas certainly understood why Bagwell was doing everything he could to be a contributor.

"This time of year, you do anything you can to get on the

field," Thomas said. "You don't worry about pain, about hurting yourself worse. If you can be on the field, you get on the field. You're a baseball player, and that's what we do as baseball players."

Bagwell, bothered by pain in his right shoulder for at least five years, finally had to submit to surgery in May. He was activated from the disabled list Sept. 9 and got a game-winning single a week later. He proved to be a decent pinch-hitter, going 3-for-12 to keep anyone from saying he didn't deserve a spot on the playoff roster.

His teammates wanted him there, and he deserved to be there. But it's one thing to be used as a pinch-hitter and another to get four at-bats a night in a World Series game.

The Astros didn't exactly feature Murderer's Row, especially not with the slap-hitting Willy Taveras playing center field and batting second behind leadoff hitter Craig Biggio. That's why Garner started Chris Burke, a converted second baseman, in center in four postseason games, using Lamb at first and Berkman in left.

Garner wouldn't tip his hand during Houston's Friday workout.

"I do have an idea of what I want to do with the lineup, and I'm not going to announce it today," Garner said. "I'll announce it tomorrow. And I'm excited to no end, I can tell you, that Bagwell is with us. ... We'll be able to utilize Baggy, and I'm happy for him."

He sounded like a guy who wasn't going to start Bagwell, at least not until Sunday's Game 2. If he was going to start him, why not end the suspense?

Big kid delivers

Sox make Astros' veterans look old as rookie Jenks slams door

When Game 1 of the World Series arrived on a reasonably pleasant Saturday night, it was obvious this was anything but another autumn evening in Chicago.

Security was tighter than ever around U.S. Cellular Field. Helicopters hovered overhead, at eye level with some fans in the upper deck. They were said to be monitoring the air quality in case terrorists picked this event to detonate dirty bombs or biological weapons.

It's fair to say there wasn't usually such concern when the White Sox played the Royals and Tigers. But this night was different.

Before the ceremonial first pitch, the great Minnie Minoso, at 82 both a great-grandfather and the father of a teenager, walked around U.S. Cellular Field like royalty. He hadn't seen a Chicago team win the World Series in his lifetime. "I can rest happy now," Minoso said. "Double happy, triple happy."

Eddie Einhorn, a partner in Jerry Reinsdorf's ownership group, was giddy with anticipation. "I just saw someone who asked if I'm ready," Einhorn said. "Am I ready? I've been ready for 25 years."

From Josh Groban's teasingly slow national anthem to the crowd of politicos in Commissioner Bud Selig's box, there was no missing the significance of the moment. But the goal for the Sox was to somehow forget that this was Game 1 of the World Series and play it as if it were Game 9, a continuation of the roll they had been on in October.

In something of a surprise, at least based on Phil Garner's comments a day before, Jeff Bagwell was in Houston's lineup as the designated hitter.

Maybe Garner had no choice but to play Bagwell. Maybe he was managing more with his heart than his head. But the Sox were happy to see the Astros starting Bagwell instead of Chris Burke, who was hitting .348 in the playoffs.

Garner made that decision while acknowledging that Bagwell's arthritic right shoulder kept him from being the same hitter who had piled up 449 career homers, 27 as recently as the 2004 season.

"He doesn't have the power that he had, and he will have more power next year as his ability to work [out] like Jeff likes to work out gets better," Garner said. "But he can still put the bat on the ball. He can still give you good at-bats."

Garner said Bagwell was "excited" when he told him he was starting for the first time since May 3, but he did not want it to be the manager's version of a Lifetime Achievement Award. "He wanted to make sure this was a baseball decision," Garner said. "It definitely was."

◆

For Sox hitters it was mission accomplished, from the moment Jermaine Dye ripped a 3-2 fastball from Roger Clemens for a home run in the first inning until Scott Podsednik's triple off Russ Springer in the eighth inning. They had played like it was Game 9, not Game 1, and won 5-3, thanks largely to two great defensive plays from third baseman Joe Crede and lights-out pitching by relievers Neal Cotts and Bobby Jenks.

But the Sox didn't just win, they got a bonus. Clemens, who got the call to start the World Series opener in part because of questions about Game 2 starter Andy Pettitte's bruised knee, lasted only two innings before leaving with more of the hamstring problems that had dogged him since an unbelievable first half. ESPN radio commentator Rick Sutcliffe said he wouldn't be surprised if the Rocket was grounded until 2006, if not—scary thought here—forever.

"We'll have to see how he is as we go along," Garner said.

In winning seven of eight games in the postseason and 12 of their last 13 overall, the Sox's hitters had consistently come through in big at-bats while their pitchers frustrated the opponents. The Sox entered the World Series hitting .333 with men in scoring position in the playoffs, and Juan Uribe delivered a long double to left-center off Clemens in the second inning. It came in the first chance with a runner on second or third.

Nice way to turn down the heat.

Clemens left after the second inning, having thrown 25 pitches in the first inning and 29 more in the second, including 10 after getting Podsednik to an 0-2 count. It was announced that he had a strained left hamstring, leaving him uncertain for a possible start in Game 5. But Clemens' pride was strained too.

A 341-game winner, Clemens was more than just a future Hall of Famer. He was almost without question the greatest pitcher of his generation. Some historians ranked him alongside Walter Johnson, Christy Mathewson, Warren Spahn, Sandy Koufax and Bob Gibson on the short list of the greatest pitchers ever.

But Clemens had more mileage on him than any of the trucks in Astros owner Drayton McLane's fleet. He had turned 43 in August, which made his 1.87 season earned-run average an amazing achievement. But Clemens had won only 13 of his 32 starts, with his teammates too often becoming as mesmerized behind him as the hitters facing him.

There was a pattern here too. Clemens would get himself in terrific shape at the start of the season but wear down, especially in his legs, as he piled up innings. This season his ERA had been 1.48 in the first half and 2.42 (still great, but not historic) in the second half.

October has always been a cruel month for aging starters, with the demands of the regular season leaving them without their normal killer instinct. No starting pitcher in his 40s had ever won a World Series game, with Clemens having failed once previously, in Game 4 of 2003 against Florida, to become the first.

The postseason had rarely been kind to Clemens. He had a .665 regular-season winning percentage but only a 12-8 record in 24 games in the postseason. He had been fortunate enough to work the playoffs for seven years in a row since orchestrating a trade that sent him from Toronto to the New York Yankees in 1999, but he hadn't been truly dominant in a postseason game since 2000.

That year he followed a one-hit, 15-strikeout shutout of Seattle with eight shutout innings against the New York Mets in the game remembered for his heaving the jagged barrel of a cracked bat toward Mike Piazza as Piazza ran up the first-base line. Clemens had said he thought he was throwing the ball, even though few have ever confused those two pieces of equipment and previous bad blood between him and Piazza might suggest motive. Either way, it showed how fast his mind sometimes runs in the biggest games, how he psychs himself up like Bill Romanowski before a Super Bowl game, and sometimes just loses it.

Clemens had said he was probably going to retire after his last season with the Yankees, in 2003. When he worked a World Series game at Pro Player Stadium, the huge crowd there turned the night sky white with their flashbulbs in what fans thought would be the last appearance of his career. But he wound up signing with his hometown Astros after Pettitte, also a Houston resident, shocked baseball by leaving the Yankees to sign with the Astros in December 2003.

Some felt Clemens was risking embarrassment by coming back at his age, but he gave McLane two of the greatest seasons of his career. He hadn't had his mojo in October, however, failing to protect a one-run lead in Game 7 of the 2004 National League Championship Series in St. Louis and lasting only two innings against the Sox on this night.

Clemens, normally not camera-shy, vanished abruptly from the Cell after the game. His only interview had been with television, practically on the run, as he was heading out.

"I had the problem in the second inning and fought my way through that inning, got through that inning," Clemens said. "I came up here as quick as I could to take my sleeve off and have them check it and see if there was anything I could do so I could continue. The fluid already started to build up in my leg. So they gave me some medication and I'm going to treat it, and that's all I can tell you from there."

◆

The Sox were ninth in the American League in scoring, but this was the fifth time in nine playoff games they had bounced an opposing starter before he had finished five innings. "We should have scored a little bit more," Ozzie Guillen said. "We did a good job against Roger, made him throw a lot of pitches. You just saw a Chicago baseball game."

Jose Contreras was not as sharp as he had been in his three previous playoff starts. He gave up a second-inning home run to Mike Lamb, who started at first base with Lance Berkman moving to left field, and then a two-run double to Berkman in the third, failing to protect early 1-0 and 3-1 leads.

But Contreras and the bullpen got all the big outs after Crede drove a high 0-2 fastball from left-hander Wandy Rodriguez into the seats for a solo homer in the fourth inning, the fourth time in the last five games Crede had put the Sox ahead or tied a game.

With the Sox clinging to that 4-3 lead, Crede saved Contreras runs in the sixth and seventh innings.

In the sixth, with Willy Taveras on third and one out, Guillen played his infield in, an automatic call with Taveras representing the tying run, even though the hitter was Houston cleanup man Morgan Ensberg.

Crede made a backhand stop of a dart down the third-base line and threw across his body to get Ensberg at first. Taveras had no chance to advance and was stranded at third when Lamb grounded out.

"They're in a situation there where they're just putting the ball in the air or a ground ball gets the run in," Crede said. "But I was fortunate enough to get enough on the ball and make the play.… We were playing aggressive defense out there."

In the seventh, with runners on first and third and two outs, Crede dived to his right to backhand a smash by Craig Biggio. He pushed himself off the ground and made an off-balance throw to Paul Konerko, beating Biggio to the bag to end the threat.

For longtime World Series watchers, Crede's sterling plays brought back memories of Brooks Robinson.

"I'm just fortunate to be in the right spot at the right time," Crede said. "As for the magnitude of the game, I mean, there's no bigger stage. To be able to perform on this stage and to be compared to all those great players, it's definitely an honor."

Hard to believe this was a guy many Sox fans wanted replaced back in July, when his batting average was down and his team was having trouble scoring runs.

"It's been an awesome ride," Crede said. "This year is definitely one of the years I'll always remember."

◆

Crede's plays would not have meant as much without the work of Cotts and Jenks in the eighth inning.

Taveras, who had doubled off Contreras in the sixth, led off the eighth with another double. Guillen called on Cotts, his best left-handed reliever, to face Berkman, who went the other way with an 0-2 pitch, lining a single to left field. Taveras had no choice but to throw on the brakes at third, putting runners at the corners with no outs.

Guillen wanted Jenks to face Lamb, but he had to get through Ensberg first. Cotts struck out the All-Star third baseman, blowing a 94-m.p.h. fastball past him.

That was a telling pitch, as Cotts' fastball normally topped out at 91-92 m.p.h. There had been talk before the Series that the White Sox's bullpen was especially vulnerable because Guillen had allowed his starters to work 44 1/3 of the 45 innings against the Angels in the championship series. But maybe giving tired arms some time off was a good thing.

"I said a couple of days ago, I'd rather have them real rested rather than real tired," Guillen said. "We have power pitchers. We're not control-type guys from the bullpen. We attack people, and I think that helped those kids throw the ball the way they did."

Lamb had almost no chance in a lefty-lefty battle with Cotts. He fouled off a two-strike pitch but went down swinging on the next one, making it two outs with the tying run still at third base.

Bagwell, batting sixth in the order, was next up. Guillen went to the mound and gave one of the strangest signals ever, first putting up his right arm and then using both arms to form an oversized circle. It was the signal he had been using since late in the season when he wanted the 24-year-old Jenks, who stands 6 feet 3 inches and is listed at 270 pounds.

In the stands, Gordon Lakey, a veteran scout for the Philadelphia Phillies, could hardly believe his eyes. He had seen Jenks pitch in Arizona during spring training, when his 98- and 99-m.p.h. fastballs were all over the place, and did not envision him as a guy anyone would trust to save a World Series game.

"I didn't think he could throw enough strikes," Lakey said.

Imagine the surprise of Bill Stoneman, the Angels' general manager. He had dropped Jenks off his 40-man roster after the 2004 season, and Sox GM Ken Williams scooped him up for the $20,000 price of a waiver claim.

Moved to the bullpen, Jenks somehow learned to control the lightning God put in his right arm. He split the season between Double-A Birmingham and the big leagues, showing tremendous maturity for a guy with a long rap sheet for acts of drunkenness and stupidity.

Along with injuries—his right elbow had been screwed together in the summer of 2004—it was immaturity and a suspected lack of character that caused the Angels to give up on Jenks, whom they had selected in the fifth round of the 2000 draft.

Guillen broke him in slowly but was unafraid to expand Jenks' role when veteran Dustin Hermanson was limited by back problems in August and September. Jenks did not back away from ninth-inning responsibility, which pleased Guillen and astounded some of his older teammates.

Because of his 100-m.p.h. fastball and snapdragon curveball, Jenks had become a cult favorite at U.S. Cellular, where fans chanted his name. But few of those fans had an appreciation for how far this guy had come from his dirt-road roots in the outback of Idaho.

Jenks' parents didn't care whether he went to school or not, so he stopped going. He was ultimately rescued by Mark Potoshnik, a coach with the Northwest Baseball Academy in Lynnwood, Wash., near Seattle. Potoshnik had heard about Jenks' powerful arm and recruited him to pitch on his summer team. He wound up serving as Jenks' mentor, if not a surrogate parent.

Even with Potoshnik in the picture, Jenks had no high school career. He attended Inglemoor High School in Bothell, Wash., graduating in 2000, but was academically ineligible to pitch there. In order to help him pursue a professional career, Potoshnik arranged showcases for Jenks, one of which attracted 30 scouts. They left talking about the new Steve Dalkowski, telling colleagues Jenks had been so wild they worried about their safety. One San Diego Padres scout, according to legend, was almost decapitated.

But when you can throw the ball harder than anyone in the country, you get the benefit of the doubt.

Potoshnik said Jenks was "far and away the most talented individual I've ever been around in terms of arm strength," but something was always holding him back, either his health or his self-destructive tendencies.

"Everyone who saw him when he was younger, it was never a matter of ability," Potoshnik said. "It was whether he was going to be healthy. And with his background, is he going to be able to overcome some things and learn how the rest of society works and be able to flourish in that environment?"

In his third professional season, the world beyond the low minors learned about Jenks. The messenger was ESPN the Magazine, and the message was this: Stay out of this guy's way.

The article told of Jenks' potential but detailed his binge drinking and recklessness. It talked about him being suspended for repeatedly bringing beer on minor-league buses and how "in a drunken stupor, he took a lighter and burned the backside of his pitching hand, opening a wound the size of a silver dollar. He then torched his left hand and the underside of both forearms before passing out."

Matt Soshnick, an agent who had once represented Jenks, painted a bleak picture in the story.

"Imagine being in the top five in the world at what you do, and your demons are so terrible that your ability is dwarfed," Soshnick said. "That's Bobby Jenks. The worst thing that could happen is if he gets to the big leagues. If he gets to the big leagues, he'll free fall. He can't handle success."

The Sox claimed Jenks, figuring they had nothing to lose. But their scouts also had been told he was turning his life around. He married a woman he had met at a Seattle restaurant and was a young father, trying to support his family.

"That would settle anyone down," Jenks said during the playoff run. "Knowing when I come home, even if I had a bad game, my daughter and son will still come over and give me a big hug."

When asked about the bad-boy side of Jenks, Sox coaches didn't know what to say.

"There's never been a smudge on his slate, as far as I'm concerned," pitching coach Don Cooper said. "I don't judge anybody until we get him. He's been great. There hasn't even been a question. Anything in the past is simply that: the past."

Jenks had already earned two saves in the playoffs, nailing down Games 2 and 3 against Boston. But after U.S. Cellular fans cheered him running into the game, they held their collective breath. This was the World Series, and who knew how the kid would react?

After walking from the left-field bullpen to the mound, Jenks seemed to have trouble getting comfortable. Jermaine Dye and Aaron Rowand talked nervously in center field as they watched him warm up.

"He may have thrown one strike in warmups," Dye said. "We were out in center field like, 'What's going to happen here?' "

Bagwell swung through the first pitch from Jenks, a fastball clocked at 99 m.p.h. He fouled off the next one, also clocked at 99, and then worked the count to 2-2 by taking the next two pitches, both fastballs, one clocked at 100, and then fouled off a two-strike fastball.

Jenks had thrown five straight fastballs. Would the next one be the hard curve? Nope. The heat, again, this time at 99. Bagwell swung and missed, and the rally was over.

"If you'd seen me warming up, you'd see I didn't throw anything but a fastball," Jenks said later. "I couldn't find anything else. Going off the scouting report and 0-2 counts, he chases fastballs up above the zone, so I was sticking to what I was doing best, going [with] my strengths and his weaknesses."

Jenks was money in the ninth. He fanned Jason Lane, retired Brad Ausmus on a grounder and struck out Adam Everett, preserving the win for Contreras.

The White Sox celebrated the victory, but not for too long. There was another game to play on Sunday, Game 10.

Chicago Tribune photo by Scott Strazzante

Left-fielder Scott Podsednik is swarmed at the plate after belting a walk-off home run against Houston closer Brad Lidge in the ninth to win Game 2.

Chicago Tribune photo by Scott Strazzante

Ozzie Guillen uses his unique signal to summon rotund closer Bobby Jenks from the bullpen in the eighth. Jenks struck out Jeff Bagwell to end the inning and worked a 1-2-3 ninth.

Chicago Tribune photo by Nuccio DiNuzzo

Bobby Jenks lets out a shout after finishing off the Astros to earn the save in Game 1.

Chicago Tribune photo by Nuccio DiNuzzo

Chicago Tribune photo by Scott Strazzante

With Joe Crede and Scott Podsednik nearby, shortstop Juan Uribe charges into the box seats along the third-base line to snare a foul ball in the ninth inning of Game 4. When Uribe followed that by turning a grounder into the third out, the Sox had won the World Series.

Geoff Blum is congratulated for breaking the 5-5 deadlock in the 14th inning with a solo homer. Blum had not played since the first game of the playoffs.

An emotional White Sox Chairman Jerry Reinsdorf is surrounded by his team, his staff and family members as he clutches the World Series trophy, which had not made its home in Chicago in 88 years.

Chicago Tribune photo by Charles Cherney

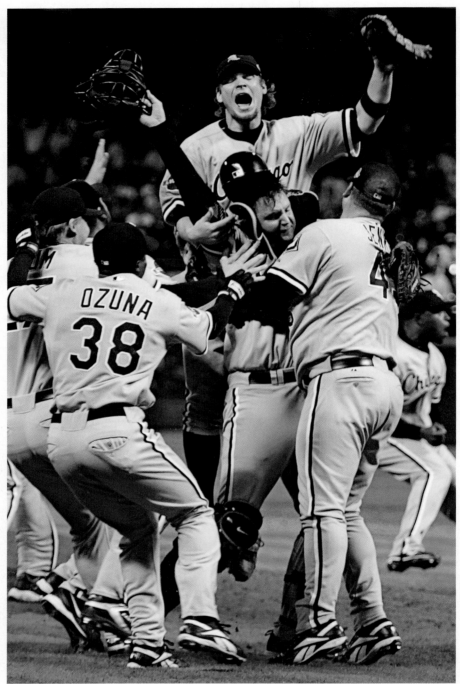

The Sox—who began to take shape last winter in Tucson—celebrate on the field in Houston as World Series champions.

Pods' power

Slap hitter stuns Lidge in 9th as Sox pick up Buehrle

Tracing the origins of the 2005 White Sox was easy. The amazing, crazy and ultimately historic run they were on began on two days in a span of six months in 1998 and '99.

The first was Nov. 11, 1998, when Ron Schueler traded young center fielder Mike Cameron to Cincinnati for Paul Konerko. Cameron had talent, but he frustrated Jerry Manuel and the Sox brass with his inconsistency.

The second date was May 21, 1999, when the Sox signed Mark Buehrle, keeping the anonymous young left-hander from going back into the 1999 draft.

Based on reports from scouts Nathan Durst and John Kazanas, the Sox had used a 38th-round pick on Buehrle in the 1998 draft. Yes, the 38th round—only five higher than where the Sox once selected Carey Schueler, the general manager's daughter.

The way Buehrle's career has evolved, you'd figure he might have been the 38th pick overall, and even that would have been low. But the surprising reality is this cornerstone of the championship rotation was never recognized as an excellent pitcher until he began to retire hitters such as Jim Thome and Alex Rodriguez.

When the Sox drafted Buehrle, he was pitching for Jefferson (Mo.) Junior College, not exactly one of baseball's leading factories. He was identified as a prospect there and claimed in a quirky process known as draft-and-follow, which allows organizations to select junior-college players one year and then decide whether to sign them after seeing how they develop the next year.

It's a no-risk situation for clubs, and it extends a carrot to fringe prospects. Buehrle wasn't complaining when the Sox explained it to him.

After all, this is a guy who was twice cut from his high school team. Buehrle had the misfortune to be undersized in a culture that wants its athletes buffed. He remembers his freshman year at Francis Howell North High in St. Charles, Mo., for two things: being stuffed inside lockers by senior boys and being told he wasn't good enough to pitch on the freshman baseball team. He was cut again after trying out his sophomore year.

"I fired that [sophomore] coach and almost got fired because of it," said Bob Donahoe, the Francis Howell North varsity coach. "I was a very unhappy camper. Now I make all the final cuts myself. We call it 'The Buehrle Rule.' "

Donahoe says he always knew Buehrle was a quality pitcher because of his unusual command, but other coaches discounted him because he didn't throw very hard. For two years, while lesser pitchers worked for the school team, Buehrle was limited to summer baseball. It's a wonder he continued to go out for the team.

"To Mark's credit, four days before tryouts for his junior

year, I saw him in the hall and told him to make sure he came out and he just said, 'Coach, I'm there,' " Donahoe recalled. "I said, 'That's good because I just want you to know—shame on me for what's happened in the past.' He just kind of smiled. God, I love him. He's really special."

Buehrle said he almost gave up on baseball after those two cuts. His father had to talk him into trying out again.

"He was disappointed and embarrassed," John Buehrle said. "Not making the team hurt, but I told him, 'Buddy, that's life. Life is often disappointment and hurt, but if you take that disappointment and turn it around into something positive, you can learn from it. Your mother and I didn't raise any quitters and we're not starting now.' "

Suffice it to say Ozzie Guillen and Ken Williams are happy Buehrle didn't quit. It was Buehrle, not Cuban legend Jose Contreras or 18-game winner Jon Garland, who was picked for the Wheaties box after the World Series.

"Sports has enough egos to fill the gossip columns," Williams said. "It's not often a guy remains the same. If anything, Mark has become more humble and more of a team guy. He's a pleasure to be around. It's refreshing to have a guy like that on board."

Schueler recognized Buehrle's potential the first time he saw him pitch, with Burlington (Iowa) in the Midwest League playoffs in 1999. He saw enough to invite him to big-league camp in 2000, Buehrle's first spring training as a pro.

Buehrle acted as if he'd been a big-leaguer forever that first spring. Nothing bothered him, including big-league hitters. The White Sox, on their way to 95 wins and a division title that season, promoted him from Double A at midseason of his first full season as a pro, giving Jerry Manuel another lefty in the bullpen.

Equipment manager Vince Fresso gave Buehrle a linebacker's number when he arrived. Instead of complaining, he stuck with it, turning No. 56 into a fashionable one around Chicago.

The Sox cruised into the playoffs in 2000, but only after surviving a test from the reigning power, the Cleveland Indians, in early September. On Sept. 8 at Jacobs Field, Manuel brought Buehrle into a game with the Sox clinging to a one-run lead. The Indians had already scored once in the inning on singles by Kenny Lofton, Omar Vizquel and Manny Ramirez, and now had runners on first and third and one out for Thome.

The powerful first baseman, who was on his way to a 37-homer, 106-RBI season, was noted for his eye at the plate. He struck out a lot, but he also walked a lot, seldom putting the first pitch he saw into play. This at-bat was no different. Thome worked Buehrle to a 3-2 count, then hit a grounder to second baseman Ray Durham, who started an inning-ending double play.

Buehrle was the winning pitcher as the Sox pushed their lead over the Indians to 8½ games instead of 6½. It was the last gasp for a Cleveland team that had won five straight division titles, twice advancing to the World Series.

After reporters had cleared out of the clubhouse, one doubled back to ask Buehrle a question. "The 3-2 pitch to Thome: Was that a changeup?" he asked.

"Yep," Buehrle said.

"Do you throw a lot of 3-2 changeups?"

Buehrle, a stoic even by rookie standards, cracked a little smile. "No," he said. "That might have been the first one I've ever thrown."

Major-league rookies aren't supposed to throw changeups on 3-2 counts. That's a veteran's pitch. But then, Buehrle wasn't a typical rookie. He was a natural.

Buehrle finished his rookie season working out of the bullpen in the playoffs. Only 14 months after pitching for the Jefferson County Vikings, he faced Rodriguez and Mike Cameron in the ninth inning of a playoff game against Seattle.

He gave up two singles in a three-batter stint in a 5-2 loss but was notable, as always, for his poise. Ten of the 12 pitches he threw were strikes, including the first pitch to each hitter.

"I wasn't nervous at all," Buehrle said. "I was more nervous pitching to Jim Thome in Cleveland. This just seemed like a normal game. I had to come in and get guys out."

Not much bothered Buehrle, the king of keeping it simple. This is a guy who proposed to his hometown sweetheart in a deer stand on 1,100 acres Buehrle had bought near his boyhood home in St. Charles, Mo.

"A lot of people said, 'Man, you're a redneck for proposing in a tree stand,'" Buehrle said. "I was like, 'I like to be out in the country, I like to hunt.' If people want to say I'm a redneck, whatever, I don't care. That's my nature."

His fiancé, Jamie Streck, wasn't put off by the location of Buehrle's proposal. "It was completely his personality and how he and I are," she said. "I don't care about flashy stuff. When we hang out, we go ride four-wheelers."

Just as when Buehrle pitches, he throws strikes.

When Buehrle beat the Indians 1-0 in only 1 hour 51 minutes to start the 2005 season, no one was surprised. He had long ago earned a reputation for working faster than anyone in the big leagues. His crowning achievement in that regard came two starts later, when he beat Seattle 2-1 in a game that lasted 1 hour 39 minutes, the quickest in Seattle's history and the fastest for the Sox in 21 years.

"I just go out there, do what I can do and get everybody out of here as quickly as I can," Buehrle said afterward.

Buehrle gave up only three hits in that game, all by Ichiro Suzuki.

"Buehrle's the best to play behind," Paul Konerko said. "He just grabs the ball and fires it. When he's throwing his game, you know exactly what it's going to be."

Buehrle shakes off his catcher like he pays his taxes—once a year, even if it kills him.

"You can call the wrong pitch as a catcher and he still gets them out because he locates so well," said Chris Widger, a back-up to A.J. Pierzynski. "When you have four pitches to choose from at any pitch in the count, it makes a catcher's job easy."

Buehrle rolled up 16 wins during the 2005 regular season, not including the All-Star Game in Detroit, which he started and won. He made at least 32 starts and worked more than 220 innings for the fifth consecutive season.

Buehrle was on track to be the Sox's No. 1 starter in the playoffs until two things happened: Jose Contreras turned into the hottest pitcher in the majors, and the rotation fell naturally with Contreras working in front of Buehrle, which meant it would have to be reshuffled to get Buehrle into his customary role at the front.

The Sox knew Buehrle wasn't going to complain about working behind Contreras in any situation, especially not the World Series. Eighty-five big-league wins and more than $10 million later, this was still a guy who was happy to be on the varsity.

◆

Jeff Bagwell visited the interview room at U.S. Cellular Field before Game 2. For the second night in a row, he was in Phil Garner's lineup as Houston's designated hitter.

At 37, Bagwell was 11 years removed from his MVP season and six from the last of his four seasons as a National League

All-Star. He still cut a dashing figure in his baseball pants, his brown Astros sweatshirt and his thick brown beard, but something about Bagwell was different. He seemed to be shrinking as he was aging, his shoulders not quite as broad as in his prime. He looked more like Kevin Costner playing Jeff Bagwell than the Bagwell who had hit 366 home runs in one decade.

Bagwell had never ducked a challenge, though, and he wasn't going to start now. His motivation in accepting an invitation to the interview room, at least in part, was to answer criticism that he should not be in the lineup. He had gone 0-for-2 in the Astros' Game 1 loss, flying out deep to left field in his second plate appearance and getting blown away by Bobby Jenks in his fourth and final plate appearance. Contreras had hit him with pitches the other two times.

ESPN's Jayson Stark asked Bagwell the question he had been waiting for.

"There has been some second-guessing of the decision to play you last night, mostly on the strikeout by the guy throwing 100 m.p.h.," Stark said. "What did that tell you about where you are?"

Bagwell smiled.

"That's interesting that I get second-guessed for striking out on a 100-m.p.h. fastball," he said, pausing as the reporters laughed. "I'd like to see people hit that one. I'll tell you what, if anything, for me it went a long way. As I said after the game, my only fault in that at-bat is I didn't get the ball down as much as I should have in the first couple of swings. But my bat head was there, which means I can get the bat head to it. I just need to get it down."

Bagwell continued.

"Anytime you face a guy who throws that hard, you have to try to get the ball down, because it's so hard to hit an elevated pitch. So I'm very happy in that fact. If I get in that opportunity again I will really, really concentrate on getting the ball down. I think that went a long way for me."

A couple of questions later, another reporter brought Bagwell back to the subject of his diminishing abilities.

"Some of the second-guessing about your striking out on a 100-m.p.h. fastball is also the fact that there is a belief that you are on the team because of your emotion," the reporter said. "If you didn't feel you could be capable of helping your team, would you tell the manager that? Talk about that."

Bagwell was happy to oblige.

"When I came back [from shoulder surgery], we decided to give it a try to see how I would do. I went down to Corpus Christi and had a few at-bats down there. We came back to the team and said, 'Let's go, I can give you a good at-bat.' … I think I can help the team, I really do. I'm a lot stronger now. I can hit a home run now. I can hit a base hit to right. And I have been in these situations, big situations where I've got guys in scoring position. I can do whatever it takes to try to help this team win.… Phil Garner believes in that, and my teammates do too.

"Second-guess all you want. It's easy to do that in this situation, but it's a little unfair too. You have to look at the situation and what happened. But I think Garner feels comfortable putting me in the lineup, and I think all my teammates do too. And that's all that matters."

When Sox scouts concluded that they wanted to face a lineup that had Bagwell in it, as opposed to one with Chris Burke and Mike Lamb, they had taken emotion out of the decision. Garner and others who had watched Bagwell through his by-the-book career did not have that luxury.

While Bagwell might have been a hot-button item elsewhere, including talk radio in Houston, his presence was a given for those who best understood how Drayton McLane's franchise worked. The Astros may have waited 44 years to get to the World Series, but that didn't mean they were going to abandon their civility.

If Bagwell wanted to play, many thought he deserved to play. And besides, this wasn't exactly like letting Doug Ford and Arnold Palmer compete against Tiger Woods and Phil Mickelson in the Masters.

Houston Chronicle columnist Richard Justice had written that Garner had no decision to make on Bagwell.

"He has to be in there," Justice wrote before Game 1. "For all the years and all the big hits and all the victories. For all he has meant to a franchise and a city. For how he has conducted himself. For the teammates who revere him still."

He quoted shortstop Adam Everett, Lamb and general manager Tim Purpura high in his column.

"He's the leader on this team," Everett said.

"He deserves this," Lamb said.

"We're here as a franchise because of Jeff Bagwell," Purpura said.

Concluded Justice: "If this is Bagwell's goodbye, so be it. Give him a going-away gift he'll remember. The Astros may never have a greater player. They almost certainly will never have one who is a better teammate, player and citizen."

◆

When Buehrle threw the first pitch of Game 2, U.S. Cellular had taken on the feeling of a deer blind in winter. It was 45 degrees, a 10 m.p.h. wind was blowing from the northwest and rain showers were falling intermittently. It wasn't too uncomfortable in the dugouts, but it was brutal in the exposed parts of the ballpark, such as the right-field bleacher seats that the

White Sox sell as field boxes.

Because of the rain, the game started seven minutes late, the first rain delay for a World Series game since Game 3 of the 1993 Series in Philadelphia. But in the postseason, delays of one kind or another become the norm, not the exception. Buehrle had talked earlier in October about how hard it is for him to slow his pace to allow for the additional time between innings on nationally televised games, and no games have more time between innings than World Series games.

Buehrle would never make an excuse, but between the weather and the pace, he seemed to have a tough time getting comfortable on the mound. Houston took a 1-0 lead on a lead-off home run by Morgan Ensberg in the second inning but was denied more when Buehrle struck out Everett to strand runners at the corners.

The Sox came right back with two runs, as they had done often in October. Consecutive singles by Aaron Rowand, A.J. Pierzynski and Joe Crede at the bottom of the order, along with Craig Biggio's drop of a Juan Uribe popup (scored a fielder's choice because right fielder Jason Lane was able to force Crede at second base), gave Buehrle a 2-1 lead.

It was gone three batters later. The Astros tied the score 2-2 on a one-out triple by Willy Taveras—him again?—and Lance Berkman's sacrifice fly. They took a 4-2 lead in the top of the fifth, the biggest blows doubles by Brad Ausmus and Berkman. An infield single by Taveras, the rare play Crede and Uribe couldn't make, also played a role.

But Buehrle's teammates picked him up.

Scott Podsednik had set the tone for the Sox's hitters with a 10-pitch at-bat to start Andy Pettitte's night. It ended with Podsednik lining out to Burke in left field—Burke was in the lineup, Lamb was out—but contributed to Pettitte having to throw 98 pitches in six innings. That wasn't an overly high total, but Garner had been handling Pettitte with kid gloves since he was hit on the inside of his right knee by a liner during batting practice before his Game 1 start in the National League Championship Series.

Pettitte had thrown 103 pitches in Game 5 against the Cardinals, but Garner decided to lift him before the Sox seventh began rather than let him face the two right-handed hitters scheduled to start the inning, Crede and Uribe. He brought in Dan Wheeler, his top setup man for closer Brad Lidge.

It was the right move, but in baseball, that's never a guarantee of success. After Crede hit a foul pop for the first out, Uribe lined a double off the left-field wall. Wheeler struck out Podsednik for the second out, but Tadahito Iguchi worked him for a walk as Wheeler missed with a 3-2 pitch.

That put men on first and second for Jermaine Dye. Wheeler fell behind 3-1 but threw a strike that Dye fouled off, running the count full. Dye fouled off the next pitch, and Wheeler came back with a fastball inside that just missed Dye's left elbow on its way to hitting the handle of his bat.

There was no reaction from Dye, but plate umpire Jeff Nelson pointed toward first base, ruling that the pitch had hit Dye. Replays showed it was a bad call, that the ball had hit Dye's bat rather than Dye and should have been a foul ball, the count remaining 3-2. Instead the bases were loaded for Paul Konerko.

Garner decided not to allow Wheeler to get out of his own mess. He called in reliever Chad Qualls, a move that had some scouts in the stands scratching their heads.

"Wow, what a tough thing to do any pitcher, let alone a young pitcher," a scout for a National League team said later. "It's freezing outside, and raining like midnight in Moscow, and Phil brings in a kid with Paul Konerko batting and the bases loaded. Wow. That's all I can say."

The first pitch to Konerko was a belt-high fastball, and Konerko had been locked in for a month. He wasn't missing many fat pitches, and he didn't miss this one. He drove the ball into the stands above the left-field bullpen for the Sox's first-ever grand slam in a postseason game. Quick as that, the 4-2 lead Pettitte had held turned to a 6-4 lead for Buehrle.

Not that it would last.

Cliff Politte worked a perfect eighth inning in place of Buehrle, who was lifted after 100 pitches, seven innings and no walks. Guillen called for Jenks in the ninth, but this time he didn't have it.

Bagwell had failed to get the ball out of the infield in his three at-bats off Buehrle, though in fairness, he had been robbed of one hit by Iguchi. Given a second chance against Jenks, he found a way to get the bat head on the ball and drop a single into center field, the ball falling with the gentleness of a pigeon coming to roost.

Down two runs in the ninth inning, the Astros needed a baserunner as much as a leadoff home run. Bagwell had delivered a hit that had to come with a lot of satisfaction, given the criticism he'd heard and the way Jenks had owned him a night earlier.

After striking out Lane on three pitches, Jenks walked Burke on four pitches. If the Sox were going to win, it was not going to be easy.

Looking to advance the runners, Ausmus followed with a grounder to Konerko for the second out. Bagwell and Burke moved up a base, putting both in scoring position. Jose Vizcaino, pinch-hitting for Everett, lined the first pitch Jenks threw him into left field. A great throw from Podsednik might have had a shot at Burke, but he didn't make a great throw. The Astros had tied the score 6-6.

Guillen called on Neal Cotts to get Jenks out of further trouble when Garner pinch-hit Lamb for Eric Bruntlett, who had entered as a defensive replacement for Biggio in the seventh inning. The lefty preserved the tie, retiring Lamb on a fly to Podsednik to end the Houston ninth.

◆

Podsednik, a solid fielder and a pesky leadoff hitter with speed, was the personification of the changes Ken Williams had orchestrated after the 2004 season. His acquisition in the Carlos Lee trade with Milwaukee, basically finished on the way home from the winter meetings in Anaheim, had not seemed like a turning point for the franchise. In hindsight, it had been. The trade freed up the money that allowed Williams to be active later in the winter, when players such as Pierzynski and Iguchi were available, and it did more than that. It gave Guillen the leadoff man who was the link to the 1959 Go-Go Sox.

Podsednik's electrifying first half—.369 on-base percentage, 44 stolen bases in 53 tries—changed the personality of the Sox from passive to aggressive. He became a one-man rallying point for his teammates in July when he was included in the goofy online balloting for the final spot on the American League All-Star team.

Not much gets big-leaguers excited, but the chance to get Podsednik on the All-Star team did. Buehrle was in the middle of a grass-roots campaign to get Podsednik elected, distributing T-shirts that he and his teammates wore during the voting. They went on every radio show they could, urging fans to vote early and often—the Chicago way—for the little sprinter from the central Texas town of West, who had spent eight years in the minor leagues before establishing himself as a big-leaguer in Milwaukee. During that crazy week, it wasn't uncommon to see a player sitting in the dugout with a laptop computer, checking the latest voting results.

Podsednik was honored to be included in the selection process but figured he had no chance to beat out Derek Jeter, who joined Torii Hunter, Hideki Matsui and Carl Crawford on the ballot. Podsednik was blown away when he won the election, collecting almost 4 million votes.

The Sox were hardly alone in the effort. It was a cause celebre in West, a town of 2,692 with Czech roots, located along Interstate 35 between Dallas and Austin. Podsednik remained a very visible part of his hometown, spending off-seasons as a substitute teacher there as recently as 2001.

"He was a good teacher and we'd ask him all about baseball," said Luke Bullock, a junior at West High School, where Podsednik had been prom king in 1994. "All the girls loved it when he subbed."

Asked by the Tribune's David Haugh about his hometown, Podsednik had said West was "a lot of bars, a couple of banks" before turning serious.

"Even during the grind through the minor leagues, I know they were keeping tabs on me and wondering how I was doing," Podsednik said. "So to know those guys are watching now means a lot to me."

As a young player, Podsednik was held back by self-doubt, especially after an injury-plagued run in which he had hernia surgery, broke his wrist and hurt his knee.

"He'd come back worried, like, 'I don't think I'm going to make it, so what am I going to do to make a living?' " his aunt, Rhonda Deiterman, said. "He was a tightly strung athlete. He struggled with that. That makes it so much better to enjoy now."

Growing up in West, Podsednik wasn't much different from the other kids in town. He ran a little faster, but other than that he was just like his neighbors. He picked up his work ethic from his father Duane, a worker in a glass plant in Waco, and mother Amy, a school secretary.

About the only time anyone remembers him straying was when he and a friend marked their nicknames on an electrical tower they were painting on their summer jobs. You can still see "PODS" written on the tower.

West held its first Scott Podsednik Day in January 2005, giving him the red-carpet treatment after the trade from Milwaukee to Chicago. The town honored him because he honors it with his presence on a regular basis.

"An Escalade will pull into town and the kids will see it and start saying, 'Scott's in town,' " said Kim Smith, who once taught Podsednik world history. "And nothing about him has changed except maybe what he drives. That's the way he was brought up."

◆

Brad Lidge, who had entered Game 2 to get Crede for the last out of a perfect eighth inning by Houston's bullpen, started the ninth by getting Uribe to fly out. That brought Podsednik to the plate.

Lidge's concern was keeping him off base. He knew the Sox's leadoff man was almost certain to attempt a steal if he got on. He had served notice with a steal in Game 1, giving him four steals in the last three games as he once again ran like the guy who had created havoc before straining a groin muscle in late July.

But Lidge's night was reminiscent of Game 5 in the NLCS against St. Louis, when he walked Jim Edmonds to bring Albert Pujols to the plate. Lidge wasn't at his best. He did not have command of his fastball, which he uses to set up his "slider from hell," as one scout called his best pitch.

Lidge started Podsednik with ball one, then ball two. He came back with a strike, which Podsednik took. He then left the 2-1 pitch up in the strike zone, over the middle of the plate, and Podsednik crushed it. While the crowd of 44,712 turned instantly silent—who could believe this?—the ball kept carrying and carrying in the heavy, damp air. It carried all the way into the seats in right-center field.

Podsednik, who had gone 523 at-bats without a home run before hitting one in Game 1 of the division series against Boston, had delivered his second of the playoffs. This one gave the Sox a 7-6 victory.

The ball was barely in the seats before the U.S. Cellular public-address system was cranking the schlock-hit song by Journey that had become the Sox's theme song.

"Oh, the movie never ends," went the lyrics, belted out by Steve Perry, who had joined the White Sox for the World Series ride. "It goes on and on and on and on … Don't stop believin' … Hold on to the feelin'."

◆

Back in West, the crowd watching Game 2 at Wolf's Bar on Oak Street, including Podsednik's uncle, Duane Deiterman, was as ecstatic as anyone at the Cell. Maybe even more so.

Men and women hugged. Everyone jumped up and down. Their man, that little Pods, had become the 14th player to hit a walkoff home run in a World Series game, joining the likes of Hall of Famers Eddie Mathews, Bill Mazeroski, Mickey Mantle and Carlton Fisk.

"Nobody expected Scott to jack it out," said Tom Wolf, the bar's owner. "And when he did, people were so genuinely happy and shocked for him they started crying."

Deiterman was able to reach Podsednik on his cell phone in the Sox's clubhouse only a little while after the home run.

"He sounded like a little kid," Deiterman said. "He was so excited, happy for him, happy for us."

Blum dinger

Sub's 14th-inning homer puts
Sox on verge of Series title

Minute Maid Park was born under a bad name, if not
a bad sign.

Known as Enron Field for its first two seasons, Minute Maid
is the Houston Astros' publicly funded playground. It was nar-
rowly approved by Houston voters in a deal that also gener-
ated funds for the Houston Texans' Reliant Stadium and the
Houston Rockets' Toyota Center, which is just south of Minute
Maid—known as the "Juice Box"—in downtown Houston.

On the one hand, it's an awesome facility, one of the best
parks in the major leagues for fans to watch games. That says
a lot given the building craze in which 17 teams moved into
new parks between 1989 and 2004. On the other hand, it was
built with quirky dimensions, in part because of the site and
downtown streets, and an artificially quirky playing surface.

It was built as a hitter's ballpark, with only 315 feet from
home plate to the left-field foul pole at the edge of the so-called
Crawford Boxes, which are among the most easily reached
bleachers in the major leagues. It is only 364 feet to the left-

field power alley because Crawford Street runs directly behind the left-field wall.

In 1999, the last season they were based at the pitcher-friendly Astrodome, known as the Eighth Wonder of the World when it opened, the Astros won 97 games behind a pitching staff that compiled a 3.84 earned-run average. Jose Lima was the staff's leader, going 21-10 with a 3.58 ERA. But the move into Enron, where subsequently disgraced Enron boss Ken Lay threw out the first pitch on Opening Day, did not go well.

Houston's victory total plummeted from 97 to 72, and its staff ERA soared to 5.41. Though the pitching staff was largely the same one that had allowed 128 home runs in 1999, it served up 234 homers in 2000, including 48 by Lima. He was broken mentally by Memorial Day and finished 7-16 with a 6.65 ERA.

Along the way, Lima hung a good nickname on the new ballpark. He called it Ten Run Field.

Gerry Hunsicker, Houston's general manager when the park opened, acknowledged that Astros owner Drayton McLane wanted games to be more exciting but said no one expected Enron to join Colorado's Coors Field as places where slumping hitters went to get healthy.

"We're still perplexed at why the ball carries like it does," Hunsicker said in 2001. "We've had engineering studies done here, and we still haven't come up with a reason why the ball carries like it does."

Because he couldn't handle the ballpark's character, Lima was traded halfway through 2001. But those who stayed behind learned to pitch to the ballpark. "We've had to adjust, especially coming from the dome," former Houston pitcher Shane Reynolds said. "You just have to realize there are going to be a lot of high-run games here."

Over time, the Astros came not only to tolerate their home park but to thrive in it. They had gone 53-28 in the 2005 regular season at Minute Maid, which was renamed after Enron collapsed amid a financial scandal that cost many who had worked there or invested in the company their life savings. The Astros also had won seven consecutive playoff games there before Albert Pujols' ninth-inning homer in Game 5 forced the 2005 National League Championship Series back to St. Louis.

Like the SkyDome in Toronto, Safeco Field in Seattle, Bank One Ballpark in Phoenix and Miller Park in Milwaukee, Minute Maid was built as a convertible. Ballpark operators had the option of playing with the roof open or closed, which in Texas generally was a hedge against scorching summer temperatures.

But Jeff Bagwell and his Houston teammates had noticed it was a whole lot louder in the Juice Box with the roof closed. They believed that provided a home-field advantage, especially in the playoffs. Even when autumn weather arrived, the Astros kept the roof closed throughout their postseason run and figured they would keep it closed for the World Series.

If not for Curt Schilling, they probably would have been able to do so. But when Schilling was with the Arizona Diamondbacks during the 2001 playoffs, he had made a major issue of wanting to have the BOB's roof closed when he pitched. He knew the ball carried better with the roof open there, as was also the case at Minute Maid, and he did not want to risk losing that benefit when the Diamondbacks advanced to the World Series.

Unfortunately for Schilling, Phoenix had mild weather that October. Sandy Alderson, then in charge of baseball operations for Commissioner Bud Selig's office, declared that baseball was meant to be played outdoors and ordered the roof open for Game 1, when Schilling was Arizona's starter.

The day before the White Sox-Astros Game 3, the question was whether MLB would follow that precedent and order Houston to close the roof.

No fair! screamed the Astros, who should have had more important things to worry about. "I think it's ridiculous that [MLB] is involved in this," said Houston catcher Brad Ausmus, a Dartmouth graduate. "It's a little bit dictatorial."

Manager Phil Garner agreed. "We've played with it closed most of the year, I want to say about 85 percent of the time," he said. "I find it strange that somebody would say we have to open it now."

Morgan Ensberg used a column he was writing in the Houston Chronicle to grouse about outside involvement. During the season the Astros had gone 38-17 when the roof was closed and 15-11 when it was open. "The bottom line is with it closed, it generates a lot of noise and it's a lot of fun," Garner said.

Especially for the Astros, who figured to gain a slight edge over the Sox if the ball wasn't carrying as well as it might if the roof were open. But at the end of Monday's workout day, no one was sure what call Selig would make. "The roof," Astros GM Tim Purpura said, "is day-to-day."

At least Purpura still had his sense of humor.

◆

With the sky clear and temperatures in the 70s a day later, it was obvious Selig was going to order the roof open. He had almost said as much to Houston Chronicle columnist Richard Justice a day earlier, and he explained himself at a pregame news conference Tuesday.

"In these types of situations, [in] anything, you try to be fair and consistent," Selig said. "I know there have been some people who have said, 'Why does MLB interfere in the World Series?' It's true in all sports, by the way. And what you try to do is to be fair. We've studied weather, winds, we've studied humidity. There isn't a cloud within 800 miles of here. And the thing we have said to all clubs with roofs is weather is the determining factor. Let me say that again so there's no doubt: Weather is the determining factor. We don't let clubs do other things that will affect or disturb [the] balance."

At times, Selig's news conference took on an almost adversarial tone, with Houston reporters badgering him and others from MLB about dictating policy for the Astros. They talked about the comfort of fans, as if sitting outside in temperatures in the mid-60s was a hardship. After all, the forecast was for 68 degrees at game time, dropping no lower than 60 by game's end.

"With all due respect, in the city I come from you're lucky to get that by July 4, and that's true in other places," said Selig, former owner of the Milwaukee Brewers. "Using the criteria we've always used and the team has always used, I want to suggest the decision is a fair one, and that's all we can try to do. Is it popular? Well, I understand. I understand people—they think they want [it closed], but we've got to use some established criteria here, not just [go] off the top of our head."

Selig said McLane and the Astros' executives had accepted the ruling without rancor. "They could not have been nicer," he said. "They were worried that there were people mad at me. I said, 'This is not the first time, and I'm sorry to tell you it won't be the last time.' "

Bob DuPuy, MLB's chief operating officer, jumped in with a thought. "Whether the roof is open or closed," DuPuy said, "the team that scores the most runs tonight will win."

Selig smiled. "Very good point," he said.

◆

Though Sox rookie pitcher Brandon McCarthy had been so disappointed over being left off the World Series roster, there was little question it would stay as it had throughout October: 11 pitchers and 14 position players. The shift to Houston had caused Ozzie Guillen to take special care with his reserves—outfielder Timo Perez, infielders Pablo Ozuna, Geoff Blum and Willie Harris and backup catcher Chris Widger—during batting practice, as he would be more likely to use them without a designated hitter.

Rust would figure to be an issue. Ozuna was the only one of the group who had played since Oct. 4, Game 1 of the Boston series, and he had been used only as a pinch-runner since then. Harris had the bench's only hit of the postseason, and it had come two weeks earlier, in that 14-2 Game 1 laugher against Boston. Widger had not played at all in October, last getting into a game Sept. 30, the final Friday of the season in Cleveland.

Yet life had gone on for all of them, with Blum especially challenged. His wife Kory had given birth to triplets (all girls) in May, when he played for San Diego. They were among seven children who had been born to the wives of Sox players during the season, the latest being Nicholas Konerko, born to Paul and Jennifer on Oct. 19. Freddy Garcia's wife Glendys had given birth to Sofia during the ALCS. Joe Crede had left the team the final week of the season to take care of his wife Lisa after the birth of their second daughter, Lucy, on Sept. 27. A.J. Pierzynski's wife Lisa had given birth to Ava Jordan on Sept. 5.

Talk about your late-season call-ups. This team was loaded.

◆

What little pregame energy the Astros had left from the consternation over the roof—a red herring if ever there was one—was spent worrying about Roger Clemens. He threw in the bullpen at some point during the afternoon, hoping he would feel good enough to be listed for a possible Game 5 start, but continued to experience pain in his hamstring.

Garner was left to ponder whether he'd be better off bringing Andy Pettitte back on short rest or trust an X-factor such as rookies Ezequiel Astacio and Wandy Rodriguez. He could at least feel good about his starter that night: Roy Oswalt, the Astros' ace, if not their biggest name.

Oswalt was last seen blowing away Albert Pujols and the St. Louis Cardinals in the NLCS clincher, his 44th win in the last two seasons. He figured to be a good bet to get the Astros on the board in a series that was on the verge of slipping away from them.

The Sox were excited about the challenge. "It would mean a lot [to beat Oswalt]," Jermaine Dye said. "We already faced two of the best pitchers in baseball. Our main thing on the road is to score early, take the crowd out of it and let our pitchers go out there and pitch."

Konerko, cautious by nature, acknowledged a creeping sense of confidence. And why not? The Sox had won nine of 10 games in the playoffs and 14 of 15 overall. Hard to believe these were the same guys who had inspired that Guillen tirade in Kansas City.

"I like the way we're playing," Konerko said. "I feel like we're getting the best of what we have. It remains to be seen whether it's enough to be world champions. But I see our team playing the way we played during the regular season. We're loose. We're not intimidated by the World Series. We're playing our game, and guys are doing what they should."

◆

Oswalt came out firing, hitting 98 on the stadium radar gun with one fastball in the first inning. But while the White

Sox were staying on their game in the World Series, Oswalt
seemed a little too amped. He shut down the Sox in the first
four innings, taking a 4-0 lead to the mound in the fifth as the
Astros scored once in the first, twice in the third and once in
the fourth against Jon Garland.

The early innings had been reasonably easy for Oswalt,
who needed to throw more than 12 pitches only in the second. A leadoff double by Konerko and Crede's eight-pitch
walk-a masterpiece of an at-bat in which he worked his way
back from 0-2-were the centerpieces of an inning Oswalt was
lucky to escape. He got two outs on Aaron Rowand's liner to
shortstop Adam Everett, who flipped to Craig Biggio before
Konerko could get back to the bag.

But the bottom dropped out for Oswalt in the fifth. Crede,
perhaps locked in after seeing so many pitches two innings
earlier, led off by lining a home run to right field. Oswalt followed with the automatic out, striking out Garland, but he
needed six pitches to get him.

He then retired only one of the next eight hitters, with his
fastball dropping into the 92–93 range from its early peak of
98. This was what often happened in the playoffs, when the
workload caught up to a pitcher. Credit the Sox for exploiting
Oswalt's vulnerability.

The first nine hitters of what wound up as a five-run, 11-
batter inning took the first pitch they saw. Five were patient
enough to take the first two. Dye delivered a run-scoring
single on the eighth pitch of one plate appearance. Rowand
walked on the seventh pitch of another.

"We executed," said Guillen, referring to the approach hitting coach Greg Walker had emphasized. "We approached
him real well, Oswalt. This kid is one of the best in the league.
We made him throw strikes. All of a sudden his pitch [count]

went up, his velocity was a little down.... Our ballplayers did a tremendous job to get one of the best pitchers out of the game. That was the key for us, to get him out of the game."

The top of the order, Scott Podsednik and Tadahito Iguchi, had contributed singles after Oswalt struck out Garland. Iguchi's hit scored Juan Uribe with the second run. Dye's hit scored Podsednik. Pierzynski followed with a two-run double that split center fielder Willy Taveras and right fielder Jason Lane, scoring Iguchi and Dye to give the Sox a 5-4 lead.

When Pierzynski pulled up at second base, he banged his hands together in joy five or six times, more like a Little Leaguer than someone playing the game for money, but why not? The Sox might not have knocked Oswalt out of the game, but they had forced Garner to start warming up a reliever.

"He tried to find the strike zone, [and] we took advantage," Guillen said. "He was a little wild that inning. This kid can shut them down real quick, because he's that good. He left a couple of balls over there, and I think A.J., he was the key."

The five-spot turned out to be the only runs the Sox scored in the first 13 innings of Game 3, but it was enough to get them to the 14th. That proved to be a very good thing.

◆

Garland protected his 5-4 lead through the seventh inning, retiring nine of 10 hitters and allowing only one ball out of the infield. Garner opted to give up an out to move the tying run into scoring position after Garland walked Ausmus to start the seventh inning, but Garland then did what Sox pitchers had done so often: He got the outs he had to have.

Jeff Bagwell, pinch-hitting for the pitcher's spot, ran the count to 3-2 but hit a pop to Konerko for the second out. Garland then made Biggio look his age, throwing a called third strike past him for the final out.

Garland had thrown 93 pitches, and Guillen figured it was time to turn the one-run lead over to his bullpen. He probably would have been better off getting another inning from his starter, but the move looked wise when Cliff Politte got Taveras to fly out and then struck out Lance Berkman, who'd had two singles in three at-bats against Garland.

But Politte walked Ensberg, and Guillen called for left-hander Neal Cotts to face Mike Lamb, who had been among the Astros' most dangerous hitters in October. Cotts couldn't get comfortable on the Minute Maid mound, walking Lamb on four pitches to bring the right-handed-hitting Lane to the plate.

Guillen, for perhaps the first time in a month, then let his emotions get the best of him. At least that's the way it looked on the surface. Rather than stick with Cotts, who had better stuff than anyone in the bullpen except Bobby Jenks, Guillen summoned Dustin Hermanson, an All-Star candidate in the first half of the season but a non-factor at season's end.

Hermanson hadn't pitched with a lead or a tie in a game that mattered since Sept. 20. He hadn't been in any kind of game since Sept. 30 in Cleveland. He was working on an amazing 24 days' rest. For a relief pitcher, that might as well be an entire off-season.

Why Hermanson? Why now?

"Hermanson was ready, loose," Guillen said. "We [needed] one inning to get [Orlando Hernandez] ready to go, because this guy never was a reliever, just until this year. I didn't want to take a chance. He's got to start an inning, so at least he has the opportunity to get loose."

Why not just go to the hammer, Jenks, for the last four outs?

"No Jenks, because I was afraid what happened is what happened, tie game," Guillen said. "And then I've got my hands tied because he is the best pitcher I have."

It was an odd move any way you looked at it, and this time Guillen wasn't on a magic carpet ride. Lane, a .267 hitter during the regular season, pulled Hermanson's first pitch—a get-me-over fastball—past Crede for a game-tying double. Lamb, representing the go-ahead run, stopped at third. Hermanson then faced Ausmus, who had been a tough out in the playoffs. He used all his experience to strike him out.

That was the first of eight at-bats on which a Houston hitter failed to get a winning or potential winning run home. The next six innings turned into Scary Movie Theater for Guillen and the Sox.

Hernandez, pitching for the first time since his electrifying outing against Boston in the first round, replaced Hermanson to start the ninth. Guillen pictured him working at least two innings, if necessary, but would be lucky to get one scoreless inning from him.

El Duque wasn't right, experiencing some stiffness in his neck, and his pitches were all over the place. He walked pinch-hitter Chris Burke on four pitches with one out, then made a wild pickoff throw, allowing Burke to move to second. Hernandez forgot about Burke once he was on second, and Burke stole third on a 1-0 pitch to Biggio, who coaxed a walk to put runners on the corners with one out.

Taveras was due to hit, and Garner did not pull him back for a veteran pinch-hitter, say, Orlando Palmeiro or Jose Vizcaino. It was a bad decision, and it quickly became apparent.

Taveras couldn't lay off Hernandez's collection of curveballs out of the strike zone. He went down swinging on five pitches, taking only two. That brought Berkman to the plate, and Guillen ordered him intentionally walked, taking away the last of Hernandez's cushion.

Ensberg came to the plate with two outs and the bases loaded, and the remarkable Hernandez fanned him on six pitches, including two swinging strikes. The game rolled into extra innings.

Hernandez stayed in to face only one more hitter, walking Palmeiro pinch-hitting for the pitcher's spot to start the 10th. Guillen went to get him, bringing in Luis Vizcaino (no relation to Jose), who hadn't pitched since the last game of the regular season. This seemed another curious move, given that Jenks had not been in the game. But as impulsive as Guillen often seemed, he was capable of extreme patience. This was the ultimate example.

Vizcaino retired Lane on a pop to Pierzynski and Ausmus on a flyout, but Adam Everett worked him for a seven-pitch walk, moving Palmeiro to second base with the winning run. Burke, who had walked earlier, was hacking this time but could only hit a grounder back to Vizcaino, whose flip to Konerko got the Sox through the 10th.

Guillen finally played the Jenks card in the 11th, but as Game 2 had proved, this wasn't exactly a guarantee either. Jenks blew away Biggio for the first out but then hit the speedy Taveras on a 1-2 pitch. Fearing Taveras' speed, Guillen called a pitchout on the first pitch to Berkman, but nothing was going on. That 1-0 count led to a walk, again moving the winning run to second. Ensberg, who had struck out with the bases loaded in the ninth, popped to shortstop. Palmeiro hit a grounder back to Jenks, ending the threat.

Jenks, knowing his manager must need a break, worked a 1-2-3 12th.

The Sox hadn't had a whole lot going against Houston's bullpen but did get Podsednik to second when he singled and stole a base with no outs in the 11th. Chad Qualls, who had just taken over for Brad Lidge, retired Iguchi on a flyout to right and then struck out Dye. After Konerko was intentionally walked, Perez pinch-hit for Vizcaino and grounded to first base.

After the Sox failed to score in the top of the 13th, Guillen had another decision to make. He felt two innings was all he could get out of Jenks—after all, there might be games the next two days—and he wanted to bring in Damaso Marte.

Because the pitcher's spot was due up third in the next inning, Guillen brought in Marte as part of a double switch. He put Marte in for Iguchi, who had made the last out in the 13th, and called on Geoff Blum to take over at second base, hitting fifth in the order, where Jenks had been.

"You keep seeing names getting marked off and marked off the lineup card, and eventually it gets down to the bottom of the totem pole," Blum said. "I was near the bottom."

Harris, normally the backup to Iguchi, had already been used as a pinch-runner in the eighth inning. But Blum still wasn't Guillen's only choice. Pablo Ozuna, who had played six games at second during the regular season, was still available. Guillen's initial thought was to put Ozuna in the game, but he ran the scenarios through his mind again and called for Blum.

"I had Ozuna in the double switch," Guillen said. "I had it and all of a sudden I looked at my lineup [card] and I see Blum, and he's a switch-hitter, and I think he plays a little bit better second base than Ozuna does. I switched my mind, and it worked for us."

Marte naturally walked the first man he faced. But he came back to strike out Biggio and Taveras, then used his lefty-lefty advantage to get Berkman to hit a grounder to Uribe.

After pinch-hitting for Qualls, Garner had gone through his top five relievers. He turned to someone who at least looked scary, Astacio. The tall Dominican had not pitched since working one scoreless inning Oct. 12 in a 5-3 loss to St. Louis in Game 1 of the National League Championship Series.

Dye greeted him in the 14th with a single, but Konerko hit into a double play. That brought up Blum, a switch-hitter, who was doing well to remember to go to the left side of the box against Astacio. Blum was batting for the first time since Oct. 4.

He gave himself the take sign on the first pitch. It was a ball. Astacio also missed with his second pitch, falling behind in the count.

"The first pitch definitely was taken just because I hadn't seen a pitch in three or four weeks, so I wanted to gauge the velocity a little bit, see if I was seeing one ball or three," Blum said. "But I was fortunate enough to get a 2-0 count, and I was trying to work the count a little bit."

The 2-0 pitch was a fastball, over the middle of the plate and a little above the belt. Blum, like Podsednik two nights earlier, drove it into the seats down the right-field line for a most unlikely home run. Blum's mind went blank as he circled the bases.

"Make sure you hit the bases," he said when asked what he was thinking. "As soon as I hit it, I knew it was hard enough to get out. As soon as it got out, [first-base coach] Tim Raines' face lit up and he stuck his hand up. Hitting his hand and touching the bag was a little tough.... The first thing is how am I going to hit Tim Raines' hand and give him a high-five and make it around the bases? I don't think I blinked or looked at anybody until I made it to home plate and knew it was for real."

Before the top of the 14th was over, the Sox scored a second run, on Widger's bases-loaded walk, which brought home Rowand. The Sox still needed three more outs, and, of course, getting them wasn't easy.

Marte struck out Ensberg but then walked Palmeiro on five pitches. Lane popped up for the second out, and the 7-5 victory appeared secure when Ausmus hit a grounder to the sure-handed Uribe. Oops. He booted this one, putting the tying run on base for Everett.

Guillen went to the bullpen for the eighth time, a good trick given that he had only seven relievers on the roster. Mark Buehrle, who had started Game 2, had sneaked down to the bullpen in case the game just kept going and going. "He told me if you need somebody, I'll be ready," Guillen said. "I wanted to get my best pitcher on the mound, and it worked."

Indeed. The game already was the longest by time in World Series history, but Buehrle kept it from going and going. He challenged Everett, as he always challenges hitters, and the Houston shortstop hit a high pop to Uribe. Just like that, the Sox were one victory away from winning the World Series.

◆

You could find more conventional World Series heroes than Blum, the new father of triplets who goes through hair colors and styles faster than Madonna. But you would wait a long time to find one any more like a little kid with the key to a candy store. Watching Blum enjoy his Andy Warhol 15 minutes was almost like experiencing it yourself. Here was a guy who was easy to relate to, and he didn't mind taking others along for the ride of his life.

"It means the world right now, even more if we go in and close this out tomorrow," Blum said after the game-winning homer. "It's the stuff dreams are made of. I've had about a hundred of these at-bats in my back yard playing Wiffle ball with my younger brother. But to do it on this stage and in this situation...."

Blum, 32, a seven-year veteran, had joined the White Sox

on July 31 in a trade from the San Diego Padres, costing the Sox only 26-year-old minor-league left-hander Ryan Meaux. General manager Ken Williams had been talking to Padres GM Kevin Towers about a Sean Burroughs-for-Joe Borchard deal but was surprised to learn the more versatile Blum was expendable.

Blum had signed with San Diego, his fourth team in three years, over the winter in part because his wife was expecting the triplets. He wanted to play close to their residence in San Clemente, Calif. But it hadn't been the best of seasons, with him hitting only .241 in playing time limited by the Padres' acquisition of Joe Randa. Blum said he wasn't disappointed by the trade to the Sox, but he was surprised.

"I signed in San Diego to be close to home," he said. "The triplets were on the way. It was an incredible situation. Family was close by, friends were close by. And I thought it would be a good situation for myself personally to be in San Diego. I played with a great ballclub with a great group of guys. The day of the trade was interesting. You see the GM and assistant GM scurrying around the clubhouse. And things are going on, and you're wondering what's happening. You turn around and put your shoes on, and you get a tap on the shoulder and your number has been called. My heart was torn to leave the family. But to get to a ballclub like this now makes it all worthwhile."

Blum had spent two happy seasons in Houston. It was weird-"surreal," to use Purpura's word-to be in a World Series against so many old friends.

"It's tough, it's interesting," Blum said. "There are a lot of things going through your head when you find out you're playing one of your ex-teams in a city that treated you so well. The fans took me in for two years and spoiled me rotten, and so did the guys in the clubhouse. I learned a lot about the game and how to handle myself, how to go about playing every day and things like that.

"These guys down the line still give support. I still have support for them. We still keep in touch. There's a strong tie here with a good group of friends."

When Blum arrived in Houston, having come in a trade from Montreal for third baseman Chris Truby in the spring of 2002, he was wearing black hair with white streaks. "I took a beating for that from them," Blum said. "It was a first impression-type thing. It seems to be an ongoing joke, what it's going to look like and what color it's going to be. It's a way to break the ice and get things going a bit. I enjoy it. I know those guys will get after me about my hair."

Before Game 3, Biggio had teased Blum about his hair, which now was blond-streaked and piled high. A reporter asked if Biggio had said anything to him as he circled the bases. "Not a word was said on the basepaths," Blum said. "It got pretty quiet."

Blum was asked what had been his biggest hit before the home run. "Good Lord, have I had any big hits?" he asked, incredulous. "There's a lot of mileage in between that swing right there and some of the other ones."

For the White Sox it was a huge hit, a monstrous hit, a franchise-turning kind of hit. It was their biggest in, oh, two days.

Believe it!

Heroes abound as Sox win
1st World Series title since 1917

Ozzie Guillen awoke Oct. 26 in a position no White Sox manager had been in for 32,153 days, not since Pants Rowland sent Red Faber to the mound against John McGraw's New York Giants at the Polo Grounds. That was Game 6 of the 1917 World Series. This was Game 4 in 2005, some 88 years and zero titles later for the Sox.

With one more victory over the Houston Astros, the Sox would end a drought two years longer than the one the Boston Red Sox had famously halted with their sweep of St. Louis in the 2004 World Series.

Guillen could not have been more comfortable in this situation. His starting pitcher would be his buddy, Freddy Garcia. "Ozzie is a really good friend," Garcia said. "But we're playing ball. He does his job, I do mine. It's all about respect."

Garcia had been brought to Chicago from Seattle 497 days earlier to pitch in big games, though only a dreamer could envision one this big.

Ken Williams, the general manager who had acquired the

pitcher Guillen most coveted, said he was thinking of two words when he agreed to give up three top minor-leaguers for Garcia: Nineteen seventeen. Williams was referring to the last year the Sox, or any team from baseball's wasteland of Chicago, had won the World Series.

Williams viewed his mission only one way: to win it all. That meant he had to take some risks, which he did by acquiring Garcia. He felt Garcia was worth the risk, and Garcia was proving him correct.

Garcia, at 6 feet 4 inches and 250 pounds, certainly looked the part of an intimidator. That's what the Seattle Mariners had in mind when they demanded that Houston include Garcia, then its top pitching prospect, in the 1998 trade for Randy Johnson.

All Garcia had ever wanted to do as a child in the barrios of Caracas, Venezuela, was play baseball. The son of a truck driver and a nurse, he lived with his siblings in a rough cement-block home owned by his grandmother and at times occupied by more than 30 family members.

"I was always alone," Garcia said of his childhood. "I didn't want to go to school. I wanted to play baseball. The parents, they don't like that. They want you to work in school first, then play baseball. But that's what I wanted to do, and that's why I'm here."

Garcia was one of many future major-leaguers discovered by scout Andres Reiner, who later persuaded the Astros to open a baseball academy in Venezuela. Bobby Abreu, Richard Hidalgo and Magglio Ordonez were among the others who came through Reiner's program.

"Everybody saw the potential with Freddy," Reiner said. "He let himself be polished, and now he is who he is. He wasn't a hard worker, but he learned."

Garcia climbed to Triple A shortly before his 22nd birthday, making only two starts at New Orleans before the Astros acceded to the demands of then-Seattle GM Woody Woodward and included him in the deal for Johnson. The Astros saw the Big Unit as the final puzzle piece for a team with World Series potential. He did help them win a franchise-record 102 games, going 10-1 in 11 starts down the stretch, but then he lost twice to San Diego as the Padres upset Houston in the first round of the playoffs.

Garcia probably didn't mind seeing the Astros lose. But he could hardly blame anyone for trading him in a deal that brought Johnson.

"They called me and said, 'Hey, you got traded,' " Garcia recalled.

" 'For who?' "

" 'You and Carlos Guillen and John Halama for Randy Johnson.' I was like, that's cool. It was a really big deal. People wanted to talk to you about the trade."

Garcia and Guillen, a shortstop, grew into centerpiece players for the Mariners in the years after the franchise abandoned the star power that carried it into Safeco Field—the troika of Johnson, Alex Rodriguez and Ken Griffey Jr.

Garcia was part of two playoff teams in his six seasons with the Mariners, going 18-6 for the 2001 team that won 116 games. He had three playoff wins for Seattle, including two against the Yankees in the 2000 American League Championship Series.

In his year and a half with the White Sox, Garcia had gone 23-12, raising his career winning percentage to .615, almost exactly the same as Mark Buehrle, the other half of the 1-2 combination Ozzie Guillen envisioned building around before the season.

"Freddy isn't about numbers," Guillen said. "He's about winning."

Garcia approached his Game 4 start having made eight previous playoff starts and figured to be one cool hombre. In his head, it was really Game 12 of the run the Sox had begun three weeks earlier, with that 14-2 laugher against Boston. As he always does, Garcia ate his pregame pasta and sat in front of his locker, listening to Latin "bachata" music on headphones.

◆

Jerry Reinsdorf felt like pinching himself all day. When he arrived at Minute Maid Park, he hardly knew what to say to Eddie Einhorn and the other investors in his ownership group, which had been together 25 years, awaiting this day.

Once the stadium gates opened, it was clear this was not just an Astros crowd. One of every 10 fans, maybe more, was wearing White Sox colors, with jerseys representing Paul Konerko, Frank Thomas and Buehrle mixing with those bearing Roger Clemens' No. 21, Craig Biggio's No. 7 and Jeff Bagwell's No. 5. There were at least 3,000 Sox fans in Houston, maybe as many as 5,000.

Back in Chicago, crowds gathered on both sides of town wherever beer was being served, with the biggest get-together at the United Center. Reinsdorf had made the Bulls' home available, and big crowds turned out to follow the games on the arena's giant screens.

◆

While Garcia was starting for the Sox, Astros manager Phil Garner would have to turn his season over to the unsung Brandon Backe, a former quarterback from Ball High in Galveston who not long ago had been a minor-league outfielder for the Tampa Bay Devil Rays. The matchup appeared to favor the Sox hugely but had the potential to turn into something of a setup.

One of the best-pitched postseason games in recent years had been Game 5 of the 2004 National League Championship Series, between St. Louis and Houston. Backe and Brad Lidge combined on a one-hit shutout, with Backe and the Cardinals' Woody Williams keeping the game scoreless into the ninth, when Houston's Jeff Kent won it with a three-run homer.

Backe hadn't even been in the Astros' 2004 rotation until a run of injuries claimed Andy Pettitte and Wade Miller, and he entered the '04 playoffs having started only nine big-league games. He hadn't pitched more than seven innings in any of his previous starts.

"You wouldn't have known this guy hadn't pitched in 10 World Series games if you'd been over here watching," Garner said. "He was focused, locked in and wasn't expending a lot of unnecessary energy."

Backe credited Clemens with teaching him how to succeed in big games. "He told me to relax and channel all of my [energy] toward the catcher and what I'm supposed to be doing out there," Backe said.

Backe was 10-8 with a 4.76 ERA during the 2005 season, a showing that would have fit with the trio of Boston pitchers the White Sox had roughed up in the first round. But he held the Cardinals to one run in 5⅔ innings in Game 4 of the NLCS. The Sox could not count on pounding him.

"It's great when you are in this position," Guillen said before Game 4. "It's great when you have that feeling, like, 'Wow, we are so close.' We are so close to doing something we all want to do. But I'm not coming here just happy or rah-rah, here we are. You look at my players, they get excited before the game starts. But before that they do the same thing. And coming in this position is really hard. It's hard when you get here, it's harder to win in the playoffs, it's harder to win in the World Series. We need one more game, and that's the toughest game you want to win. You win a hundred-something games, this is the hardest to win."

◆

Garner arrived with some fence-mending to do in his clubhouse. Angry after the Game 3 loss, he had heaved a chair down the tunnel between the dugout and the clubhouse when Geoff Blum hit his 14th-inning home run, then castigated Houston's hitters in his postgame visit to the interview room.

"I'm really ticked off," Garner said. "It's embarrassing to play like this in our hometown."

Garner seemed incredulous that his hitters had gone 1-for-11 with runners in scoring position in Game 3, failing to get the ball out of the infield in five chances to drive in the winning run between the ninth and 13th innings.

"That's some pretty poor hitting, absolutely rotten hitting," Garner said shortly after the 7-5 loss. "We had our chances. It's amazing. I don't know how you win a ballgame when you can't hit the ball. We didn't hit the ball good except for Jason Lane. We managed to stay in the ballgame, but we might have played 40 innings and it didn't look like we were going to get a runner across. Very frustrating."

But Garner did not backtrack in a return trip to the interview room before Game 4.

"Whatever sleep you've gotten, have you tempered your feelings at all?" he was asked.

"No, I'm ticked off," Garner said. "There seems to be a lot of trying to figure out what that means. The question, I think, was what are my emotions at the time. And my emotions are I'm ticked off. Those who have known me, been around me, I don't like to get beat, and I don't like to get beat in my own home.

"They're having their way with us right now. So I'm ticked off. That doesn't mean … Listen, I'm proud of my players. We're battling with everything we've got. I just don't like to get beat, that's my emotions."

At least Garner didn't blame the roof. "Yeah," he said, "the roof wasn't a problem last night."

Biggio was asked about Garner having said it was "embarrassing" for the Astros to play the way they had in Game 3.

"The tough part about last night is it was a long game and we lost," he said. "It would have been better if we won. It's all about momentum. I don't read the paper, so I don't know what was said. The guys in the clubhouse, we all look in the mirror, and we're all honest about it and it's all about a team. So maybe a little better pitching, maybe picking each other up offensively and making plays defensively. It's all about a team."

Like Bagwell, Biggio had waited a career for this chance, and it was not turning out the way he had dreamed it would.

"I don't think there's a letdown … maybe from a fan's perspective," Biggio said. "They've been three great games that could have gone either way. We could be very easily 3-0 and they could be down by three. But unfortunately it's the other way around. I don't think it's a letdown. It's been three good games. But we're 0-3 in the loss column, and that's the disappointing side."

◆

Once again Guillen was asked about his statement Sept. 21 that he might retire if the Sox won the World Series. "Were you joking?" a reporter asked. "Is that something you would consider?"

Guillen didn't blink.

"I was not joking," he said. "I think about it. I just try to make a point.… I just signed a new contract, and I said I'm not coming here for the glory, not for the money. I come here to win. If we get to the World Series, give me an opportunity to say I can go home with the gold. This is not my dream to be in the World Series; this is my goal."

The reporter asked again if he would consider retiring if the Sox won.

"Well, Bobby Cox called me last night and said, 'You'll never retire from baseball. Make them retire you.... You're too good a man, a baseball man. We need people like you. Make those guys fire you. Keep taking the money from them.' And I said, 'Skip, I already signed the contract.' He said, 'Make them renew the contract now.'

"I want to show people in Chicago what I want and that I'm doing what I want to do. It's not because I want to manage the White Sox. I just want to win in that city, and hopefully we do it for them, for the fans."

◆

Fans at Minute Maid Park were armed with white Thunder-Stix but weren't making much of a racket, especially not after Jermaine Dye's first-inning double off Backe. But Backe made a good play on a comebacker by Konerko, getting out of the first inning scoreless. The Sox also failed to take advantage of a two-out triple by Scott Podsednik in the third.

Unfortunately for the Astros, however, they were making Garner's statement about playing 40 innings without scoring look like a self-fulfilling prophecy.

Biggio led off the first inning with a single to left, then was bunted to second. But Garcia struck out Lance Berkman and retired Ensberg on a check-swing tapper to the mound. Ensberg, the Astros' cleanup hitter, had been 1-for-9 since a solo homer in Game 2.

Mike Lamb led off the second with a double to right field. But Garcia again did the thing that had made the Sox so hard to beat since mid-September: He got the outs he had to get.

Lane took a called third strike, and Garcia threw a swinging third strike past catcher Brad Ausmus. That gave Garcia the chance to pitch around Adam Everett to get to Backe, if he wanted to, but he went at the Houston shortstop and got him to hit a grounder to Joe Crede for the final out.

The game moved along looking like a flashback to the Williams-Backe duel in the NLCS a year earlier. Backe wasn't quite as sharp, but the Sox rarely threatened. And while Houston had runners in five of the first six innings, Garcia consistently frustrated the Astros.

In the sixth inning, a Willy Taveras single and a Berkman walk put a runner in scoring position with one out. But Garcia struck out the frustrated Ensberg for the second out (perhaps Ensberg was spending too much time writing his column for the Houston Chronicle) and then tried to get Lamb to help him out. When Lamb wouldn't chase the first two pitches, getting ahead 2-0, Guillen hustled out to the mound to talk to his friend. They decided they would rather go after the next hitter, Lane, than challenge Lamb. So catcher A.J. Pierzynski stood up behind the plate, signaling for an intentional walk, which loaded the bases.

Was Guillen crazy? He had moved a second runner into scoring position in a scoreless tie. It was a huge risk. But it would prove to be another winning move by a manager who was riding a tsunami of good karma.

Lane took Garcia's first pitch for a strike, then swung through the second one. All the pressure had shifted from Garcia to the hitter. Lane fought a good fight, fouling off four two-strike pitches and taking another for ball one, but in the end Garcia struck him out on a 92-m.p.h. fastball that was up and in. For the Sox, a scoreless tie had never felt better.

They got two-out hits from Aaron Rowand and Crede in the

top of the seventh, Rowand lining a single up the middle and moving to third on Crede's double off the wall in left-center. Because of the park's small dimensions and the ball's hard carom, Rowand had no chance to score and was stranded at third when Backe struck out Juan Uribe.

But those hits were significant. They convinced Garner to lift Backe after 100 pitches and play his supposed trump card, Lidge, in the top of the eighth. Bad move.

◆

Podsednik and Blum had hit heroic home runs in Games 2 and 3. But if there was one at-bat that had set the tone, one moment that had told them World Series baseball was still just baseball, it was Dye's homer off Clemens in the first inning of Game 1.

The homer came on the ninth pitch of the at-bat, after Clemens had Dye in an 0-2 hole and couldn't finish him off. "Jermaine has had great at-bats," Pierzynski said. "He is our 3-hole guy for a reason."

Certainly no one on Guillen's team was calmer than Dye, a gifted athlete from Northern California who turned down a football scholarship to Brigham Young and a basketball offer from Nevada-Las Vegas to pursue his dream of playing big-league baseball. It first occurred to him watching the Giants play at Candlestick Park, often with his father Bill, who had briefly been a Detroit Piston before a knee injury ended his basketball career.

Like Pierzynski and Japanese import Tadahito Iguchi, Dye had the playoff experience many of his teammates lacked. He was only 22 when he played in his first World Series, with Atlanta in 1996. That had started promisingly, with the Braves winning the first two games at Yankee Stadium, but ended with a thud as Atlanta lost the next four, including three in a row at home.

"I go about my business, do what I can to help the team win and don't get caught up in all the hoopla if I have a good game," Dye had said earlier in October. "This is my fifth time in the playoffs. I know what it takes."

Dave Wilder, an assistant general manager, had been instrumental in bringing Dye to the White Sox as the free-agent replacement for Ordonez. Wilder was scouting California for the Braves when he got to know Dye in his time at Cosumnes River College in Sacramento.

"So smooth, so natural, and he always has been that way," Wilder said of Dye, now 31. "He never has been an 'I' guy. Jermaine does his job. That's why we got him. And that's the way he's always been."

Dye had followed a friend to Cosumnes, where he had been primarily a pitcher. He had a low-90s fastball and a good breaking ball, but his career path changed the day coach Rod Beilby had his pitchers take batting practice. Dye hit the ball better than any of the position players.

"I leaned over to one of my coaches and said, 'We have to find a spot for this kid to play every day,' " Beilby recalled. "I told my closest friends that this guy is going to be a major-league hitter one day."

The Dyes, strict disciplinarians who had challenged their children, would not be an easy sell for Wilder. He knew Jermaine wanted to play pro ball and had figured he could sign him quickly after the Braves took him in the 17th round of the 1993 draft. But it took multiple trips to the family home to get the Dyes to accept a $35,000 bonus.

"I usually went into a guy's house and signed him within an hour, but I had to go to Jermaine's house three times," Wilder said. "I finally told his mom, 'I'm not coming back there until you've got something ready to sign.' The dad was good cop, the mom was bad cop. They had it down."

Dye was considered one of baseball's top young outfielders while he was in Atlanta's farm system, which is why Kansas City insisted on him in a deal for outfielder Michael Tucker and second baseman Keith Lockhart in the last week of spring training in 1997. He became a top run producer with the Royals, driving in 106 or more runs for three years in a row beginning in 1999. The last of those seasons was split between Kansas City and Oakland, with the Athletics getting him in a three-way trade before the deadline.

But Dye's luck turned bad in a first-round series against the Yankees in 2001. He made the mistake of trying to hit one of Orlando Hernandez's exaggerated curveballs and fouled the ball down on his right leg, just below the knee. His tibia snapped. He worked his way back from the broken leg to play in 2002, but in April 2003 he tore cartilage in his right knee diving in the outfield, and later that season he hurt his shoulder crashing into Bengie Molina at the plate. Dye had a relatively unimpressive 2004 season for the Athletics, hitting .265 with 23 home runs and 80 RBIs.

Research by White Sox officials, including Wilder, revealed he had stayed in the lineup despite a thumb injury that would have sidelined many other players.

"That's a gamer," general manager Ken Williams said. "People questioned his injuries, [said] he's always hurt. But he has been a quality guy to keep the clubhouse headed in the right direction, so it was not really much of a stretch for us."

Based on Wilder's recommendation, Dye was high on Williams' list of options to replace Ordonez. Once again, Wilder tried to sell Dye on his organization. Williams turned it into a full-court press during a round of golf with Dye in Arizona, explaining how well his opposite-field power would fit at U.S.

Cellular Field, which had turned into one of the best places to hit in the American League.

"We went after him and told him the White Sox do it a little differently," Wilder said. "We have what we have. If you fit here, you fit. If you don't, you don't, but you have to want to play for us. If you don't want to play for us, it's not going to work."

Dye was sold. He turned down a handful of better offers to sign with the Sox for two years plus a third-year option.

"There were a couple of teams that came in at the last minute and kind of blew Chicago out of the water, which a lot of people wouldn't have turned down," Dye said. "But my heart was already set, and I gave my word to Kenny Williams that I was coming to Chicago."

Dye said the potential of the Sox's pitching staff was among the factors that sold him. He picked the Sox hoping he could have an October like this.

"When you're a free agent, you just want to put yourself in a position to get on a team that can make the playoffs and play in the World Series, and I really thought we had a chance," Dye said. "I felt this club was the best fit for me ... where I could come in and be myself. I'm not an outspoken guy. I try to lead by example."

With that nine-pitch at-bat against Clemens in Game 1, he had done exactly that.

◆

Willie Harris, a left-handed hitter who had lost his second-base job to Iguchi, was Guillen's choice to bat for Garcia when the pitcher's spot came up to start the eighth inning. Harris had pinch-run in Game 3 but hadn't been to the plate since the garbage-time innings of the 14-2 victory over Boston back on Oct. 4. Facing Lidge would be a huge challenge.

Like Blum against Ezequiel Astacio, Harris took the first

pitch to try to get a little more comfortable. Umpire Derryl Cousins called it strike one. Harris fouled off the next pitch, putting himself in an 0-2 hole.

A free swinger throughout his career, Harris had somehow sharpened his approach watching this postseason run from the bench. He laid off the next two pitches, which were out of the zone. Lidge, incredulous that Harris hadn't helped him out, didn't want to walk him. Instead he threw a fastball that Harris slapped into left field for a leadoff single. Podsednik bunted, moving Harris to second. Carl Everett, pinch-hitting for Iguchi, then grounded to Biggio for the second out, Harris staying at second base.

That brought Dye to the plate. He punched a 1-1 slider up the middle, past Lidge, for a single. Taveras had no chance to stop the speedy Harris from scoring, and the Sox had a 1-0 lead.

◆

Now it would be Uribe time.

Cliff Politte, taking over for Garcia, pitched himself into trouble in the eighth. After retiring Biggio for the first out—Pierzynski and Crede let a foul pop fall between them, extending the at-bat—he hit Taveras with a 1-1 pitch, putting a fast runner on base as the tying run. Making matters worse, his sailed his next pitch past Pierzynski, allowing Taveras to move to second. With the count 1-0, Guillen ordered Berkman intentionally walked.

Like Guillen's decision to put Lamb on base in the sixth inning, this move went totally against The Book, baseball's unwritten strategy rules. Among the first of those commandments is Thou Shalt Not Put the Go-Ahead Run on Base, and Guillen had just done that. Shouldn't lightning come out of the clear Texas sky and strike him?

Not this night. Not this month. Not this year.

Politte fell behind the underproductive Ensberg 2-0 but was saved by the spacious center field. Rowand had to retreat to catch Ensberg's fly, allowing Taveras to move to third, but the Sox now had two outs. Guillen called on Neal Cotts to face the left-handed-hitting Lamb, and Garner countered with Jose Vizcaino, who had delivered a game-tying pinch single in the ninth inning of Game 3.

Cotts fell behind Vizcaino 2-0 but came back with two strikes. The Houston pinch-hitter then hit a slow grounder toward short, breaking his bat. Uribe charged, grabbed the ball and fired to Konerko to get Vizcaino and preserve the 1-0 lead.

Pierzynski led off the ninth with a double. But Lidge, getting a break when Rowand bunted foul on three consecutive pitches for an easy strikeout, would not allow the Sox to score an insurance run. That put the ball, and the 88-year history of failure, in the hands of the big man, rookie Bobby Jenks.

Lane worked the count to 3-2, then dropped a soft single into center field. Again, the tying run was on base. Garner gave up one of his last three outs to have Ausmus bunt Lane to second, and Uribe would take it from there.

Chris Burke, pinch-hitting for Everett, took the first two pitches from Jenks for balls. But Jenks came back with smoke in the strike zone, evening the count at 2-2. Lane fouled back the fifth pitch, then hit a high foul toward the seats behind third base. Uribe raced over from shortstop, never taking his eye off the ball. When his feet hit the dirt track in front of the wall, he launched himself into the stands, catching the ball just before he landed in the first two rows of Section 110.

Uribe then scrambled to his feet, keeping Lane from advancing to third. The White Sox were one out away.

As Garner called on Orlando Palmeiro to hit for Lidge, millions of Sox fans in Chicago and Illinois, and those scattered around the globe, looked at each other in confusion. What happens now? What do we do if they win?

Who knew?

Palmeiro took Jenks' first fastball for a ball. He then fouled off two in a row off, giving the kid from the Idaho outback a 1-2 edge. Palmeiro would have to be defensive on anything close. He put a short, make-contact-please swing on the next pitch, and the ball one-hopped over Jenks' head.

It appeared headed up the middle, on roughly the same course as Dye's run-scoring hit an inning earlier. But enter Uribe from stage left. The shortstop was moving just as quickly to his left as he had gone to his right to catch up to Burke's foul. Uribe put on a quick burst of speed to reach the ball, then grabbed it with exquisite smoothness on a tiny hop and, on the dead run, fired to Konerko with the relative pace of Jenks' fastball.

The ball beat Palmeiro to the bag by a step. Umpire Gary Cederstrom raised his right hand, and Jenks raised both hands over his head and jumped in the air just like the kids do at Williamsport in the Little League World Series.

Chicago had its first hardball champion since 1917, when Faber got Lew McCarty to ground out to the great Eddie Collins for the final act in a drama that had captivated the ancestors of many who would shed tears in Chicago bars this night.

The Sox had started their season with a 1-0 victory. Now they were ending it the same way.

"We built this team around defense and pitching," Guillen said. "When you've got good defense, your pitching staff is going to be better because they're not going to make that many mistakes. When I saw Uribe make the last play, I knew he was going to make it. The one before, I was down in the dugout, and everybody jumped out and I didn't know what's going on. But that's the reason we bring this kid here. Our defense, it was one of the biggest reasons we win the World Series, no doubt about it. I knew we were going to play good defense all year long."

White, indeed the new Red.

◆

As he had done after the American League Championship Series and the division series, Guillen stayed in the background as players mobbed each other on the field. This was the players' time, not the manager's time, and Guillen had grown up into being one terrific manager. By now, no one should have been surprised he would act the part.

"It's a great feeling," Guillen said later, his hair wet with champagne. "It was a great competition. The four games could go either way. They played real tremendous baseball against us. A good thing happened to us. That's the reason we win it.

"Jerry Reinsdorf, one of the biggest reasons I wanted to win this thing was for him. I just needed people in Chicago to be so excited about the thing. I just wanted to accomplish it in my life. I wanted to win this thing for Jerry. He deserved it. He worked so hard in baseball. I think Kenny Williams did a tremendous job. Not only put the best players on the field but put the best team players on the field."

Guillen talked about the home-field advantage the Sox had held in the World Series. They had that because Terry Francona's AL team had won the All-Star Game.

Because his team won the pennant, Guillen is scheduled to manage the AL All-Stars at the 2006 game in Pittsburgh. He talked about his responsibility to win, as he wanted the AL to keep home-field advantage in the next World Series.

If he was planning ahead to the All-Star Game, didn't that mean an end to his threat of retiring?

"I can't," Guillen said, smiling. "I'm not retiring until the All-Star Game."

In the end, after 99 wins in the regular season and 11 more in October, after the stress of seeing a 15-game lead reduced to only 1 ½ games, after the joy of eliminating four of baseball's best teams in a span of 24 days, after Ozzie Guillen had threatened to walk away only to realize there's no way he could leave the team that had done all this, after they had captured the attention of a nation, not just the city that so often had taken them for granted, the White Sox were left with two things:

A reason to throw a great party, and the Holy Grail of artifacts for Chicago baseball fans: the Rawlings "2005 World Series" game ball that Juan Uribe fired into Paul Konerko's glove for the 4,764th and final out of a trip that carried the White Sox from Opening Day to a sweep of the World Series.

They had carved a niche that would last forever with arguably the greatest postseason run in history. They had won a title by leading from wire to wire, they had led their league in victories and they had swept the World Series.

Only one other team had ever done those three things in

the same season: the 1927 Yankees, who did it behind Babe Ruth and Lou Gehrig.

But that was hardly the only way to quantify their achievement.

They outscored Boston, the Los Angeles Angels and Houston by a total of 33 runs, the greatest run differential ever in the postseason. Their 11-1 run through the playoffs equaled the 1999 Yankees for second-best record since division play was implemented, behind only Cincinnati's Big Red Machine, which went 7-0 in 1976. Their 16-1 finishing kick matched the 1970 Baltimore Orioles as the best ever, and it included 11 wins on the road and 11 in games decided by one or two runs. They became the first team to twice hit a game-deciding home run in the ninth inning or later of a postseason series. Their six-run edge over Houston in the World Series matched the 1950 Yankees for the thinnest margin of victory in a sweep.

It didn't seem to matter to anyone, including Joe Crede, but they had at least two World Series MVPs. Jermaine Dye was given the award mostly on the strength of his eighth-inning single in Game 4 and first-inning homer in Game 1. But Crede, who saved Game 1 with his fielding, had two homers and drove in three runs in the first three games and was at least as deserving.

Two days after Dye singled up the middle off Brad Lidge, Chicago's conquering heroes were toasted in a ticker-tape parade that began near the original Comiskey Park, which had been home to Chicago's last World Series-winning team in 1917, and headed north toward the city's center—but only as far north as the southern bank of the Chicago River.

These were the South Siders, after all.

Ozzie Guillen rode at the front of one of the double-decker tour buses carrying team members and their families. He had a Venezuelan flag wrapped around his shoulders and looked like a real-life Horatio Hornblower sailing into port as a conquering hero. Konerko, proud father that he was, held his baby, Nicholas, in a blanket as he rode along the Chicago streets.

Konerko had protected the ball he had caught from Uribe two nights earlier in Houston as if it were one of those eggs handed out in Life class to represent a baby. His motives were totally different from those of Doug Mientkiewicz, who had been playing first base a year earlier when Keith Foulke fielded Edgar Renteria's grounder to bring Boston its first championship since 1918.

Mientkiewicz, for years a member of the Minnesota Twins team that had bedeviled the White Sox, had quietly slipped the game ball to his wife as the Red Sox were celebrating their victory in St. Louis. He placed it in a safety-deposit box the next day and was holding on to it to one day put on the auction block. He said he would use the proceeds to pay for his children's education ... not exactly what fans want to hear from a ballplayer earning millions.

Konerko, in a gesture befitting the spirit of the 2005 White Sox, proved much more magnanimous.

After taking the podium at the victory celebration, he called for Sox Chairman Jerry Reinsdorf to come forward.

"Everybody kept asking me the last couple of days, what did I do with the ball from the last out?" Konerko said, reaching into the pocket of his letterman-style World Series jacket. "It's going to this man right here because he's earned it."

Fans cheered for Reinsdorf, who couldn't hold back tears after Konerko handed him the ball.

But the fans' loudest cheers had come earlier. Konerko had neatly summed up the odyssey, with a tease to 2006.

"I've got to tell you, all year we had to listen to people saying we didn't have the team to do this," Konerko told the crowd. "We were in first place at the break and people didn't want to believe. We won the division and people were saying we're going to get beat by the Red Sox, the wild card, and it didn't happen. We go into Anaheim, play Anaheim, and I have to hear umpires' calls and I have to hear about all the other stuff. It didn't happen. The World Series, and I had to hear about domes and all kinds of different stuff. I'm trying to think in my mind what would make people think we're a good team, and the only thing I could come up with is we'll have to do this again next year."

◆

A week after Game 4, Commissioner Bud Selig was on the telephone from his office in Milwaukee, talking about the amazing ride of the 2005 Sox, who came together to show why baseball remains our best game.

As a commissioner, Selig knew he was supposed to be neutral, and that was how he operated. But it was impossible to ignore his feelings. He and Reinsdorf had been friends for 25 years, and often they had helped each other through hard times. Selig never got to celebrate a World Series victory in the years he owned the Milwaukee Brewers, so now a part of him was living vicariously through Reinsdorf.

"I talked to Jerry yesterday," Selig said, "and you know what he told me? He said, 'I don't believe it. I still can't believe it.' I said, 'Well, Jerry, you'd better believe it because it happened.'"

CHAPTER 1

Pat Gillick quote from "The Million-to-One Team," by
George Castle.

Jim Dowdle quote from "The Million-to-One Team," by
George Castle.

CHAPTER 2

John Kruk quote from "OzFest," by Tim Kurkjian, ESPN.com.

Jerry Krause, Roland Hemond quotes from, "What if Guillen had never arrived?" by Ed Sherman, Chicago Tribune,
Oct. 10, 2005.

CHAPTER 3

Ken Williams' quotes on Ozzie Guillen's hiring from an
"Out Loud," by Steve Rosenbloom, Chicago Tribune,
Oct. 18, 2005.

Jerry Reinsdorf, Doug Melvin and other quotes on Ken
Williams' hiring from "Promise Keeper," by David Haugh,
Chicago Tribune, Oct. 2, 2005.

Jerry Williams quotes from an interview by Ken Rosenthal
of The Sporting News, November 2000.

CHAPTER 6
"Batting around with Michelle Mangan," by Bella English,
Boston Globe, Oct. 1, 2005.

CHAPTER 7
"Red Sox rooters scarce at the Cell," by Jon Yates,
Chicago Tribune, Oct. 6, 2005.

CHAPTER 8
"Heart of the Order: Paul Konerko's gritty approach
makes him a clubhouse leader and a South Side hero,"
by David Haugh, Chicago Tribune, Oct. 4, 2005.

CHAPTER 10
"Guillen tries to win it all for his hero Carrasquel,"
by Rick Morrissey, Chicago Tribune, Oct. 21, 2005.

CHAPTER 11
"Angels' Paul once forgettable, now notable," by Paul Sullivan,
Chicago Tribune, Oct. 14, 2005.
"Pauls get caught in middle," by Dave Newbart,
Chicago Sun-Times, Oct. 14, 2005.

CHAPTER 12
"Sox respect hard-nosed Pierzynski," by Mark Gonzales,
Chicago Tribune, Oct. 14, 2005.
"Man in the middle: Trouble seems to follow A.J. Pierzynski,"
by David Haugh, Chicago Tribune, Oct. 21, 2005.

"Angels fans rail at embattled umpire," by David Haugh, Chicago Tribune, Oct. 15, 2005.

"Eddings' explanation continues to evolve," by T.J. Simers, Los Angeles Times, Oct. 14, 2005.

CHAPTER 16

"The Golden Tickets," by Brendan McCarthy, Tonya Maxwell and James Janega, Chicago Tribune, Oct. 19, 2005.

"In Cuba, pair of Sox officially don't exist," by Gary Marx, Chicago Tribune, Oct. 22, 2005.

CHAPTER 17

"Sweet redemption for Jenks," by Larry Stone, Seattle Times, October 11, 2005.

CHAPTER 19

"Hopes rise sky-high: If roof ordered open, Sox stand to benefit," by Dave van Dyck, Chicago Tribune, Oct. 25, 2005.

"Trumping an ace," by Mark Gonzales, Chicago Tribune, Oct. 25, 2005.

CHAPTER 20

"From hilltop barrio to top of the world," by Hugh Dellios, Chicago Tribune, Oct. 26, 2005.

"Freddy Garcia: White Sox's Game 3 starter tells Our Guy about pitching, togetherness," by Steve Rosenbloom, Chicago Tribune, Oct. 6, 2005.

"Dye finds he's good fit for Sox," by David Haugh, Chicago Tribune, Oct. 17, 2005.

"Dependable Dye flying under radar," by Philip Hersh, Chicago Tribune, Oct. 24, 2005.